In darkening times, people need the light. Blessed and torn by the internet, globalization, democracy, immigration and individualism, beset by inequality, division, abuse, rootlessness, alienation and uncertainty symbolized by hate-crime and fake-news, Britain is wilting. What hope for the common good?

Christianity has, for 2000 years, been about living through darkness - including its own - and seeking the light. The Church offers light from Jesus' courageous and loving way of life, search for God and truth, story, spiritual encouragement, religious tradition/s, special Services, belonging and counselling, values and moral standards, a mixed society, community, service, internationalism, musical and artistic culture - foundations for today and hope for tomorrow. Yes, all that! It is also at the forefront of practical partnership with the other world faiths in Britain, such partnerships as, for example concerning climate change, being potentially invaluable for helping save the planet.

Christianity however is little appreciated, widely wasted and even betrayed. Over 50% of the British population say they are 'non-religious'. What's going wrong? And why? And what's God doing about it? Exploration into 'God' seems crucial. This book suggests ways forward.

Author
Richard Tetlow, The Revd. M.A. (Cantab), CQSW.

Community and social caseworker, inner London; lecturer in Social and Community work, Lancaster University. Ordained in mid-life as Anglican priest - vicar of the multi-racial, inner-city parish of St John and St Peter, Ladywood, Birmingham - led the church's restoration and redevelopment as church and multi-faith arts and education centre. After 20 years, retired with his wife, Ruth, to nearby multi-faith community of Moseley. They now have two children and four grandchildren. Ruth has also long been engaged in inter faith life. Richard currently- 2018- convenes two local inter faith groups and the Birmingham branch of the Progressive Christianity Network, (PCN), Britain of which he is a national trustee. He is keen on mountain/hill walking, singing and classical music, gardening, theatre, film, most sport, politics (not Brexit) and CND.

in contemporary society where religion is becoming increasingly significant. This area could not be more important

Councillor Carl Rice
Birmingham Ladywood councillor, Lord Mayor of Birmingham, 2016-7

Richard Tetlow isn't just a religious theoretician – his Christianity is rooted firmed in the practical reality of being an intensely committed inner City Priest for over 20 years. This book is essential reading for people trying to make sense of how religious ideology fits in with the modern United Kingdom as demonstrated in the great historic and diverse City of Birmingham.

Brian Pearce, OBE
Director, Inter Faith Network, U.K. 1987-2007

A fascinating and enthralling account by an Anglican priest of his personal journey over many years as he engages with the Christian tradition and with followers of other faiths - the book offers his wide ranging and challenging reflections on a contemporary approach to Christianity and on inter faith relations, inviting the reader to share an illuminating dialogue with his own passionate concerns. Whether you agree with all of his conclusions, journeying with him will enrich you at a very deep level.

Marcus Braybrooke, Revd Dr.
Joint-President of the World Congress of Faiths and Co-Founder of the Faith & Belief Forum

The story of Richard Tetlow's book is that only if we, whatever our faith or belief, religious or otherwise, listen attentively to each other will we help to heal the divisions in society. For those Christians who have never talked in any depth to a person of another religion, this book is a great place to start. I much admire all the inter faith work that Richard and his wife Ruth have done. I hope that many will see the book's importance – and buy it!

Canon Dr Andrew Wingate, OBE,
Founding Director of the St Philip's Centre, Leicester.

I have known Richard Tetlow for over 35 years. He served as vicar for nearly twenty years in St John's Ladywood, one of the toughest parishes in Birmingham. He was a forerunner in initiating several inter faith schemes with local faiths, Jewish, Muslim and Buddhist, and showed great ability to bring people on and leave them to be the leaders.

Richard is trusted by people of various faiths, particularly perhaps by Muslims. The fruit is here in this book. A great strength is Richard's own personal testimony of his journey backed by his wide understanding of the heart of the Christian faith. The book emphasises that it is out of personal encounter that inter-faith dialogue comes alive and deepens. Richard does not try to speak for all places but encourages the reader to look at their own city, in the light of Birmingham's story.

PERCEPTIONS
OF
CHRISTIANITY
FROM PEOPLE OF
DIFFERENT FAITHS

To See Ourselves as Others See Us

Richard Tetlow

authorHOUSE®

AuthorHouse™ UK
1663 Liberty Drive
Bloomington, IN 47403 USA
www.authorhouse.co.uk
Phone: 0800.197.4150

Published by AuthorHouse 09/20/2018

ISBN: 978-1-5462-9073-5 (sc)
ISBN: 978-1-5462-9080-3 (hc)
ISBN: 978-1-5462-9072-8 (e)

Dedication

In memory of Duncan,
dearly loved son and brother
who sought justice and made music
May 1977–January 2017

LETTER TO THE CHURCH TIMES, PUBLISHED 9 JUNE 2017

Many of us are fortunate to know the comfort and support of family and friends on the death of someone dear to us. We ourselves have been greatly upheld by family, friends, and church well-wishers. Over the New Year our younger son took his own life, alone and away from the family. He was clever, stimulating, of dual heritage, studying politics and philosophy at Glasgow in his fourth year, musical, aged thirty-nine, troubled deep down, and sometimes paranoid. On 22 May, some good local Muslim friends invited us to a prayer meeting in his memory, in their mosque. We were asked to invite a few other friends. We gathered in a circle and our prayers were introduced by a senior woman. There were about thirty of us present, two-thirds Muslim women, men, and children, most of whom never knew Duncan. His photo was surrounded by candles amidst a mass of white roses. As parents, we both spoke about him. Our friends who knew him contributed, and a senior Muslim gentleman read from the Qur'an. Our son had no association with Islam. We all shared spontaneous inclusive prayers and silence. The atmosphere was serene, accepting, and beautiful. Carefully prepared food followed. As we left, we were presented with the roses, each with a prayer attached. Everyone left with a small packet of forget-me-not seeds.

At this time of Muslim–Christian uncertainty, it seems our gift and responsibility to share this deeply moving experience.

Ruth and Richard (Revd) Tetlow

Acknowledgements and Gratitude

To my broad-minded school and magnificent university, Harrogate Grammar and Cambridge (Trinity College); to the LSO and Birmingham Symphony Orchestra Choruses; more directly, to those friends and to senior friend of the world John Hick who helped me think more generously and colleagues who over the last four years have supported and guided me with this book: Grace Davie, Stephen Pattison, Alan Race, Andrew Wingate, Adrian Alker, Jan Waterson, Yann Lovelock, John Nightingale, Donald and Kerstin Eadie, Michael Hell and Marc Jobst; currently to Birmingham Ridges and Tops (Ramblers); to friends and colleagues/trustees in the Progressive Christianity Network, Britain and Birmingham and Birmingham's inspiring interfaith world, who have kept me thoughtful, light-headed and fit enough to stimulate my heart and spirit. Then my enormous gratitude to those ten contributors of different faiths who gave me their trust and experience to make this book possible.

Notable in my three careers and all now deceased have been three next-door neighbours who started me off as a youth: Bishop Henry de Candole and his wife, Mrs Bishop and Norman Goodacre; then Dr Frank Lake/ Clinical Theology, David Sheppard (my ordination sponsor), John V. Taylor, Harry A. Williams (my college personal tutor), Eric James and John Austin (my early clergy friends) and once ordained at 41, Peter Hall, Rector of St Martin's in the Bull Ring. They all inspired and encouraged me – despite being nearly all male, clergy and even bishops! It was that generation. The college friends to date, Peter Virgin who pushed me out of the nest and Francis Buxton and Denis Brazell.

Thank you to my four families. I give them my deep gratitude and love because I only exist because of them: my pantheist, professional and lonely father and my mystical, literary and loving mother and with them my - originally five - siblings, Katherine, Julian, Sara, David and Jane; to my children, three, until January 2017, Duncan, Rachel plus Paul and Daniel plus Almut; and my grandchildren, Lucia, Alma, Thomas and Phillip.

To all those hundreds of people who have contributed to my well-being, after school and university days: the local people and social and community workers, like Annie Grocott, Adeline Searson and Betty Roberts of Walworth/Camberwell in Southwark and colleagues of Lancaster University Social Work Dept . Then, following my Ordination, the people and clergy of St George's, Basseterre, St. Kitts, of St Martin's in the Bull Ring, Birmingham, St John's and St Peter's, Ladywood, especially my long-committed and dear colleague, Josephine Mason, the Progressive Synagogue with (Rabbi) Margaret Jacobi, and of the Moseley Benefice led by Duncan Strathie, all in Birmingham, and throughout all my ordained life, my/our Queens College '83 clergy cell. of 35 years. To all these I owe my deep gratitude.

Most of all, to my dearest wife, Ruth, near life-time friend, companion and mate, my admiring respect, abundant love and thanks for our lives together.

Finally, to the NHS and to God for the wonders of the world and our shared responsibility for continued creation.

Contents

Dedication ix

Notes to the Reader xvii

Foreword – Risk and Gift xxi

PART I

Introduction 1. Content 3

Introduction 2. Development 39

Introduction 3. Background 43

PART II

Chapter 1 Five Perceptions of Christianity 67

    A Hindu View of Christianity 68

    Through the Eyes of Others 75

    Christians and Christianity: A Sikh Perception 82

    A Muslim Perception of Christianity 90

    A Buddhist Perception of Christianity 99

Chapter 2 Five Christian Responses to the Perceptions 108

    Josephine Mason 108

    Maureen Foxall... 117

    Ruth Tetlow 123

    Andrew Smith 129

    Peter Rookes 132

Chapter 3   A Review of the Dialogues, Perceptions and
            Responses.. 139

PART III
Chapter 4   My personal journey; 169
            Reflections on my interfaith Journey;
            A Christian Context: God, Jesus and love;
            a Christian theology for inter faith Britain

PART IV
Chapter 5   Challenges to Christianity:..227

PART V
Chapter 6   Ways Forward...253
Chapter 7   Hopes for the Future: concluding summary in
            ten challenges..301

Questions from each chapter...315
Epilogue..323
Bibliography 329

THE CONTRIBUTORS

From left to right Muhammad Amin-Evans, Jyoti Patel, Ruth Tetlow, Andrew Smith, Pyara Singh Bhogal, Peter Rookes, Margaret Jacobi, Maureen Foxall, Jo Mason, Richard Tetlow, Sinhavacin Walsh

The Faith Contributors

Jyoti Patel	Hindu
Margaret Jacobi, Rabbi Dr.	Jewish
Pyara Singh Bhogal, Dr.	Sikh
Muhammad Amin-Evans, Shayk	Muslim
Sinhavacin Walsh, Dh.	Buddhist

The Christian Respondents

Josephine Mason, the Revd..

Ruth Tetlow,

Maureen Foxall, the Revd.

Andrew Smith, Dr.

Peter Rookes, Dr.

Notes to the Reader

Disclaimer: Every article by the ten contributors to this book has been written without any knowledge of the writing of any other article. Responsibility rests entirely with each contributor and the author. Questions of agreement or disagreement have not been relevant. Personal experience, response, and comment have been paramount.

In compiling this book, there have naturally been issues with generalisations and definitions. The words *Christian*, *Christianity*, and *Church* have been used with both separate and the same interchangeable meaning. I recognise this will rouse queries. There are evident questions as to my choice of priorities. It might well be asked, just to whom and to what am I referring, and where and what is the evidence? I hope I have given more than adequate evidence for a book that is not meant as an academic treatise. (I am no academic). I have had to take shortcuts with such a potentially large topic. Repetition has sometimes been appropriate but kept to a minimum.

Explanations

Contributors' conditions: The writers have only their own authority. Their views do not necessarily reflect those of the other contributors or those of their own faith 'councils'. The views of all the contributors, including those of the author, are their own and contributed entirely separately.

Italics: These are used for editorial commentary on what follows in the chapter's preamble, and by the ten contributors to introduce themselves; for the titles of books, for the abbreviated title of the book as *Perceptions* and occasionally for emphasis.

Word usage: The words *inter* and *faith* are used both separately *and* together depending on the contextual emphasis of their relationship. Inter is not a word in its own right – until now, except that it is used by the Inter Faith Network for the UK.

Bible references: The names Matthew, Mark, Luke and John are references to the New Testament according to their respective Gospels. All Bible quotations are from the New Revised Standard Version (NRSV), unless stated otherwise. The description *general* indicates a famous biblical passage recognised in all versions. The numbers indicate chapter and verse. They are put directly into the text when very much part of the meaning.

Figures, Statistics and Dates: This book has been with me for 5 years. I have done what I can to keep up to date. I apologize for where I have failed in this but life out there can move quicker than my reactions.

Definitions

Usages in this book come from a combination of sources:

- *Belief:* A belief is a principle or tenet of a religion or a Faith. As a verb, as in *I believe*, it means acceptance of specific meaning and terms of a religion/Faith. Belief is usually interchangeable with Faith: their Hebrew root, *aman*, is the same, as it is in the Greek scriptures, *pistis*, for both the noun and the verb. However, they have connotations of their own from usage such as when translated as trust/confidence and associated with another meaning. Flexibility would seem acceptable. For this book, faith is a way of life, religious and non-religious; belief is more specific to an idea or fact or assumed fact of life.

- *Christianity:* Many people use the name interchangeably with 'the Church', 'the British Church' or 'churches'. For example, some of the contributors have used the name Christianity when they mean the Church and generalized about both when, clearly, they are both extremely diverse. It may be known only through a particular church or a particular person or just a catch-phrase, especially in the case of people of different faiths. It may be symbolised by the church building. I generally use it as the name for the religion built on the love of Jesus Christ.

- *The Church:* is the Christian institution founded in the name of God, Jesus Christ and the Holy Spirit.

- A *faith* in modern and present usage can be a trust, a belief, or a religion with emphasis on identity, behaviour, and way of life. It can also indicate a garment or artery of identity.

- A *religion* is the spiritual, devotional, institutional and organisational means through which people practise their faith. It binds together the traditions, dogmas and beliefs of its members.

- *The relevant different major world faiths* are Buddhism, Christianity, Hinduism (not strictly a faith), Islam, Judaism and Sikhism (the original six of the Inter Faith Network for the UK). Usually in this book I do not distinguish one faith from another by their differences or their similarities. Though both are considerable they are usually secondary here. The faith contributors write from their own separate faith experience and knowledge.

ERRATA significant amendments

by page, paragraph and line

25 2 11/14   The Brexit vote ,   , was won by just ....

92.3.9   Logos to the Muslim means 'the Word of God' not 'the way of living'.

174 2 6   a truly beautiful setting for enhanced worship, musical pursuits and adult interfaith and children's educational interfaith activities - see Ch 2 pp108/9pp, 'Educating for Interfaith awareness' - which Ladywood people could be proud of. ....It included...

237 3 2   the power of words can be. 'You are from your father the devil' (NRSV., New Revised Standard Version). Such words.....

276. 4/5   that work well together. 'Footsteps: faiths for a low carbon future', is a Birmingham interfaith support group that stemmed from the Paris global warming coalition in November 2015. Christian Aid, Islamic Relief and Muslim Aid are national organisations with bases and/or roots in Birmingham which work co-operatively with similar goals. 'Faiths for Fun'

276. 3.2-4 in 2005[29] .Yet many still go it alone and Councils of Churches have declined in strength. And how many..........places of worship?.

304 2 5   In my understanding, most people from English and 'overseas' backgrounds, are slowly learning to accept, respect and appreciate one another just as human beings; and this despite the unravelling of the Caribbean ship Windrush scandal, 2017/8., which was not a faith issue. At least, I like to think so. Before attitudes .....   PTO

310 2 11-16.......of good faith. ...We might encourage one another in the cause of a new and renewed mindset, paradigm, way of life, not to be constantly ....might be; instead, aiming to put the love ethic, commandment and experience into practice by trying to understand why people might be violent and extremist - and the opposite. In my language – maybe not yours, but our basic understanding may be similar- to put God first. This is primarily........

312.1.1/2   through loving human partnerships. Sacrifice to varying degrees as a possible ingredient of our incarnation in the name of the cross of Jesus is an age-old Christian aspiration that began with Jesus. We may all...

327.1.5/6.... not the same. We have our own stories as individuals and people of whatever -hopefully- good faith, religious and non-religious. It is our responsibility to choose how we use them for the benefit of the present and, as far as we can, the future. Technological and climate changes have already created a world revolution, a new context for humanity, essential priorities on a personal and community level that await urgent application.

.

Foreword – Risk and Gift

This book has been many years in the making and it represents the fruit of the author's Christian engagement with people of different faiths, five in all – Jew, Muslim, Hindu, Sikh and Buddhist. It is written from the experience of encounter, friendship, dialogue and collaboration in the UK's second largest city, Birmingham. It is informed by deep and generous compassion.

The book can also be imagined as a theological and dialogical experiment, conducted with integrity and vulnerability in respect of self-awareness, openness and honesty about the kind of Christianity that has inspired it. Integrity leads the author to lay before the reader his own Christian assumptions, struggles, aspirations and the meanings he attaches to Christian ideas. Vulnerability takes the reader to the heart of the experiment which was, firstly, to invite five people independently from his chosen traditions to reflect on their experience and reception of Christian faith, people and churches; and secondly, to invite five Christian respondents to react independently to the accounts they were given to read. And then the author would distil from the results what was to be learned for himself and for the churches. We learn, it is often said, through experience, reflection and interaction with others. These necessarily overlapping processes are deeply embedded in this book and it is one of its strengths.

For the author Christian integrity and solidarity with people of different faiths are two sides of the same coin. This has been his ministerial lifetime's revelation. If such dual yoking is thought to be an unusual prospect by the reader, then the journey reflected in these pages will be both intriguing and challenging. Inviting the gaze of co-religionist friends on matters one holds dear involves both risk and gift. The author set out in risk but received in return a gift. At least it is possible to read these pages that way.

In 1990, the American publishers, Orbis Press, published an academic book of essays by Jewish, Muslim, Hindu and Buddhist scholars reflecting on Christian faith, entitled *Christianity Through Non-Christian Eyes*[1], and compiled by an American Christian theologian, Paul Griffiths. The aim was to facilitate better understanding between Christians and reflectors from these four other traditions. Griffiths is himself no pluralist-inclined theologian, but he nevertheless saw the need to counter the 'stereotyped images' we have of one another in order to clear the deck for a more honest dialogue about the meaning of faith itself and the impact of religious plurality in our world. The present book, based on a committed journey of patient reaching across cultural and religious divides in one English city, represents a twenty-first century people-centred counterpoise to that scholarly volume from 1990. The/Its author's openness to those who are different and his determination to face theological questions as a result of the encounters helps to span the other divide too, that between a detached scholarly discussion and the lived experience of people struggling to make sense of past traditions in the light of present new realities.

A central principle in interfaith dialogue circles is that there is no substitute for people actually meeting one another – sharing stories, histories and perspectives, listening to hurt, anger and pain, seeking to see the world as others see it. Without this real meeting and seeing, interfaith relationships are unlikely to bear fruit. Yet real seeing often seems virtually impossible. We all have what might be called interfaith baggage – colonial baggage, name-calling baggage, basic prejudice, wilful misrepresentation of that which is different, and even scriptural sanction for violence. And often we also like to hold on to our victimhood.

This book represents a bold step in the direction of real seeing. It follows the instinct and the hope that opening oneself up to seeing and hearing what others see and think about oneself, one's community, and the truths that are often unexamined – without holds barred but in respect – leads to a different future. Others' perceptions of us will inevitably contain not only some home truths worth noting but also misrepresentations – whether of historical happenings, intellectual achievements or spiritual perceptions that reside near the centre of those home truths. The good and the bad, the wholesome and the inaccurate, then become the stuff of dialogue. And dialogue changes lives, thus holding out the possibilities of a different future. So, this book believes.

There is no returning to an imagined golden age of isolationist living – in spite of political calls to pull back behind nation-state lines or of religious calls to believe that an 'in group - out group' mentality is inevitably how history has somehow been designed. When it comes to imagining what 'God' (to speak theistically) has been 'up to' through earthly time and space we have seen the need to move beyond the confrontational stance defined by 'othering' processes. Some writers in the literature have even expressed this provocatively as yielding a choice between 'death or dialogue'.[2]

Interfaith dialogue summons us towards a vision of the spiritual presence in others outside our own bounded walls. Whether we share in practical action, in religious experience, in intellectual enquiry, or simply in personal friendships, interreligious dialogue is here to stay and it heralds the next stage in what it means to live out of religious conviction. We are rapidly reaching the evolutionary time when we realise that 'I cannot be who I am without the other'. This book recognises the summons within that conviction. It is also wonderfully honest about the change in theological outlook that will be necessary if we really are going to take it to heart.

Alan Race

Notes

1   Paul J. Griffiths, *Christianity Through Non-Christian Eyes*, Maryknoll: Orbis Books, 1990.

2   Leonard Swidler, John B. Cobb Jr., Paul F, Knitter, Monika Hellwig, *Death or Dialogue?: From the Age of Monologue to the Age of Dialogue*, London: SCM Press, Philadelphia, Trinity Press International, 1990.

Alan Race is a recognised author in the Christian theology of religions and his classic book Christians and Religious Pluralism (SCM, 1983) framed the discussion of this theology for three decades and more. He has also been active in movements for interfaith dialogue, being currently the Chair and journal editor for the World Congress of Faiths. His life's work over 40 years of Christian ordination has combined theological education in church and university settings with parish pastoral practice. He is known internationally and has addressed numerous conferences around the world concerned with theology and dialogue, including at the Parliament of the World's Religions. A volume of critical and appreciative essays discussing his work was produced as *Twenty-First Century Theologies of Religions* (Brill, 2016). His own most recent book is *Making Sense of Religious Pluralism* (2013), which was produced as part of a *Modern Church Series* in liberal theology.

PART I

INTRODUCTION 1

Content

What the book is all about; five hopes; interfaith relationships; a political context; the Church's response; Christians living and working with different faiths; Christianity in Britain; the Christian Church in Britain; a theological background; on being Christian.

The core of this book is the perceptions of Christianity from five people each of different faiths and responses to them from five Christians. It formed from a seed, long germinating in my mind. I had progressively realised how much our human relationships arise from our perceptions of others; then how our perceptions can mature into learning and from there into mutual relationships and friendship worthy of one another and of our innate calling to live happily together. In this new, transformed, fraught and ever-needy world of the 21st century, that is to look on the bright side; we all know there is a dark side too. People of faith particularly, religious and non-religious, naturally live within this context like everyone else. Those who feel they have no faith at all are especially welcome to join the discussion and explore what are perhaps to them different ideas of Christianity and of faith generally. One key to this welcome aim is that we have willingness to listen to one another; then we can learn about ourselves from others as well as about others. Another key is that we learn to interpret, question and trust our experience of what really matters and discuss it with others. Increased positive and mutual relationships between people of different faiths are my vision and hope. A third is that we recognize that the world is one world, its people are all one and the natural environment is all one too.

This book is a combined effort to explore this ambition. It lays on the table ten perceptions and my own reflections as the focus of a work in process as new relationships always are. You, welcome reader, may find unclear argument and unproven statement: I trust not too much and that my main points will be clear to you. I have constantly revised my own input over several years because I have constantly developed the issues broached, for they are not by nature fixed or water-tight. I hope the book will release discussion and commitment as to how Christianity, the major faiths and any good faith might work together in trust and friendship for the common good. I enthusiastically acknowledge the rapid increase in inter faith discussions around the country since the Millennium.

I am a life- long church-going Christian and I love the Church - on the whole. I became ordained thirty-five years ago, which was about half-way through my life so far. I was soon – as I had never dreamt - to become an Anglican inner-city vicar living and working in Ladywood, Birmingham. I retired in 2008 and now still live in Birmingham but alongside people of different faith in the mixed- faith area of Moseley. I have always believed in God, that is, in my understanding of God.

I trust Christianity as a faith and a vast community blessing rather than a belief system. Its heart to me is, in the 'the greatest' Judaeo-Christian commandment, according to Jesus as St Matthew

4

records, Chapter 22.37 -39, 'to love God and to love our neighbours as ourselves'. I'm not convinced that this message gets across to most people. I therefore feel that the eternal genius of Jesus and indeed, of the Christian faith is, to a degree, wasted. I have friends within the Christian family who feel similarly. I sense there are even more people outside Christianity who share such feelings and have their own private faith, parallel to loyal Christians, and who feel angry and disenchanted about apparent Christian beliefs and present priorities. My experience is that Christian priorities are just not made clear to everyone and so multitudes miss out. That is very dissatisfying to me and maybe to you.

Such experience of Christianity led me to ask how I might write about this situation, share a few ideas and offer a few suggestions. I hold very dear the concept of the unity of body, mind and soul in relation to my life-beliefs and faith. Behind that unity I wish to perceive a rational basis for myself and others. There is far more rationality in life than we may allow for, even though our judgment may be faulty. In common-or-garden terms, my beliefs and faith and consequently responses to the above situation for me have to 'make sense'. I wish the same for Christianity and fellow Christians and their beliefs and faith particularly in communication with outsiders. (Granted the issues of definition and degree but they are for another time). I wanted my approach to be empirical in unwrapping and describing evidence and then finding a way forward to address it and follow-up with my reaction, questions, naming of possible causes and obstacles and hopes for the future. In mid-2015 I asked colleagues of different world faiths in Birmingham, of whom I knew a good number, how they see Christianity and to 'write it down'. That was rather a big canvas but I felt the Church would benefit from listening to new voices. This process took over two years. It has not been the usual way to ask people of other faiths for their opinion about Christianity rather than tell them our opinion - as Christians - of them. Crucially, it has not been to toy with the facts, you are you, Jesus was Jesus and I am writing this now, whatever perceptions we have or ourselves or others.

It was an unusual way forward to seek the experience and perceptions of these five people of different religious faith in Britain, Sikhism, Judaism, Islam, Hinduism and Buddhism, and then responses to their writing from five Christians. Thankfully, they all agreed. We shared a geographical focus because all ten, equal men and women, plus me, were living and engaged in interfaith activity in Birmingham. Naturally, another ten would be likely to very different experience and perceptions. That is the fascination of perceptions which raises the question, Why? Naturally, they could not be representative but I thought we might set a ball rolling even with our limited resources and experience. Hence this book. I've never written one before. Their ten articles make Chapters 1 and 2, and my review of them, Chapter 3.

Faith questions are not just out there but within us. Why do I have my perceptions of Christianity? Why do you? To give such questions authentic flesh and blood, I therefore relate them to my own experience of interfaith relationships and my own life story. The personal is inescapable; in a sense the world is personal. I am questioning of present-day Christianity but I aim to be informed and positive as well as critical. I trust that this Project might encourage us to aim to 'to see ourselves as others see us' with all our human differences and opinions. It further hopes that this might contribute to transformation of ourselves, our interfaith relationships - whether in reality or just in mind - our Faiths and thence of our society. At this early stage I invite you to engage with these initial five hopes that came to me shortly after reading both Perceptions and Responses.

Five Hopes

Firstly, that Christians will be encouraged to listen and, however challenged, take a fresh look at themselves, through the eyes and minds of others of different faith while taking heart that people's perceptions of others can vary greatly;

secondly, that Christians will foster mutual meeting and discussion with those of different religious faiths, the secular world and non-churchgoers on the basis that we are all equal before God;

thirdly, that the Christian church will bless good interfaith relationships through seeing people eye- to-eye, sharing personal trust and engaging in theological discussion with people of different faith;

fourthly, that it will show those of faith outside religious institutions and all those who have positive hopes for the common good, national and international, that we can live and work together for mutual benefit, with due recognition of the partnership so essential between body, mind and soul incorporating reason, emotion and spirit;

fifthly, that rivalry of faiths and surrender to human impulses of power and control are no longer a viable option for peaceful survival, for the book rests on the contrasting human instinctual imperative, necessarily backed up by the Judaeo-Christian duty, of loving other people as ourselves and the risks of not doing so.

Interfaith relationships

First, about perceptions of human relationships in general. See Introduction 2. They are, to an extent, a matter of personal choice. We bear some responsibility for them. But intellectual questions about perceptions may not get to the heart of any matter and actually be of any service to society unless their wider context is faced. I attempt therefore to explore the make-up of perceptions and give them context of how and why, and how they might be of symbolic value. They all have their contexts and meaning. Experience clearly requires analysis and learning if it is to be widely beneficial. People's perceptions and experience - including my own - can all be questioned and deemed positive and/or negative. As a personal offering, for me the most profound context is a dimension of mystery and meaning, love, beauty and holiness, conscience and vision that enlightens and empowers me and all of us whatever our faith or belief and somehow, maybe, actually creates us extraordinary human beings in the first place. I could call it 'God' but the name is less vital to me than the reality.

Many such thoughts are relevant to inter faith relationships. This book is about such relationships in Britain between Christians and people of different faith, including those who are religious but also those who are non-religious. It is also about hope for the future of Christianity in Britain amongst such faiths. The contributors' perceptions which range from the psycho-social to the theological from past and present are a guide. They all have connections and context that throw light on their background and on questions of What and why? What are *your* perceptions of say, cricket, ants, God, Muslims, the stars, child abusers, brass bands, immigrants and porridge? Why? And by what definition and on whose understanding? And who says? Our perceptions all have their contexts.

Inter faith relationships in Britain have a specific context. On the one hand, there are the major world faiths and their members, firmly established. On the other hand, there are the Christian churches within Britain's multi-faith society numerically a mixed picture of rise and fall in numbers and of loyalty, devotion and service to the community. Over half of Britain's population say they have no religion[1] at all.

Inter faith relationships were, until lately, relatively rare, as rare in the cities as they are now in some British towns and country areas. Growing up in the late 40s and then 50s and 60s I personally knew no Muslims, Hindus or Sikhs until the 1980s, not even in the inner city of London where I had lived in the 60-70s. Now, in the second decade of the Millennium, 15-20% of the population of Birmingham has become Muslim. In many cases, such growth is a product of past British Empire days and the migration of the last 50 or so years that in part defines globalisation. They are now part of everyone's general context in Britain. We cannot now avoid being affected particularly at home and away by the society in which we live. Its internet-driven communication revolution sees to that. We have the choice to ignore, to deny, to scorn or - actually - to appreciate and enjoy. The different faiths in Britain now are not going to go away. We are interdependent in all manner of ways with one another, giving and receiving.

Internationally, inter faith relationships are implicated inevitably in a vast array of modern realities, for example, the world wide web, slavery, climate change, nuclear armament, forced migration and cyber and military warfare. The Faiths, religious and otherwise can shut their doors and minds to such influences. That would be irresponsible and delusional. Our media will probably see to that anyway wherever we live, whether we like it or not. Are we to assume attitudes of

Global Morality or Immorality? We may be dominated to whatever degree and combination by joy or despair, trust of fear, or terrorism, poverty or wealth, education or ignorance, by climate change or denial, smooth democracy or political divisiveness, by Facebook, the dangerous nonsense of fake-news or fake-truth, fantasy or reality, family strife or harmony, inequality or fairness. That is a huge perhaps overwhelming list, but it is where we are. Historical and social events and issues that continued or began yesterday can have extraordinary effect on the local and personal and so potentially on everyone, whatever their faith.

The question for the Faiths is how far they seek to recognise and identify with influences about them and how they act for themselves, for each other and for society as a whole. Such decisions are their responsibility to their faith, in Christians' specific case to Christianity. Primarily, behind everything the questions are: what about God? And, what about the small question of the future of humankind? Here are three snapshots of British society amidst local and international influences. Their significance here is religious and social as well as political.

The Brexit referendum in June 2016 saw an appalling indictment of the faiths, apart from anyone else, in their lack of willingness to raise the tone of the debate while not necessarily favouring one side or the other in terms of peaceful and co-operative relationships so basic to the future of humankind. The Revd Keith Clements, Baptist minister and past General Secretary of the European Council of Churches has written angrily about what the churches failed to do together, 'Surely the church leadership, as loudly and clearly as possible, could have…. challenged the superficiality, opportunistic self-centeredness and untruthfulness of much of the public debate.'[2] This confirmed his grave disappointment at the collapse of ecumenism since the early 1990s. It is worth conjecturing whether inter faith relationships have displaced ecumenical relationships as Christian priorities. That no doubt depends on geographical and social context.

The London Grenfell Tower fire in June 2017 was an dreadful tragedy. It highlighted Britain's increasingly gross inequality and a dismissive Local Authority bureaucracy but also the presence of the Church which provided refuge for burnt-out residents and a multi-faith population - many of them recent immigrants, who showed great generosity and neighbourly love. Negative injustice, untruth and suffering became positive love, compassion and partnership from different faiths. It was simultaneous with the night-day horror, as I understand from a previous Methodist minister of the vicinity, that the ultimate value of love and human presence in suffering was experienced by some in scenes of unspeakable grief and horror.

Adverse effect on Muslim loyalty to Britain, the institution of Christianity and therefore on inter faith relationships has often resulted from recent political causes. The British and American invasion of Iraq in 2003 and the killing of thousands of Iraqis estimated as nearly 200, 000, more than 70% civilian, by the Costs of War Project (more than doubled by some estimates) and then of Afghanistan have had strong negative effect on some Muslims I know in Birmingham, besides invoking natural sympathy. After World War One, a hundred years ago, Britain indulged in sharing a carve -up of the Middle East to its own dubious advantage. Traumatic memories of loss, pain, violence, discrimination and selfishness frequently live on in human individual and community psyches across generations and, indeed, centuries.

Wisdom and commitment lie in the Faiths' choice as to where they can best contribute separately and together for the common good. In this book I look forward to times when the churches work together not just with themselves - historically and ecumenically proved hard enough - but with the different faiths and our whole society. A common claim at present, 2016–17, is that Britain has lost its bearings and a dangerous vacuum is developing through collapse of the old religious and meta political narratives.

Before being more positive with a Christian and interfaith response I want to reiterate, inevitably very subjectively in this context, the alarming but always perversely hopeful situation of British society - incorporating the faiths - in its world context in this second decade of the 21st century. In our internet age it is far from irrelevant and needs further emphasis on a second front.

A political context

Changes through globalisation mean that our world and all of us have now become interconnected and interdependent on a phenomenal scale more than ever before. This is not least in our standards, expectations, morality, way of life, relationships and our whole being. This new global society is no less value-free than our political contexts. Politics and economics are inescapable because they are inseparable from human operators with the personalities, tensions and rivalries, individually and corporately, that we all share. President Trump has already quashed any doubt of that. Human judgements, conflicts, decisions and relationships are woven into its creation and survival. Perceptions of it vary hugely; none of us are bystanders. We all play a part opting in or out, whether for humanity's practical goodness or evil, creativity or destruction and ultimately whether for life-giving or life-taking. The multitude of people's beliefs in this global world interact with the world's condition to which the British have long contributed. Feed rampant racism into islamophobia, far-right extremism - developing fast in Europe post- Brexit - violent extremism and despair then one desperation magnifies another.

British society is at a cross roads, politically, socially, morally and spiritually. So much has become apparent since the Brexit vote in June 2016. It was clear in November 2016 when the Daily Mail crashed over the fences of decent journalism by declaring three judges of a parliamentary situation, 'Enemies of the People'. It has been clear from the weekly BBC TV programme, 'Question Time' which often now hardly keeps the Queen's peace. The barbaric actions of the Islamic violent extremists of IS(is) and Syrian President Assad are a shocking, all-embracing, international context. So-called faiths are not irrelevant. TV programmes featuring unregulated barbaric human slaughter particularly of civilian adults and children in Aleppo and Eastern Ghouta symbolised overwhelming need for reconciliation and transformation in the face of traumatic human suffering.

This picture suggests a perilous brink of a volcano on which humankind is perched. Climate Change adds to the human problems. We know this 21st century is different from all previous generations because of its extraordinary powers of communication of body, mind and spirit through the internet. We may still have a chance to stay on the safe side of the brink, narrow though it may be. The choice to work with God and one another, or not, remains in human hands.

I feel need of a cheerful note. Does civilization/humanity progress? Yes and no. It depends on one's criteria. There are New Optimists such as economists/philosophers Stephen Pinker and John Norber.[3] According to the United Nations Millennium Development Goals, achievements since 2000 include massive improvement in young lives around the world from prevention of poverty. That is one symbolic reason for taking heart enough to do what we can. Points of no return are reached but hope on, God is still with us. Something must be done to confront international crises. Whatever that is, must surely be inclusive of others. Very fortunately, Britain has copious blessings and opportunities and we are not in war-ridden Syria.

This book is focussed on experience of just one city, Birmingham, Britain's second city and sticks to that without wide academic surveys beyond. This enhances as well as limits its credibility. To some Brummies and outsiders - the old name for Birmingham was Brummagen – the city itself is generally, despite its difficulties, a beacon of British social cohesion and good interfaith relationships. Grievously and increasingly since 2010, government cuts have curtailed the city council's already difficult task of interfaith support work otherwise advanced through Birmingham's faith members and faith leaders, many places of worship, innumerable groups and the new West Midlands mayor. Simple day-to-day life may be the natural glue to interfaith relationships. Despite its limitations, I think it is fair to suggest that Birmingham accepts a national role of being a touchstone for good efforts at inter faith relationships. I acknowledge the likelihood of comparable work in other cities each of which has its specific contexts on which to work.

The Church's response

Christianity's subject has always been new life, new Spirit, new ways of seeing one another as equally important before God. Christian responsibility, individually and corporately is a gift. Christianity has a mixed public history but together with different faiths it could accelerate its contribution to renewed national well-being considering its wide resources.

It is an empirical matter how we apply our observation and experience, combined with our traditional Christian heritage, to make the dramatic choice between life and death in these matters political, both local and global. It is we human beings who make such decisions, not lifeless farming machinery nor God. So, I seek out what are some perceptions of some Christians/the British Church/ churches of this overall situation? How best can it/they respond? And where do the major world faiths fit in? This may feel like a new issue for each new generation, but the ancient Jews knew it from the Hebrew Bible, recorded in the book of Deuteronomy. In verse 30.1ff, the proposition of God, surmised by the writer is that humankind must choose between life and death. The political context is no more escapable in our century than it has ever been since the 8-7th century BCE Jewish prophets in middle-eastern Judah. We should take heart, because reformation has always signalled change in need, struggle and development. A ditty I have adapted reminds me:

When from the garden, they had to leave,

To her partner, it was said by Eve,

We must realise, my dear, that we must arrange

For what is now about to change.

In seeking from the outset to discover how best the British Church is to respond, I have consulted with Christian people, who are the Church and actually part of what is called 'the body of Christ', about our priorities of life and faith in the face of this new world and Britain's present unease. To that end I am relaying my experience of those who do not accept the institutional label of Christianity with what some see as its outdated and meaningless theology but still recognise and stand by the moral principles of a Christian way of life even if they feel they cannot name them in religious terms. I have confidence that Christianity and so many people could be far more effective than they seem to be at present. We all live together and have different contexts, language and responsibilities. British society needs our moral, spiritual and community framework. Most essentially, it is my experience that such transformation has to be a corporate desire and action which re-establishes society from below rather than imposed from above. The time for the opposite has passed however appropriate or otherwise it might once have been through Church or State.

I, myself am part of the Church's response, however unofficial. You may be too. Before you might wonder, I, the author am a Christian, an ordained one, a strong believer in the Church, a critic of Church and Christian priorities and a lifelong church-goer. To encourage you, the reader, to look with your eyes at possible contexts of the Perceptions and Responses and hopes that follow and perhaps at your own contexts and hopes too for such issues, I offer, as personal context, some flesh and blood from my own life story, reality and experience of life as a Christian and what I consider to be God. Much of it is focussed in chapter 4. My faith is based on its two-way partnership with my experience of life. With the exception of a short period in the United Reformed Church my faith experience is mostly from the Anglican Church of England, amongst over 300 others, Britain's largest denomination. Primarily, I hope to interest those who have any commitment in building bridges between us all and those who may have faith in the inclusive abundance of Life, non-religious as well as religious.

As catalyst to this discussion I provide introduction, analysis and comment that arise from the evidence, particularly about perceptions. I also ask questions. Jesus asked 307 questions in the Gospels and was asked 183, to which he gave only three direct answers amid indirect replies! Some bright spark may have asked him why he always asked questions. There is quite a tension in life, emotionally and intellectually, individually and corporately. between certainty and uncertainty, even about asking questions at all and certainly about faith and the different faiths! In this book we live with the tension: questions imply and suggest need for ways forward. I hope my questions will encourage non-Christian people of different faith, religious and otherwise, to speak out confidently about how they see Christianity in our rapidly developing new 21st century context.

So do many young people by nature. Hope, as I understand it, has to be in their capacity for questioning, (why do you keep saying 'Right, Grandpa'?); endless questioning, whys, purposes and selfies, histogram likes, exam grades, money, identity and status. Adults too often fail to encourage and get the best out of them - and one another. Church/ worship communities are an endless source of identity, comfort, reassurance that all their young people are loved and of the same inherent value, not in being the same but in being courageously themselves. Their potential for forging exciting and natural interfaith relationship is enormous.

I hope my questions will encourage personal seeking as to why, psychologically, we see and believe religion as we do or not, ours as well as that of others. What is going on inside us regarding our faith or lack of it? I attempt in Chapter 4 to let you into my own self. I see my role partly too as offering observations. An observation then on experience for it is naturally subject to perception and all of us can get it horribly wrong over any matter, light or serious.; maybe that is a common characteristic of passionate youthfulness and convinced emotion that can extend throughout our lives. I have ranked experience very highly, especially on the road to trusting myself and therefore readily trusting others. This book testifies to the cry 'Here I stand, I can do no other'. 'Experience' can signify anything from single to lifelong experience of body, mind and spirit all in one. Like most good gifts though, that is dodgy and religious experience can be even more dodgy, especially if sexuality is involved. When labelled 'conversion', especially 'necessary conversion' we do have to watch it. How do we trust ourselves and others on that score, not least, say, when a prevalent atmosphere is of group positivity to be 'born again' and potential wrath and disillusionment are spiritually destructive. In a sense, I fell for it myself, twice, with no regrets at all, the opposite, as I clarify later. I imagine evangelist, Billy Graham, learnt to be wise to the problem despite or because of his passion for 'new life'. I emphasize here it is a universal gift. Risk inevitably goes with it.

As for my own involvement in interfaith life, since my inspiring university days, from which I distilled 'alternative views' of Christianity, I have increasingly identified with British multi-faith, progressive Christianity movement as a real hope for Britain. Jesus and Christianity have, in my mind, stayed firm but traditional orthodox Christianity ceased in small but very significant ways to work for me over my later years of being a vicar - a life I loved. What the ten contributors have written here has increased my own inter faith understanding and my faith in the essence of Christianity in Britain and therefore their relevance and value. The personal integrity of each of them enabled by increasing trust played a large part in our corporate vision and hope.

Christians living and working with different faiths

The foregoing picture has given an overall context of the book, of the contributors and of me. Within this context comes the question for Christians and the adherents to other major world faiths as to whether and how they are going to live and work together in order to contribute to the well-being of one another, everybody else and all God's creation and also give succour to reconciling the situation above. Once the questions and challenges are clear, resulting organisation and authority became the difficult issues with which to grapple.

While twenty-first-century world issues spell danger for everyone, each nation has varied responsibility to address whatever issue it chooses, to whatever degree it can. Similarly, every faith, in conjunction with and separate from the nation, has its own part to play according to its own specific givens. Every faith community has its own priorities at different times such as, since 2016, leaders in multifaith areas passionately seeking harmony together in an increasingly divided society. Every person of faith has responsibilities too. S/he may have special knowledge, expertise, and experience, negative and positive of inter faith relationships. Individual responsibility is to be shared within the social context of community, faith and nation, with full recognition of those with faith and principle but who are not Christian or religious by label. Difference of opinion, in a sense, is irrelevant. The human issue is mutual acceptance and willingness to learn from another.

Wherein lies current and ongoing responsibility for the Christian and for Christianity, for people of the different world faiths and for those of secular faith? In Britain, Christians have to choose which responsibilities, corporate and individual, are, in their terms, God-given. Christianity remains the dominant faith, despite its increasing institutional difficulties. Interfaith relationships in today's world are naturally Christians' business, as they are also the business of those of the other faiths. *Perceptions* has grown out of the need to take that responsibility to heart. It has developed within the context of the assets, snares and sheer reality of growing cultural and human globalisation and debate as to whether life is getting better or worse. What do you think? How would you judge? Are you hopeful or not and why? Members of different faiths themselves cannot be separated from their own personal givens and wider contexts, but they are not wholly controlled by them. Our contributors have naturally had different experience of Christianity from one another, just as Christians do whether they number twelve or five thousand. To the surprise of some devotees, for two thousand years this has been nothing new. Human beings have always been no less, human beings.

Good, just and generous relationships between faith-members do not come vacuum-packed. They are likely to be found - at least in attitude - in a much larger package of our generally good relationships with God, our neighbour and the natural world and ourselves - our perceptions can be as much a survey map of ourselves as of other people. We need our own compass. Our future is always ours. Christians and the Church have frequently shown responsibility to play their part in recognising need and seeking new life for each generation. Members of the other faiths probably no less so, but this book is primarily about Christianity and for Christians. I aim to convey my critical belief in the Church and Christianity's working in mutual partnership with the other world faiths, essential enablers of something recognisable as 'the kingdom of God' and discovering the power of God and Jesus through friendship, creativity and justice, as well as traditional stability and continuity,

In my experience, there has not been enough discussion in society about the part played by religious faith in our potential to rise above the magnetic selfish discussion of similarity, diversity and excessive individualism. Customary education does not seem to teach how to argue creatively with appropriate emotion and thought. I lament what has recently been called the jettisoning of European's Christian heritage, the 'We-don't-do-God'[4] mentality, with nothing to replace it save the religion of human rights[5], so-called 'British values' and re-established traditions despite their due importance. I recognise the extraordinary interdependence of our existence within the tapestry of our society and societies and how if two or three threads are snagged, all may unravel.

Living in harmony entails the embracing of different world faiths, and especially their theology, as neighbours, sisters and brothers based on the love of God and of our neighbour as ourselves. For me it has its own fulfilling benefit for everyone. This is not to suggest agreement or disagreement over doctrinal matters, which are often on the back of a context of past and present relationships. My most important question about faith relationships is whether it is acceptable, ever acceptable, or ever has been acceptable, to exclude anyone from such love, whether in practice or in theory, or according to religious or personal faith or theology. I recognise that practicalities and personal preferences force our hands and voices. The problem of exclusion of those who exclude is a challenge to mind and practice, but it is not for here. It is not so easy. I run the risk, like any outspoken thinker, of excluding through the themes of this book those with whom I do not agree or giving that impression. I can only say that is not my intention. Within twenty-four hours last week, in Birmingham and Oxford, I was told by two strangers that if I did not believe what I was being told that, sorry, I would 'go to hell'. I know that receiving or exerting pressure to believe and exclude is overwhelming on and for vulnerable spirits, but isn't that spiritual abuse? I don't always know when to draw the line, say with Scientology.

Christianity in Britain

Central to this book, positively and negatively, is Christianity? What is it? It's a nigh impossible question for anyone to answer simply and conclusively. It is a fair question which clergy- probably with different opinions - at least should be able to answer. To begin with, some would take it as synonymous with the Church, in our case the British Church which some would say is only one aspect of a whole faith. Most simply Christianity is the religion/faith of Christians. For Christians, all people, events and situations are said to be God-bearers, carrying the gift and call of God and the sacrament of the present moment. In Chapter 4, I offer something of my own experience, my own understanding of Christianity and my lifelong journey of joy, fulfilment and frustration with the Christian Church, brought sharply into focus by my developing interfaith relationships. Christianity and our whole world always faces death and new life; that is the human condition, different in detail in every age. The Catholic Church's promotion of interreligious dialogue marks a new life.[6] So does the 2018 Lenten Study Course of the 1701 missionary society, USPG in writing Christianity is about relationships rather than rules'[6a]

Through globalisation, the world has now become, say, in the last two decades, truly one on a scale that would have been inconceivable even to Jesus, who, according to the record of John[7] more than two thousand years ago, spoke of humanity's oneness in God. 21st century Christianity and Britain cannot be understood without reference to past, present and possible future relationships, along with the acceptance of the reality of their interdependence with the different world faiths and the wide world, secular and religious. Everything, in difference and similarity, is interdependent with God. Christians themselves have had and continue to have radically different opinions and convictions about Christianity

God, Jesus and Love are at heart the basis and raison d'etre of Christianity. The Judaeo-Christian 'greatest commandment in the law' endorsed by Jesus and Christian worship is 'to love…. God …and love and your neighbour as yourself'[7]. I believe the human need and purpose is just that too, to love God and to love our neighbour as ourselves. Updating the Trinity, I consider Christianity to be based on the threefold faith that God is love and that he loves all creation and all humanity, that Jesus Christ demonstrates God's love in all its human fullness and that all people have the gift of the Spirit of God[8]. Infinite contexts determine the expression and application of that love in goodness. Love however, remains the universal gift and the need and command of natural law. My faith is in this principle fashioned by the context. They are far too big subjects for any Introduction but they are fundamental to the practice and purposes of this book. I make reference to all three throughout the book but for specific reference please refer to chapter 4, 'A Christian Context'.

My general sadness is that Christianity is not fully appreciated by many people. I question why not. I do not think it to be Christianity's fault but rather our understanding of it and of God. It does not do itself justice, or rather Christians do not do it justice, in being seen so often to be out of tune with the world, failing to connect body, soul and spirit, traditions and present-day realities, rating doctrinal belief above human goodness and love of whatever good variety. That is tragic and somewhat bizarre, if we consider how Jesus Christ was in tune with the world, by what was known even then as his 'way of life'.

Five core biblical quotations (NRSV)

- 'God said: Let us make humankind in our image, according to our likeness' (Genesis 1:26).
- 'Love God ... and your neighbour as yourself' (Matthew 22:36, after Leviticus 19:18 and Deuteronomy 6:5).
- 'Do to others as you would have them do to you' (Matthew 7:12).
- 'I have come in order that you might have life—life in all its fulness' (John 10:10).
- God in whom 'we live and move and have our being' (Paul in Athens, Acts 17:28).

The current Christian Church in Britain

The leader of the *Anglican Church Times* on 8 September '17 stated of the Church of England that, however ironically, Christianity and churchgoing, as they are perceived, seem no longer to have much conscious bearing on the vast majority of people in Britain, nor on the great issues of state ranging from war to peace. Has the nation lost confidence in Christianity and the Church? Between 2006 and 2016, children, that is under 16, at Church of England services, fell 22%.[9] According to Baroness Warnock, Oxford philosopher, the Church's 'continuing decline should surprise no one .... For some decades, each succeeding generation has been shown to be less religious than the last'. No one doubts [the Christian Church] has now lost its dominant ... position in the lives of the majority of citizens.'[10] Archbishop Welby, speaking to the Board of Deputies of British Jews, 6 May 2015, said 'We do not as faith groups in our society always exhibit......secure tolerance to each other. Christians are as bad as anyone at this. In fact, I think we're worse'. My own understanding

24

is that traditional churches face similar conditions, except in terms of their greater numbers and, using broad terms, the evangelical ones. Professor Linda Woodhead, a sympathetic professor of religion, has said, 'Britain is undergoing the biggest religious transition since the Reformation of the 16th century,'[11]

Figures abound and vary, but they nearly all confirm decline. The major exception in, for example, the Church of England from 2006- 2016 there was an increase in 11% of parishes [9]. In the 2011 census, 59 per cent identified themselves as Christian, compared with 72 per cent in the 2001 census. In 2016, roughly 50 per cent of people, had no contact with the Church.[12] Approximately 50 per cent had belief in God or some 'spiritual power'. In 1983, 67 per cent of those surveyed by the National Centre for Social Research identified themselves as Christian; in 2016, just 41 per cent. (It is worth noting, to keep these figures in relative proportion, that many members of the British population neither vote nor join. The Brexit vote, which radically seeks to transform British politics, was participated in by just 37-9 per cent of the theoretical voting population and just 30 per cent of all registered voters.)

Young people especially are vulnerable to injustice by nature of their age, experience and resources. In 2016–17, more than usual voted on the subjects of Brexit and the British government, particularly young people, under, say, forty, but they are not generally consorting with the Church. David Kinnaman in *You Lost Me* has said their issues with it are 'access, alienation, authority and especially lack of engagement, participation and sharing'. I agree and simply add language and comprehension. Young people from children upwards are a desperately sad loss at present to the Church, not least as models for the following generation. Their absence is a likely loss to inter faith Christian relationships if not to relationships over all. With older members are not only dying out but also giving up, children may learn nothing at all about faith in their young lives, so busy are they for, example, playing sports on Sunday. Young adults likewise, for Sunday professional sport is a new feature of the last 20 years. Transmission of faith to an upcoming generation is no longer the norm, in practice or principle. Clearly, school encouragement at vulnerable ages has always been vital.

The connection between the decline of institutional Christianity with the advance of inter faith thinking and activity may be more than a chronological one. Religious Studies was the second fastest growing A-level subject after Further Maths in 2017, more than Political Science and double 2003 figures. 'Excellent preparation for living in a multi faith, multicultural world', commented the chief executive of the Religious Education Council for England and Wales, Rudolf Lockhart. Greenbelt, a Christian arts, faith, and justice youth festival, has had a programme of Muslim culture since 9/11.

It is hard to achieve, let alone evaluate, a whole picture relating to decline, fall and progress. It is clear, though, that whole pictures exist to be recognised and developed. For example, not looking on the bright side, Professor Linda Woodhead, has said that the Church's situation is 'so grave that … the whole structure needs to be reviewed from top to toe and creative and courageous decisions need to be made'.[13] Richard Chartres, recent Bishop of London, in his Christmas message of 2016, spoke of the Church of England—possibly a legitimate marker for all churches—rooted within the context of our rampaging contemporary world, needing 'to rediscover its heart'. He added positively, 'There is need for narratives capacious enough to permit development and to accommodate new themes.'

Emeritus Professor of the Sociology of Religion, Grace Davie sees a balanced picture. African and immigrant church populations increase throughout many denominations as well as separately - as we cheerfully experienced at St John's and St Peter's, Ladywood when I was vicar, 1989-2008 - and there is a juxtaposition of decline and potency, which demonstrates a 'persistent paradox of religion in Britain. Overall, church-going and religious adherence goes down while the British population goes up.'[14]

If Christianity, the Church and its members are patently still not getting across to a majority in Britain, except perhaps within Religious Studies - whether through school, the media, church itself, or society in general - then the whole Church at every level of belonging would logically appear to have responsibility to continue even harder than at present to try to determine, recognise and attend comprehensively to possible difficulties and explore causes of decline and ways forward. Every stone has to be turned, inspected. That is only rational and sensible. To my mind and that of many a progressive Christian within the Progressive Christianity Network of the UK and of Birmingham it is the theological stone that requires much unearthing. Except in academic circles, in everyday church life it seems to me rarely lifted to explore potential causes of both decline and growth in religious awareness and development. Though decline in numbers is addressed, ideally, they are secondary to meaning and purpose.

Two stories have not budged throughout much of the Church. One relates to justice. The *Church Times* series *Theology Now*, 'left the unfortunate impression that (certain) 'theology' remains unaware of the injustices and inequalities it perpetuates'.[15] Paul Bayes, Bishop of Liverpool, has referred to systemic problems of enduring inequality as between rich and poor.[16] So has Archbishop Justin Welby in a strong article stemming from a report of the Commission on Economic Justice 2017, in which he writes that 'our economic model is broken and Britain lives in a profound state of economic injustice'.

The implication to me is that we, the church, are in a state not just of poverty alongside wealth, but also of rank unfairness, which becomes a spiritual issue of well-being and motivation, accordingly one that negatively affects support for Church and faith. Ignorant and prejudiced attitudes to members of different faiths are another form of injustice in present thinking which can lead to dangerous behaviour in future practice. South Africa under twentieth-century apartheid finally had to surrender - in theory - the disparities that had caused such injustice. Maybe that gives hope for us now.

The other stone relates to theology: a massive ancient corner-stone which since the 4th century Roman Church Councils and then 16th century Reformation has upheld a particular traditional theology of Church worship - irrespective of denomination - its awesome strength dressed in robes of beautiful soft green moss. In his well-known struggle for Reformation, Martin Luther, in 1517, spotlighted the danger of concretising and circumscribing the spirit of any new life in faith which may be of God. I suspect that many apparent non-believers, like some progressive Christians (including me), if they know about church at all, may well know of that danger first-hand through being witnesses of church worship and teaching. Here is a recognisable comment: 'I'm told God loves me, forgives me, and is in my suffering in which Jesus died for me.' Response: 'That's as may be, but it does not feel like that to me.' In my experience, that kind of theological comment and all-too-human response voiced in and outside church, symbolises and exemplifies some of the unrealistic sentimental theology that may swamp new life in and outside the Church except for the relatively few. And another comment: 'I can see that all this Spirit stuff is marvellously uplifting for some, but it does nothing for me. Is that my fault? I refuse to feel guilty about it.' I sympathize strongly. Christianity tends to wallow in guilt.

Christian frameworks, among those of other religious and nonreligious faiths, are invaluable to the spirit of Britain. Religions are very powerful, mostly for good, and they symbolise much of human life. Hope is always there. The task remains: 'how does the Church have the imagination and courage to proclaim …the faith… afresh in each generation'[17] Rowan Williams, previous Archbishop of Canterbury, has hoped 'above all else that the years to come may see Christianity … able to capture the imagination of our culture … plaiting together a single strand of all kinds of diversities'.[18] According to the same leader of the *Church Times*, 8 September 17 as earlier, 'the chief task … is to encourage and equip individuals to communicate their faith in ways that mean something to the 'nones'. ('Nones' is a useful new name for those not just non-Christian but also, in their own eyes, of no religious faith). As many as 50 per cent of the British population are 'nones'. Providing a definition is difficult. Naturally this group includes immense numbers of thinking and radical people seeking justice and compassion for life. Let us say that nones may have faith in many high aspects of life and how to live but have no institutional faith.

Church communities are an endless resource for both Christian and inter faith relationships, no longer just in traditional denominational terms but also by way of attitude and approach. Whether Pentecostal/charismatic/evangelical, liberal, traditional, or of whatever mixture, we all need one another to be in good faith, irrespective of my or your particular taste, perception or even truth. And I do confess that some practices and ideas, words and tunes are almost beyond the pale for me at least. Good theology, good Spirit and practice, and therefore good discussion are all at a premium. Connection between Christianity and inter faith activity may come to bear good fruit both for its own sake and for Christian stability and progress.

Theological background

It is essential at this point to say what I mean by God. More discussion of God follows throughout the book especially in Chapter 4. Our human attempts at understanding God are basic to our human existence and it is on our human understanding of God that much of the integrity of this book depends. Christians pray, worship and follow Jesus, to lead what we may hope to be godly lives within the context of God.

The very word *God* is a turn-off for some people for whom belief in so-called 'God' is therefore a non-starter. However, I take as fundamental that there is more to life than just me, and indeed you, that there is something going on up, down, over, or out there or in here that is not just personified, personal projection but also thoroughly mysterious, ever-present and supreme. It feels like it, and in this I trust myself. Some, like me, see God as Creator and Sustainer, definition of all life itself. Some see God out there, transcendent; others, in here, within us, immanent. That is Christian tradition and my experience is both. I derive hope from the persistent evidence of the reality of death, incarnation and resurrection in daily life, immanent and transcendent, because I consider that what I choose to call God is irrevocably always with Creation and its humanity, in life and in death.

Some call this 'God', the Spirit of Life. Some prefer to substitute qualities of life that mean everything to us. Hope is a good one, used constantly in churches. Naturally, their attributes may vary in priority between different people. These qualities have been called the fruits of the Spirit, and the Spirit - presumably holy - is traditionally one persona of God which, with Jesus, helps understanding of the Trinity and its three faces or personas of God. The fruits are 'love, joy, peace, patience, kindness, goodness, faithfulness, humility and self-control'.[19] I would add truth, beauty, creativity, justice, and energy. We have to find what works for us. To my mind, these values are what the word *God* stands for and what God symbolises. Please note that when I use the word 'God' that is what I generally mean. We are not doing sums - though I like them. They are eternal values for all humanity to work for, church and state included, and preferably together. They are summed up in that proposition 'love God and love your neighbour as yourself'. To declare my own context and where I am coming from to produce this book, I offer, in Chapter 4, my own experience and understanding of God and Christianity, and my lifelong journey of joy, fulfilment and frustration with the Christian Church, brought sharply into focus by my developing inter faith relationships. Questions naturally arise about how far the world faiths already work in our times for the actual and perceived well-being, justice, peace and mutual benefit of everyone, and how well they are equipped to work on the needs outlined.

There are hopeful signs that new expressions of human unity and well-being in God are emerging, stimulated by cells of different faiths in loving relationships of friendship and respect. The invaluable Inter Faith Network for the UK, established in 1987, now with over 250 local interfaith groups affiliated; National Inter Faith Week in November; U.N. World Inter faith Harmony week, the Methodist and United Reformed Church interfaith relations group; Anglican Renewal and Reform; Fresh Expressions; Faithful Neighbours; the Church Urban Fund; Quaker literature such as *Interfaith Dialogue at the Grassroots*; the annual Islam Open Day in February /March grown from about 20 in 2013 to over 150 in 2017; Roman Catholic interreligious (faith) literature, pilgrimages and walks; Baptist interfaith activity in different towns; Baptists' positive 12 Myths symbolize their inter faith engagement. Different faiths' funeral, discipleship and digital projects;

visits to one another's places of worship, all are firm indications of new life and strength attempted by many churches, individual Christians and different faiths.

Behind all this discussion is Jesus. From a Christian standpoint, Jesus is the model for learning how to love God and our neighbour as ourselves throughout all our life. His model is enhanced by the golden rule expressed by all major faiths in their different ways and contexts: do as you would be done by.[20] The particular challenge to Christians and Christianity to be consistent and inclusive in theology as well as in behaviour, talk and practice is to avoid hypocrisy. This means recognising Christian obligation to step out actually to meet and appreciate one another with all our boundaries, differences and similarities, all our actual and potential threats and conflicts. Doors are only open wide when everyone values difference as much as sameness in one another and seeks mutual partnership on the specific difficult issues of our times. That applies with much friendship and it is friendship that we seek.

Jesus calls his followers 'friends'. His advice to them, stemming from the Jewish writers of the Hebrew Bible, we have seen already, is to love God and love their neighbour as themselves.[21] It sums up the human, democratic and Christian ethos of this book at all levels and, to my mind, Christianity altogether. The principle is acceptable to most of the world's faiths. It is basic to this book because at its root it is about our human relationships. It may be worth a reminder that it is nothing new to us from time immemorial. Yet we often publicly fail to capitalise on it. My experience is that scarcely anyone of whatever faith disagrees, particularly once the name of God is explored. But then selfishness, strife, suffering and segregation have always been strong contrary forces.

On being Christian

Christianity and the different faiths are not just about ideas, theories and doctrines but essentially about putting these into practice. What is their rationale? What does faith mean in practice? All world faiths - and most human beings - have found difficulties in the practice of their ideas and with hypocrisy. Work for justice and peace is in part their responsibility, not to seek it alone but in partnership with others and all those seeking the common good; not to be led by their prevailing culture but to lead where necessary in the Spirit of God. Their ideas and practice are intimately wrapped up in their theologies for ill as well as for good. In Christian circles.

I hear and read cries that an imperative way forward is for religious absolutism to be renounced and the whole meaning of belief and faith examined.[20] I also hear, 'I still have faith'; 'I've lost my faith'; 'You must have faith!' Just what do these statements mean not only in theory but in practice to the speaker and to the hearer? What did faith mean to those recorded as having been healed through their faith by Jesus? Transformational movement is in the air, but - it is hard for me to judge - much 'worship theology' seems in practice to me to be rigid and implacable against theological change. From the viewpoint of outsiders, the 'nones', they may want to know what to do with his or her spirit. This is by no means always realised in recognition, discussion or experimentation. The spirit of Luther might agree, for a while, about the need for the people's freedom in spirit.

My belief is that Christians' specific responsibility is to increase what they/we can do and enable with others. Here are three interdependent emphases. The first is by liberating others, nones, Christians, and would-be Christians from what, for many, stifles them in any purpose of seeking abundant life for others and themselves. For some, this means seeking to follow their spirit in the 'way of Jesus', that is the way of goodness and love. For others, like myself, it may mean recognising the human need for rationality *within* faith. For example: unselfish love begets unselfish love, in individuals and communities. A loving atmosphere at work and play is very infectious. There are naturally different levels of relationships, but an open Christian theology and process is indispensable at every level with, crucially, personal investment and control put aside. Whether short- or long-term, in daily life or just on Sundays, it is a cop-out from honesty and commitment to omit discussion and theological issues in church and out of it. A local church I know does now, to strong approval, practise regular discussions.

The second is by enlarging and deepening the scale on which Christians seek to know, accept and collaborate with members of the different religious faiths. This has to involve nurturing mutual relationships in faith and honesty and exploring theological issues - in other words, being true in word, action and thought to ourselves and to one another. If it is a mystery for some Christians to understand what on earth God is doing through other faiths, then it is worth their reflecting that those of other faiths may feel just the same about God and Christianity. That has been within my hearing. One way forward is to visit a place of worship different from one's own. Rather than a problem, it can be a reverential wonder, as it has often been to many people I know. I enormously welcome 'Open/Visit a Mosque Day' organised now on an increasing national scale. The Church has slowly learnt maybe about mutual relationships with one another, such as white and black, about which the racism of '60s and 70s, to white disgrace, was so shocking. If black Christians, black 'Brits', met with shameful white prejudice and discrimination, what is the future for society with black and brown Asian British, such as in Birmingham, where they are soon to be a majority? 'They' are not even - as might be said - Christian? A very serious question! Patterns of behaviour are possibly being set now for the whole century, especially amongst young people. Preventive relationships are of utmost importance for the future.

The third is working together with others of whatever faith or belief on urgent internal and external, local and international, crises, to be met, and met so much better, in partnership, possibly by campaigning together. Issues exemplified earlier, climate change, pollution, refugees, food banks, child abuse, homelessness, street crime, nuclear warfare, immigration, democracy, interfaith relationships, are examples of urgent topics on which the Church will always require a mind, several minds uniting, if it is to be taken seriously as a player on the British and even the world scene. Primarily they will require love in whatever form is possible and appropriate and willingness to nurture it. Audiences may be learned or ignorant of any response to the question, 'what would Jesus do?' It is heartening when world and national British religious leaders put denomination behind them, take up such issues, and even take the lead. Pope Francis with his book on climate change, *Laudato Si'*, and Archbishop Justin Welby's book on the economy, *Dethroning Mammon*,[23] are notable examples. It is to be hoped that faith differences will also be submerged in search and delivery of 'one justice' as perceived through applied theology and universal recognition.

Such a mysterious and precious word as love can be used loosely; we could ask ourselves how it differs from 'liking'. This book seeks to explore love[24] and recognise the necessary balance between loving ourselves and loving our neighbour, particularly if of different faith, looking after ourselves by giving others a stake in life too. We could all agree that hospitality, both religious and secular, is a supreme test of love in all faiths. A vision of love in action between members of different faiths can spur us on, as for example, the common reality in most British city hospitals. The following is an illustration from the Birmingham interfaith world.

Annually since 2007, fifty-plus people have gathered in various places of worship for a meal and a celebration. Each time, this event has included individuals from the six major world faiths: Judaism, Islam, Sikhism, Buddhism, Hinduism and Christianity. It is a reminder of the Christian Pentecost. They come together for the awarding of the Institute of Tourist Guiding certificate to a dozen or so people who have worked together for three months on a course to become faith guides. They have learnt to interpret and express their own faith to visitors of other faiths in terms that they can understand and therewith learn to respect one another's ways of understanding faith. Their tutors, examiners, organisers and friends are invited.

This event is the annual culmination of the Birmingham Faith Guiding course.[25] It is notable and possibly unique because it nurtures dialogue, friendships, learning skills, practical action and theological discussion with involvement from all six major faiths. It is an inspiring event for all involved: safe but alive, welcoming, hospitable, companionable, instructive, liberating and jubilant. It is a glimpse of how the Lord's Prayer, especially 'thy will be done on earth', can be realised as a present reality. The celebration does not emphasise religious practice, doctrine, conversion, or belief, but demonstrates the potential effect of religious faith on the ethical and political transformation of society through meeting and partnership. It is an example of the collaboration and social cohesion sought by Church and State.

In whatever language and form, in times of great change, we all need some tangible examples to inspire and direct our aims towards our own heaven on earth in the name of God. The Faith

Guiding course has stood as a visionary symbol of what is possible in interfaith relationships. Its nature and composition illustrate the kind of activity that other Christians might seek, share and celebrate with people of different faiths. It demonstrates that change can have good consequences and that we can aim to love one another to different degrees whomever the other may be- if we are prepared to unbutton ourselves.

All projects have different direct givens and broad contexts, but the best ones foster visions of something better - a something created that is more than the individual parts, something with eternal value. Visions that are built on imagination, creativity, rationality and mutual respect *have* been realised and can be realised again. This project is a powerful example of the work I consider as being of the Holy Spirit and being Christian in a universal sense acceptable to all.

1   Some evidence with authoritative statistics is essential, but this is not a sociological treatise; it is a book of perceptions. I therefore include intuitions, so-called 'common knowledge', and insights alongside hard evidence. In the West Midlands, hate crime increased from 2,677 reported incidents to 3,450 from 2014–15 to 2015–16, while rough sleeping increased three times from 2010 to 2016 (West Midlands Mayor's Faith Conference, 27 Nov. 2017).

2   Keith Clements, Look back in Hope, Wipf and Stock, Resource publications, 2017, p399

3   Stephen Pinker, The Better Angels of Our Nature (New York: Viking, 2011), and John Norberg, Progress: Ten Reasons to Look Forward to the Future (Amazon, 2016).

4   'We don't do God', said by Alistair Campbell, Prime Minister Blair's spin doctor, 4 Apr. 2003.

5   Sir Roger Scruton, philosopher, on A Point of View (3 Sept. 2017), Radio 4.

6   Catholic Bishops' Conference of England and Wales, Meeting God in Friend and Stranger (2010).

6a. United Society Partners in the Gospel.

7 Matthew 22.37-39 based on Deuteronomy 6.5 and Leviticus 19.18

8 Manifesto of St John's and St Peter's Church, Ladywood, based on Matthew 22:37, 39, that I wrote in 2004.

9 Church of England Statistics for Mission, 2017.

10 Mary Warnock, Oxford and public philosopher, in her Introduction to Dishonest to God (Continuum, 2010).

11 Linda Woodhead, professor of the sociology of religion, Lancaster University, British Academy Lecture, January 2016.

12 From a survey of the international research agency YouGov, 2016.

13 Linda Woodhead, letter to the Church Times, 4 Mar. 2016 following the Church Times series, 4th March

14 Grace Davie, emeritus professor of the sociology of religion, Exeter University, Religion in Britain: A Persistent Paradox (Wiley Blackwell, 2015).

15 Linda Woodhead at the Westminster Debates, 17 Apr. 2017, and in a Church Times article entitled 'Questionable Statistics'.

16 Paul Bayes, Bishop of Liverpool from 2014, in the Church Times, 11 Aug.

17 Church of England 'Common Worship' Declaration of Assent' at Ordination Services

18 Quoted by P. P. Shortt in Rowan Williams: An Introduction (Darton, Longman, and Todd, 2003).

19 Galatians 5.22

20 The golden rule in all religions including Matthew 7:12.

21 Leviticus 19:18 and Deuteronomy 6:5, quoted in Matthew 22:37.

22 Beyond the Dysfunctional Family: Jews, Christians, and Muslims in Dialogue, ed. Bayfield, Race, and Siddiqui (Manor House, 2012).

23 Dethroning Mammon, Justin Welby, Bloomsbury Continuum, 2016

24 See 'Love', in Chapter 4, 'A Christian Context'.

25 See Ruth Tetlow, 'Faith Guiding', its initiator and leader, Chapter 2.

INTRODUCTION 2

Development

Writers are usually given a brief introduction on the fly-leaf and little more may be known of their context. In this book, a short description of the contexts of the five people of different faith accompanies each of their Perceptions on the basis of its relevance. Then because my own context and personal experience have a major influence on the book, I have described in chapter 4, my own journeys, personal and inter faith, in addition to my understanding of 'a Christian context'. This approach is concerned with integrity, the contributors', mine and that of the book itself. I also encourage us to take our own religious/life experience seriously as our sheer reality alongside other approaches that may be pronounced from the Church as essential traditions and doctrines. We are all young in learning both about the outside world and ourselves. Your own context and integrity as reader are as important to all our different understandings of perceptions as are those of the contributors. We are interdependent.

I describe the book's practical processes and perceptions in general in Introduction 3. In order to make connections with our daily living I write briefly here about the processes in my mind for the reader to discern what lies behind all our perceptions and hopes and the extent to which they may be products of our own interior world, fulfilment and trauma combining body, mind and soul.

It was late in 2017 that it dawned on me, in addition, that perceptions are a way of addressing big issues of the mind. It seemed to me only fair and honest to start with my own. It has made sense to me to try to integrate body, mind and spirit, which effectively means integrating my experience of life with any knowledge I've acquired. Now in the space of retirement, *Perceptions* seem to me a practical outcome of this combination, a subject worth exploring. In pursuing it myself, stimulated by others I have been raising questions as to why we and I do and see people and situations as we may and do, and why we believe as we do. 'Love of God and our neighbour as ourselves' in relation to people of different faith, is the central ethic I've chosen. Why? Because its most pertinent questions, therefore, are about why we love and do not love, how our contexts, past and present, affect that ability and motivation and the extent to which we are all interdependent in our loving of God and our neighbour.

I have usually enjoyed crossing bridges of the mind. I have had to balance ten other people's particular perceptions of Christianity with descriptions of the context of the subject and the purposes of the book doing so along with my inevitably personal choice of material. This book, though, is neither autobiography nor a vast spiritual or psycho-sociological dissertation. There are different levels to work on. It aims to bridge the personal and the academic, experience and hand-me-downs. It was never part of the bargain with the contributors that I explore their perceptions in a personal way except through their own brief introductions, however important they may be to them. What I could do was explore my own perceptions and put before you, the reader, some analysis of the reasons for my own perceptions that have contributed to book's intention and content. They follow explicitly and implicitly in Chapter 4. We might all benefit from understanding and sharing reasons for our own perceptions.

A general comment about content: some of the sub-titles overlap, God, Jesus and love for example. There are overlaps but I hope not undue repetition.

My own personal experience, our society and Christianity are the context for five questions that focus on encouraging relationships between Christians and people of different religious world faiths. The questions are rhetorical and not addressed methodically within the text. They are here and not in my personal journeys in Chapter 4 for the reader to be aware of them from the start, find them lurking throughout the book and respond at will. Other questions follow at the end of the book. The five questions are as follows:

- If we accept the ancient Judaeo-Christian claims that *all* people are made in God's image and therefore equal in God, and if we accept the Judaeo-Christian commandment to love God and love our neighbour as ourselves, how might Christians aim to live out this principle of human equality before God in a theological and practical sense?
- Why will many respond to the Church differently today and in the future compared with how people responded in the past, both ancient and recent, to its saints, sinners and leaders, Martin Luther King and Martin Luther in contrast for example and their perception of the will of God? (By chance, this very day I write, 31 October 2017, five hundred years ago in Wittenberg, Germany, Luther is known for having nailed up his Ninety-Five Theses symbolising the Reformation of the Roman Catholic Church.)

- How are Christians and Christianity to address the fact that approximately half the British population is neither churchgoing nor claiming to be Christian (and now called nones) or of another faith? What do you think may be their perception of Christianity and Christians?

- What is your perception of what Christianity reveals to those who are not Christian, when Church leaders in church refer to 'we Christians' in what could be exclusive language, as for example when they proclaim, 'We are the people of God' and when biblical literal truth proclaims that Jesus was followed to Bethlehem by a star?

- In today's context, what does it mean to us as Christians to think for ourselves, to have radical trust and to have the freedom in the Gospel to let go and trust God's Holy Spirit, *all of which* were recommended and expedited by Martin Luther, Martin Luther King and one named Jesus?

INTRODUCTION 3

Background

Readership; process; dialogue; perceptions;
listening; Birmingham; core biblical quotations

Readership

This book is addressed to Christians in Britain, to those of no institutional
faith and who may reject religious labels and to those interested
in Christianity and faith of whatever nature, religious or otherwise.
In critical times for Church and State, religious and secular, it is for
those concerned about relationships between Christians and those
of different faiths. I particularly hope to deepen future discussion and
understanding amongst Christians and anyone else interested in actual
and potential relationships with those of different faiths. Everyone is
welcome as a reader, especially those with an open mind who want
to trust or test their own experience and want to listen to those they
may not have heard before. This especially applies to young people and
those of whatever age, young or old, in faith or not.

I hope that it will also be of interest to members of different
religious faiths who have their own experience and knowledge of
Christianity. The book is for those interested in God by whatever

defensible definition and in our interconnectedness with others, our born interdependence and our human relationships as members of our one world. Its ideas are broad, the knowledge on which it draws, including my own, inevitably limited as in its focus on the Church of England and parts of Birmingham. My own experience is broad too, but I am only one!

I label my source of energy and love as *God*, so I refer frequently to God as the 'ground of my being, in whom I live and move and have my being'.[1] You may well not. I still invite you to join in any discussion that I hope this book provokes, particularly if you might call yourself atheist, agnostic or secularist. I aim as a Christian to write as responsibly and rationally as I can. For the record, I see science and religion as two wings of the same great albatross.

Lastly, this book's core of perceptions is for those who think they know about *them* but may not know what *they* think of *us*. This rightly implies it is for seekers of justice amongst us all. It is not written to seek agreement or disagreement with particular viewpoints on religious faith. It is not written either to play up or play down firmly held views about the Truth itself that all the contributors have expressed, including myself. We all have rights to our own views about ourselves and our own truth that we may or may not consider better, superior to others'. We may assume we have choice and perhaps we have pride in our choice - although in practice that may not be so, because our own culture and society, our own givens, are so very powerful. However, so do others. That has to be acknowledged and coped with within the bounds of justice and human fallibility. Agreement or disagreement are just not relevant here except within the moral position of love and justice for all others.

You as reader may believe that you do not have religious faith, though I would be surprised if you do not have faith in anything. The book is intended to encourage anyone who wishes to join in discussion about matters of faith and about listening to 'the other' - who may indeed, to 'the other', be you. It expresses strong views arising from honest experience. There is no reason that these experiences will be yours, but that might make them all the more interesting. They may ring bells with you.

As this book is largely offered to Christians and those interested in faith generally, the theology to be expected is Christian and not of the other faiths. Many parts of Britain are not multicultural or multi-faith. They may assume different faiths are not their issue. However, Britain overall, and London and most of our cities - Birmingham being a good example - are all multicultural and multi faith. We may think or assume or judge that we know one another, smiles, grimaces and all, whether through living side-by-side with each other or just through the media. We may not know one another. However, in principle, we are one another's responsibility to know and be bothered, to help make the world human, if our lives are to work at all in happy or dangerous and dodgy times. Germany in the 1930s was a tragic human disaster to learn from.

There is opportunity for us all to learn from one another. Although the book comes essentially from Birmingham it is not just for Birmingham readers. It is also for those who live elsewhere in our multi-faith world, amidst circumstances perhaps similar to those of us here in Birmingham, who might welcome an example of Christians in Britain seeking broad ways forward for themselves and for Christianity in relation to different faiths. I see Britain still as one country; that is its essence and its unique integrity. I wish it to remain so, *without* walls, national and international in reality, where people share and value faith of different kinds and take responsibility for one another and for the common good. *Them* and *us* are to work together or we may all be in serious trouble.

Process: gathering perceptions and responses

I felt urged to write this book for three concerns. As I explained in Introduction 1, the first was the British social and political climate of this decade 2010-20 and the second was the present struggling state of the Christian church. The third was my growing conviction of the great actual and potential value of good mutual interfaith relationships for British society nourished particularly by Christians' insights into themselves and Christianity through *listening* to those of different faith.

I shall expand on that third reason because the resulting process has been significant. It has grown out of my lifetime of enjoying mutual relationships across many a boundary but especially between Christians and non-Christians. Since moving to multi-faith Birmingham in 1981 I have found here members of different faiths wishing to nurture God's Spirit or, differentially, the Spirit of Life in us all just as ordinary human beings and make sense of what this might or might not mean for each of us. This experience has given me immense satisfaction. It has encouraged me to offer my own perceptions of Christianity and why I might have them in the hope that they might be relevant to shared understanding of our interfaith and life convictions. This book is for anyone of who likes to cross boundaries of whatever faith, religious or otherwise, interested, involved and seeking hope in the globalised revolutionary state of our world. That has become my conviction, the need for Christians to relate with people of different faith as equal in God. This idea progressed to my articulation of the importance of people 'listening to the other'.

None of the five faith contributors was to read what the others wrote, nor were the five respondents to read the responses of their colleagues. Our agreed-upon aim was spontaneous honesty

46

without conferring. Trusting our own experience as writers, practitioners, listeners and human beings was priority.

I visited each likely faith contributor and to my pleasure the contributions that I requested actually came in from each one. They were written over many months at different times and obligingly reordered after our dialogues, as the writers and I agreed. Only after they had completed their work did the faith writers meet together. Then the five Christian writers met together with the faith contributors.

None of these participants have known what I have been writing myself, except knowing I was basing my reflections on the ten contributions. Perhaps my asking all contributors to write in the dark was a failing, but I felt the book's integrity would depend on our honest individuality. All of us, contributors and consumers, naturally have different experience of our extraordinarily beautiful yet tragic world. Nobody is likely to see it the same, whether through different Christian eyes or the eyes of whatever faith. Why and how could we or should we? In good time, our perceptions and responses may or may not change as we discover new wisdom.

The process has been built upon perceptions[2] which are authentic, different and well meant, in no way seeking to be representative. They are not wild guesses that read like 'post-truth', despite this being a serious danger of many perceptions elsewhere. They could be judged right or wrong and may indeed, in certain strict cases, be one or the other. They are necessarily limited and different in style. As the journey of the book has not been about seeking agreement but rather about experience, integrity and mutual trust, all the faith contributors have had the chance, under the heading 'This is my perception', to be honest in desire and appraisal, pain and joy. They represent no one except themselves either in hierarchy or institution.

47

Inspiring leaders tend to act as individuals not representatives or delegates, whether in the arts, politics or religion, though probably with some personal support. Think of Jesus and Shakespeare, they represented no one. Think of whoever has influenced you, an individual parent, teacher, writer or person of whatever faith. The contributors play their part with openness, trust, integrity and collective responsibility for the entire project.

I am asking you as the reader to listen to and take heed of five perceptions and five responses from people who are strangers to you. You have the chance to discover for yourself elsewhere how far these might in reality be representative or not and what your own response might be. I believe they are symbolic voices that cry out to be heard by Christians for Christians' very own benefit, for the sake of interfaith relationships and for the common good. Of course, you do not have to agree with them or with my previous statement. If that is the case, please simply say to yourself, *I differ*, and shake your head.; otherwise, nod wisely. Recognition and acceptance of difference and similarity, disagreement and agreement, uncertainty and certainty and tensions between each pair, have been dear to the process.

I have greatly valued professional and friendly help which became increasingly invaluable - in fact, indispensable - to the whole process. For this, I am completely indebted. What I came to read in the perceptions spoke quietly and strongly to me on similar wavelengths to what were my most trenchant questions and suppositions but I have needed assistance throughout.

Dialogue – see Chapter 3, 'A review of the dialogues….'

'Inter faith dialogue' in Britain has been experienced, enjoyed and analysed particularly throughout very recent decades. It is 'not so much an idea to be studied as a way of living in positive relationship with others', according to Pope Paul VI.[3] To place it in context, we can start by imagining the dialogue between Adam and Eve or between God and Moses, which the storyteller herself imagined; the constant questioning dialogues of Socrates from the fourth century B.C.; or admiration for the interfaith initiative of Paul in the marketplace in Athens in the first century AD.[4] Notable experienced writers, academics, pastors and practitioners have all contributed to the richness of the scene. Shakespeare's Shylock dialogues are an old and modern example. We have merely continued an age-old human way of life in a modern way. The perceptions were written after dialogue then discussed in dialogue with me, then final versions agreed. The five dialogues were specific to our situation. Dialogue happened variably with the respondents but it was secondary to their responses.

I quote from Hans Kung: 'There will be no peace between the nations without peace between the religions. There will be no peace between the religions without dialogue among the religions.'[5] More is said about dialogue in the review following the perceptions and responses. It is fundamental to the processes and philosophy of this book.

Perceptions

This is a book based on perceptions. Perceptions of the weather, of the well-known elephant by a blind person and of a sports team all depend on our stance. Their meaning is open-ended. In this multi-faith context, our perceptions of one another are crucial to our daily lives and to our theological reflection. Perceptions of religious experience are also a crucial element in the quest for truth and open interfaith relationships. They have a crucial function because they can have their own honest integrity. It is useful to analyse them. Richard

Dawkins[6] has them, Gary Neville[7], England's football coach, has them, I have them, you have them, Pope Francis has them. We all have them. That's obvious but we benefit from recognizing the fact and ask why we have them and what they are about. Crucially, as I have said, they do not change the facts.

I am taking a *perception* to mean an intuition which employs both the mind and the senses. A perception introduces cultural and emotional feeling on the tandem with the rational, all learnt from past experience and observation. The feelings and the experience may be beyond words, just as the descriptive words of concert programmes often inevitably fall pathetically short, being in a different category to the moon, the music and the mountain being experienced.

To perceive and *to see* can be synonymous. Take four people in discussion, each saying one of the following:

- 'I perceive God as one.'
- 'I don't; I see God as three in one.'
- 'I see God as ineffable' (i.e. beyond words or definition).
- 'I don't see God at all.'
- All I can see is an elephant.'

We have here five different perceptions. Any number of different people, even the same person, may have different perceptions of the same subject, from God, to a parliamentary debate to yesterday's curry and rice. So much depends on context, date, time, audience, motivation, knowledge, relationship and state of mind both of the perceiver and of the perceived. Hamlet exclaims to himself, 'What a piece of work is man! How noble in reason! How infinite in faculty!' and then almost in the same breath he utters, 'And yet, to me, what is this quintessence of dust?'[8]

A perception is not a belief, though it may arise from or give rise to a belief, and then to a deep knowing by the perceiver of what is perceived. It is an insight, an interpretation of information, a symbol of human qualities. A perception, in principle, does not primarily produce combative argument about presumed 'right and wrong' as might a belief - although it may do so. It may symbolise a far greater truth, feeling, experience and commitment than is at first apparent. Perceptions are the stuff of literature, mysticism, drama and poetry, of music, art and architecture. They are as varied as human experience, imagination and interpretation.

Perceptions are also the stuff of scripture. Revelation has the weight of history and of tradition, but it was ever founded on human experience from which perceptions and stories resulted. Some, like me, would say that was the case with God. The conduits of our brain have evolved to filter everything. As in literature, huge variety arises from the complexity of the human situation, according to character, interpretation and the naming of experience—whether the terms chosen are religious or secular. Religious perceptions are easily turned into private and public assumptions and beliefs.[9] They can colour our sense of reality for years to come because of prior or simultaneous convictions and purposes. Consider, for example, someone's perception of Jesus which first maybe was a feeling, which became an assumption, which became a belief and then a certainty became a literal 'seeing' of Jesus resurrected and later for others an experience.

The distinction between perception and belief is important in relation to scripture. The two are easily confused. Christian beliefs are a distillation of Christian perceptions that vary greatly, despite a common assumption from inside and outside the faith that they do not or should not. Christianity - indeed every religion as a whole - is made up of the following:

- perceptions, signifying personal experience;
- beliefs, signifying tradition, authority, stability, commitment, conformity, and framework; and
- interpretation of words and trust of their meaning.

All of these may demonstrate compatible and essential realities that include the inevitable differences, similarities and interpretations of life. Combined, they may lead to a version of truth or at least a perception of truth by holder and beholder. The theological significance of perceptions is that they and their perceivers are in principle open to change and transformation by the ever creative and renewing Spirit of life.

In a more secular context, as David Eagleman argues in *The Brain: The Story of You*,[10] relevant questions are endless but equally relevant. Why and how do we decide what we perceive? How do we decide what to recount of what we perceive? By what criteria do we decide our priorities concerning our perceptions? How do we see others' perceptions of our perceptions? What is our motivation for making such perceptions? Such questions are relevant to all that is written in this book. My over-simplified response is to suggest that the first step is to attempt our own self-awareness and self-understanding.

Perceptions are necessarily limited and different in style. I have said that this venture has not been about seeking agreement with the other but rather about trusting that the other contributors are honest in desire and appraisal, pain and joy, under the heading 'This is how I perceive/see it'. Agreement and disagreement are not relevant. Whether we like it or not, perceptions and beliefs change. I change too, not just for bed. When I look hard, I realise that my understanding of human reality is made up of changeable perceptions which are what they are - loving and beautiful, brutal and unkind, all aiming to accord with my reality, however finite or infinite, however open or closed my doors. What we do with our perceptions is our shared responsibility, expressed in our relationships as human beings. In my social work once, years ago, I met a doctor in Brixton prison who had murdered his four children (as I remember). I perceived him as like anyone else, but a lost tragic figure, but I did not know a fraction. I suggest there are two priorities to learn about and appreciate: our own different perceptions of others and why perhaps we have them and may mean so much to us; and the perceptions others may have of us and what we stand for. This book is founded on such perceptions of perceptions.

You would be already justified in questioning some of my own perceptions. In retirement, I do have enviable space to make such assessments on my experience and interpretation of available knowledge, public and private. Many of us have to create the space to reflect when it is not a natural given in our lives. Prayer needs that. What though are my criteria? Have I really listened with clean ears? What am I trying to prove, unconsciously maybe? Where do my perceptions come from whether superficially or profoundly? As author with a theme and a passion, I have had to contend with these issues; my colleagues too. More is said in Chapter 3.

'Givens' are literally that: just what has been given to us with no credit by life, some say 'by God'. They illuminate why different people, even with apparently similar backgrounds, make different decisions and have different ideas, life journeys, personalities and outlooks—not least different religions and different approaches to religion. Givens are relevant to perceptions. They can give clues as to what influences us, why we may have different perceptions and what we think of them; clues about our perceptions of our own connections and relationships, of our own strengths and weaknesses. They can suggest why, for example, we might think and feel so differently about sex, politics and religion. Our recognition of them in ourselves may enable us to be honest with ourselves and others and be trustful.

Givens can be simply matters of fact with or without interpretation. Increased personal age can encourage their recognition and due thanks for what others have given us. Givens here are more personal than contexts.

Listening

Pope Francis has said 'The most need of humanity is to listen to one another …. People have to learn to listen more if they want there to be peace in the world' [11]

I listened to what has been both said to me and written down. For this book, five Christians have commented on five perceptions as the first formal listeners, symbolically representing future readership in hope of expanding the dialogue. All ten writers are to be *listened* to.

The art of listening can take a lifetime truly to learn. 'What are you trying to say?' 'How are you?' 'Wait a minute - and I'll tell you!' I usually had to listen to my father! I learnt more about listening through hitch-hiking, when the driver and I were there for one another— except when a lorry limited in those days to twenty miles per hour in those was too noisy. That tended to stop the listening but not the talking. My becoming a social caseworker followed naturally, almost. I've never been a 'terrorist', but had I been, I would have wished to have been listened to and asked why I was adopting such an extreme maybe violent position. We may not be able to choose much in our lives, but we can always choose our attitude to listening when in so doing we can be true to ourselves. Listening may also be the most respectful thing we ever do for another. We may take it in turns with one another. That would be symbolic justice.

In common life, listening and hearing are both necessary for dialogue's sake, mutuality and friendship. Christian interfaith relationships improve if they are grounded in this human skill. It is all the more imperative, but it appears to me much less practised in that arena. In my listening experience, Christianity is often perceived negatively by some members of the different world faiths. By listening to such people, Christians can improve relationships to redeem this perception but also have a better understanding of ourselves and the attitudes of mind that encourage us at least to become willing to listen to 'the other'. Jesus's Sermon on the Mount had words written about making peace with those who might have a grievance against us before we go to the altar. Strong advice! This could result in ever-deepening interfaith relationships and friendship.

Listening may be harder to do than it sounds, which is probably why it is so neglected. An intriguing test of our openness to listen is to ask ourselves who we mean at different times when we say 'we'! I've a particular problem because I sometimes can't hear in the first place. Meanings of words differ from translation to translation, age to age, place to place, feeling to feeling, voice to voice, relationship to relationship and of music from instrument to instrument and also voice to voice. Members of other faiths attempting dialogue with Christians are not immune to their own listening problem. We need to nurture one another in the art. A valuable route is via the art of scriptural reasoning amongst members of different faiths especially amongst Jews, Muslims and Christians and if open to questioning about sources and literalism.

Human bridges require building, but no one is marooned without God, because by my understanding, God is always with us. God, in this context creatively described as the Spirit of God, the go-between God,[12] is the bridge-builder between Christians and people of all other faiths. This Spirit, through scrupulous listening to the perceptions of others, enables exploration of a vision for what some Christians consider pursuit of 'the kingdom of God'. A dialogue is two-way, but somebody has to start it, like chess. A model for listening comes from the prophet Micah, only twenty-five hundred years ago. He saw his job as speaking for God to whom people had, in theory, to listen. 'And what does God require?'[13] Micah has first to presume to listen to God in his understanding and famously passes on his answer, which is to encourage his audience to 'walk humbly with [our] God'. Humility is a prerequisite for listening. We can show the heart of God in us to one another, if we listen.

When I am not sure of what to do, think, or say about something, I am not good at asking others for their advice, and worse at listening to instructions, especially finding which way to go in a Welsh forest. Christians as a whole are somehow not renowned for stepping back and asking others their views. A learned and seasoned Muslim recently said to me words to the effect that the problem with Christians is that they always think they are right so they think they don't need to listen. As anyone might cheekily add, so might those of other faiths! Of course, listening is a common issue in human affairs, not least in bringing up children with their questions on sex or religion or both at once. But how often did I look at myself as a parent? Listening has theological significance too with all faiths. the bible's book of Revelation, 3.20, Jesus is given the words: 'I stand at the

56

door and knock. If anyone hears my voice and opens the door I will come in'. Have a look at Jesus at the door with a lantern in Holman Hunt's painting.

When peace is really desired, conflict and warfare have finally to end in listening; better to listen first before hope is lost. If only it had happened in Syria in 2010–11! Or back in 1914! Christians, especially those in authority, have a moral and practical duty to listen to our congregations, and now particularly to members of the other world faiths. The listening Church may hear that it, too, has to consider changing, seemingly faster than its natural evolution. Some may not like that. Listening is usually best facilitated through eye-to-eye meeting. This is all likely to mean, at least internally, that the Church would benefit from prioritising its aims and efforts. Change, such as through immigration, can increase reluctance and necessity to change with it. Increased dialogue and listening resulted in the five perceptions which together may lead to possible approaches within the Church.

Birmingham

The context of Birmingham is crucial for understanding something of the roots of these perceptions of Christianity. They might well have been different in a different city with its own different culture and faith relationships. A few further notes then about Birmingham itself, with its multi-faith context. Figures quickly become outdated but they give an indication of reality.

Census figures for 2011 reveal that Birmingham is, after London, probably the most diverse city in Britain. Traditionally, Birmingham - proud to be Britain's second city - has had a strong record of immigration, welcoming migrants and fostering endless change and development[13b]. Of all British towns and cities, it has one of the longest histories of seeking meaningful interfaith relationships. Professor Andrew Davis of Birmingham University has said Birmingham 'cannot be understood without understanding of the role of Faiths'.[14] Birmingham Museum's exhibition of Birmingham Faiths records that 75% of the population considers itself religious. Serving Birmingham's 1 million people are 493 Christian, 105 Muslim, 24 Sikh, 10 Buddhist, 6 Hindu, and 4 Jewish places of worship or religious gathering, as well as others of different faith traditions. It is Britain's most culturally diverse city. Census figures for 2011 can be contrasted with those for 2001 (in brackets). Birmingham has a population of 53.1 per cent (66 per cent) white majority and 46 per cent (34 per cent) ethnic minorities; 46 per cent (60 per cent) are Christian, and 22 per cent are Muslim.[15] 46% are under the age of thirty (UK 36 per cent). By 2019 the city council estimates that black and ethnic minorities will in fact be in the majority in Birmingham schools. In 2017, of roughly 75 per cent of over 78 parishes supported by 'Presence and Engagement" – since around 2001, one of the roots of the national Anglican interfaith initiative, at least 10 per cent of the population are of different faith. Potential implications of such figures in the future speak loudly of the need for inter faith education and practices and for listening to one another.

With over one million people and more than 25 per cent of those of religious faith being other than Christian, Birmingham has increasing experience in constructive handling of intercultural and interfaith relationships There are - not least in the churches synagogues, mosques, gurdwaras and temples - many people who work at conversations across work disciplines and common barriers to achieve stable and infectious bonds. Members of Birmingham Christian churches are often foremost on the city scene for initiating mixed-faith groups. Birmingham, under its Anglican bishop since 2006, David Urquhart, is currently (2016–17) the only Anglican diocese with a full-time interfaith advisor, despite the times of severe austerity and budget cuts. For the last sixteen years, the three most recent bishops of Birmingham have all maintained such an appointment. The present bishop and advisor have organised four markedly progressive series of six-month 'conversations'[16] with and amongst people of different faiths and backgrounds from across the city spectrum. This is one of countless examples of organised interfaith work in the city. In 1998 we began the Ladywood inter Faith Education Project, the LIEP, based at St. John's Church and three other places of worship. See Jo Mason's account in Chapter 2. The imaginative inter faith Faith-guiding project - round respective different faiths' places of worship- was begun in 2007, through local initiative. Places of Welcome[17] is a new movement based on Birmingham and the Black Country since 2014 that offers wonderful support and comfort to all comers of whatever faith and background in just being allowed to be themselves. 'Faiths for Fun' has for ten years been primarily organised by Birmingham Scout Association and the Council of Faiths for all young people of different faiths. KSIMC mosque Clifton Rd Interfaith group in 2018 began 'Exploring Global Conflicts' affecting the Ummah, that is the supra-national Muslim community. Early in 2018 a mixed interfaith group of Muslims, Jews and Christians organized their own trip to Israel/Palestine for 24 of us.

Since 9/11—which back in 2001 immediately inspired the new Faith Leaders' Group—nationwide government schemes have been sown in Birmingham, mostly because of its experience and willingness to be a signpost for Britain's interfaith relationships. 'Presence and Engagement' has a growing network of interfaith activities round the country including in Birmingham. 'Near Neighbours' is a government-funded interfaith initiative also in Birmingham using parishes to bring people of different faiths together. In 2014, Birmingham City was the first to respond to the all-party government request for councils to have a 'faith covenant' signed annually.

The city council has usually been very willing - in theory - to collaborate, and 25 per cent (2015–16) of its councillors are of black or Asian origin. However, its funding of joint voluntary collaboration and therefore inter faith support has, especially since 2016, been severely curtailed by government 'austerity'. Birmingham Council of Faiths (BCF) is one of the very first, dating from 1974; I was chairman in 1994 and then trustee until 2010. Some of that wider experience has been particularly useful to me in being convenor of two city interfaith groups since 2010 and 2012 and in creating this book. The newly elected mayor of the West Midlands - which includes Birmingham - Andy Street, held his Mayor and Faith Conference in November 2017 to discuss the issues that most concern faith communities. I attended among 400 other guests and found it worthwhile delving into how to enable faith communities to meet together across faiths. Many places of worship have managed that with imagination and commitment for the last 20-30 years. We were one of those forerunners at St John's and St Peter's, Ladywood, from 1989 -2008. See Chapter 4

I think all such inter faith opportunities contribute to public well-being, however much they vary in personnel, place and time. Likewise, shops, local institutions, hospitals etc. Natural interfaith relationships at work, home and leisure may do the most of all to benefit interfaith relationships of society generally, but their good quality is not to be taken for granted when, perhaps in the future, economic and social underprivilege and rivalries come to the fore.

It is sickening to hear some of the negative views of the city written and voiced by outsiders in some of the national media, particularly about the Muslim community. To label Birmingham as 'the jihadi capital of Britain', as did the *Daily Mail* on 23 March 2017 because the sick criminal who committed the Westminster murders bought his vehicle in Birmingham and apparently lived here for four months, is not only absurd but also offensive to the open-minded and generous good name of the city. Shortly afterwards, I attended a meeting of faith leaders in the Birmingham Central Mosque in partnership with the 'Hope not Hate' campaign which was clear about that. The meeting managed to be both phlegmatic and restrained in its natural anger. Such nasty incidents caused by tiny minorities of disturbed young people and reportage do not give confidence to those considering new interfaith relationships with a view to lessening inequalities in the future. Minorities can too easily become majorities. Political, social, and religious organisations require a joined-up strategy to tackle problems inevitably facing the separate but linked Birmingham communities.[18] To date, Birmingham has not been subject to a major terrorist attack. We all know how death, violence and fear can change perceptions, as can the kindness and compassion of resurrection that can be shown in the aftermath such as in Manchester and central London. It is very unifying when an inter faith meeting begins with a two-minute silence together.

Inspiring interfaith stories, unknown to me and many others, must abound in Birmingham. This is a small but instructive one for Ruth and me. For about a year, a Muslim family consisting of parents and three children recently lived next door. The mother, a teacher, always wore a niqab - that is a full black veil across her face - when she went out. At a lunch to which they invited us we asked her why this was so. She replied that she was fearful of Muslim men and that it gave her a sense of solidarity with other Muslim women. Many local mothers with children at our neighbouring school choose to wear a niqab. It does deter personal access from chatty passers-by like me but also creates at least my respect for personal preferences. In our large cities, many people of religious faith live side-by-side and come face-to-face with people of different religious faiths. Even if that is not so for some, because many live in the country, the issue of British people living together peacefully is hard to avoid, not least because it is a constant obsession of the media. Everyone of whatever background responds to some degree to the other, whether their faith is religious or secular. The focus of this book is specifically about Christians' response to this national opportunity. That does not preclude those who are not Christian, because first and foremost Christians are like everyone else, all created equal, whether as deemed by Christians and Jews 'in the image of God'[19] or not. One does not have to be Christian to seek to love one's neighbour as oneself.

1   Acts 17:16–29.

2   See Chapter 1.

3   Encyclical letter, 1970, quoted in 'Meeting God in friend and stranger', Catholic Bishops' Conference.

4   Acts of the Apostles, 17:16ff.

5   Hans Kung, ibid.

6   Richard Dawkins, The God Delusion (Random House, 2006).

7   England's new football manager since 2016

8   William Shakespeare, Hamlet, Act 11, Scene 2

9   Elaine Graham, Between a Rock and a Hard Place: Public Theology in a Secular Age (London: SCM, 2013).

10 David Eagleman, The Brain: The Story of You (Canongate Books, 2015).

11 Catholic News Service, 14 Mar. 2017.

12 John V. Taylor, The Go-Between God (London: SCM, 1972).

13 Micah 6:6–8.

13b Our city: migrants and the making of modern Birmingham, Jon Bloomfield, to be published

14 Professor Andrew Davis, head of theology, University of Birmingham, Conversations, 23 Sept. 2016.

15 Census figures, 2001 and 2011, and Birmingham City Council Faith Map, 2010–12.

16 Under 'Conversations 2016', Practical insights for faith communities and policymakers, Birmingham Diocesan publication, 2016.

17 The website Places of Welcome, at placesofwelcome.org, developed out of Birmingham city's social inclusion process.

18 Karamat Iqbal, Dear Birmingham (Xlibris/Kindle, 2013).

19 Genesis 2.7

PART II

CHAPTER I

Five Perceptions of Christianity

Hindu: Jyoti Patel   Jewish: Margaret Jacobi

Sikh: Pyara Singh Bhogal

Muslim: Muhammad Amin-Evans

Buddhist: Sinhavacin Walsh

Preamble

The contributors' personal givens in the form of bios precede each perception and response in chapters 1 and 2.

It is basic to the philosophy of this book that all ten contributors and I accept that everyone has both their own unique and common context comprised of every experience of their lives. Our perceptions and responses arise from our context as well as their more individual givens. The perceptions of Christianity that follow come from a Sikh, a Buddhist, a Muslim, a Jew, and a Hindu. All contributors have chosen their own title and mode of expression, and they all introduce themselves in their own manner and without censorship.

A Hindu View of Christianity

Jyoti Patel

I was born in Kampala, Uganda, the youngest of five children, and I have memories of a colourful and vibrant life. My parents had emigrated to Uganda from Gujarat, a state in the west of India, and my father worked for the Ugandan government in the Department of Treasury while my mother looked after us. I was nine when we moved to Britain, where I started attending Clevelands Junior School in Ilford, Essex. My mother learnt to wear Western clothes for the first time in order to work in a tea factory, whilst my father worked in a few factories before getting a job with an insurance company. My schooling continued in London, until I qualified as a dentist from London University in 1987. I married Rajan, who is a surgeon, and we lived in Cardiff for two years before settling in Birmingham. We have three children, all of whom are pursuing a career in medicine.

At school, I participated in singing hymns and reciting 'The Lord Is My Shepherd'; I particularly enjoyed singing Christmas carols. My children also regularly went to church services from their schools. My Hindu upbringing has taught me to believe that praying is still praying whether I do it in a temple or a church, or whether I sing bhajans or hymns. I encouraged my children to think in the same way.

My religious beliefs initially came from my parents and my community. As I grew older, it became important for me to discover them for myself, so I undertook a course of academic study with the Oxford Centre of Hindu Studies. This gave me insight into the vast breadth of belief systems and philosophies within Hindu Dharma and helped me to proceed in my spiritual quest.

Jesus and God

My knowledge about Jesus comes mainly from scriptures I studied at school. The nature of Jesus is confused by the doctrine of the Trinity because 'Son of God' is not the same as 'God the Son,' and yet when I ask Christians about Jesus, they tell me that he is the Son of God and has divine powers but he is not God. One Christian revealed that he does not even believe in the divinity of Jesus. In my view, Jesus is everywhere in Christianity, in statues, paintings, and crucifixes, in celebrations of the Passion play and the Nativity play, so it seems logical to conclude that Jesus is God the Son, because if Jesus is not God the Son, then who is? This then leads me to speculate why the personalities of God the Father and God the Son are so different.

God depicts himself as a jealous God who would punish children for the sins of the parents, even to the third and fourth generation of those who hate him. This is from Exodus 20:5. This God tested people's faith and was cruel to them if they failed. It seems odd to me that God should be jealous at all, because jealousy is not a quality worthy of him, and neither is punishing the innocent. On the other hand, I have often read and heard of Jesus being described as the epitome of forgiveness, even towards Judas, who betrayed him. There are many quotations in the Bible of Jesus's forgiving nature, such as Matthew 9:2, Mark 2:5, Luke 5:20, and Luke 7:47.

The Christian concept of heaven and hell illustrates eternal damnation and, therefore, a lack of forgiveness of some people. The Hindu viewpoint is that all souls will continue to be reborn in order to have the chance to become perfected and then gain freedom from rebirth. Hindus believe that a soul can only remain in heaven and hell for a limited time, after which it is reborn to continue its spiritual progress, because one lifetime is usually not enough to achieve absolute perfection. Since speaking to a few Christians, I have found a difference of opinion about Jesus, and this has been a surprising revelation to me.

Responsibility

I understand that Christians see the story of Adam and Eve as an example of free will, but to me it seems to be more about being obedient to God. A huge amount of importance is placed on determining free will within the religion, which is something that is not a concern for Hindus, since it is evident from the law of karma that one has free will. Also, in the Bhagavad Gita, Krishna—who reveals himself as the Supreme God to Arjuna—teaches Arjuna philosophical wisdom. He concludes in verse 63 of the eighteenth chapter by saying, 'I have now revealed to you this wisdom, which is the deepest mystery. After fully considering what you have heard, you should then act as you see fit.' Krishna does not tell Arjuna how to act, but he does give him the knowledge to help him make up his own mind.[1]

Christians believe that Satan is the root of evil in the world and that he lures them away from God. It is not clear why Satan is so powerful that he is described as the Antichrist, a term which implies that he has equal powers to God. Hinduism does not have an equal and opposite of God, although there are stories of several much less powerful asuras, or demons, so I am unclear about the purpose of Satan. I understand that Christians believe that Jesus died for the sins of humankind, and I take this to mean that Jesus paid the debt of humans' sins by undergoing crucifixion. This disturbs me, as I want to have faith in God out of love and not because of guilt that he died for my sins. As a Hindu, I believe that I am responsible for my actions and will eventually have to pay for them myself.

The practice of Christian principles

I have come across the phrase 'loss of faith' many times in books and on television in relation to Christians' understanding and I understand that losing faith is very problematic for a Christian because those who doubt the faith are not regarded favourably, as exemplified by Doubting Thomas, who was seen in a negative light. This is very different from Hinduism, which encourages inquiry and self-thought without fear of condemnation. The Sanskrit word *vivek* means 'the ability to discriminate between what is true and what is not'. In order for a Hindu to progress on the path to self-realisation, he or she must have *vivek*. There is no Hindu expression for 'loss of faith', since it does not seem necessary. There has been a lot of conflict, even bloodshed, between science and Christianity because of the latter's dogmatic stance. Again, this has not been a problem for Hindus, because there are scriptures on science and health.

The majority of Christian principles—such as charity, respect to all, forgiveness, not holding grudges, being non-judgemental, not being hypocritical, and in general living a moral life—are excellent, but they are also found in all religions, as well as amongst nonreligious people. We all know people who do not follow any religion but who are very morally upright. In fact, some are vastly better than those who are affiliated with a religion. Hindus believe in an eternal soul (Atman) that carries this sense of morality. It can be refined with each birth by one's actions, the guidance of parents, communities, experiences, and thoughts. One does not need to be 'religious', to make progress, although religions can be immensely inspiring, as can be seen in the number of religious charitable organisations.

Christians have often criticised Hindus for idol worship, yet I cannot see a difference between an idol and an icon. I have seen many images of Jesus on a cross or of Jesus as a baby with the Madonna in churches. The cross itself is an image representing the religion. Christians argue that they are not worshipping God's image directly but are worshipping through Jesus Christ, their Lord, but then you can argue that that this challenges the divinity of Jesus.

I think that many Christians have a simplistic and misplaced view of Hindu worship of sacred images. Hindu belief is that God is omnipotent and omnipresent and, therefore, unlimited in form (sakar) or no form (nirakar). God with a form provides a focus for some people to build a loving relationship, whereas other Hindus are more drawn to an abstract God and may not carry out worship but meditate instead, or pursue a path of self-realisation.

Barriers to good interfaith relationship

Christianity has been internally challenged in recent times by people questioning the Christian views towards homosexuality, equality for women within the church structure, the religion's incompatibility with science, and abortion, among other issues. Christian views have become more liberal in Britain in line with modernity, but there also seems to be a decline in the number of active Christians. I have noticed a few beautiful churches that have closed, sadly. Sometimes I feel that in Britain, Christians are needlessly apologetic about being Christian, whereas people of other faiths are quite proud of their religion. The whole religion does not necessarily have to be rejected if there are differences of opinion about aspects of the faith.

There are many Christian charitable organisations that help people across the world, and the majority of these have no agenda but to help the needy. Some, however, do wish to convert non-Christians to Christianity, even if the former already follow a religion.

My view is that Christianity is let down by those groups who insist on proselytising. That shows a lack of respect for other religions and cultures and is not helpful in achieving world peace.

I was alarmed when I learned that some Christian missionary groups have used major disasters as an opportunity to convert people to Christianity. I came across this in a newspaper article which read that 'a missionary, interviewed by the Telegraph newspaper, who didn't want his surname to be revealed, explained in frank terms his motive for being in the worst hit part of Indonesia: "I'm not here to do relief work," said John. His purpose was missionary, he admitted. "They (the disaster victims) are looking for answers," he said, describing them as extremely good candidates for conversion.'[2] This example is not representative of the attitude of all Christians but of a few ill-judged groups, and yet much distaste can result from this type of behaviour. When Jesus said 'love thy neighbour' in the Christian Gospels, I would like to believe he did not reserve this solely for Christian neighbours. Now we are befriending them and giving them food aid, clothes, and other stuff. We need to make friends with them first rather than telling them of the concept of salvation. Long-term, that's where we are heading towards—to save their souls.

Power-hungry politics exemplified by European colonialism have played a large role in the spread of Christianity by forceful means. Even if this element is taken out of the equation, it is wrong to impose one's religion on others on the assumption that it is the only true religion.[3] This behaviour is underpinned by arrogance and ignorance, and therefore evangelism is one aspect of Christianity which I dislike. A Christian colleague told me that he believes that I, as a Hindu, will not get salvation and will burn in hell, in eternal damnation. I understand salvation to mean that a Christian will be saved from hell by the grace of God. It is ridiculous that some Christians believe that an amoral

Christian is better than a moral atheist or a 'heathen' simply by the virtue of being Christian—and that they use this to convert non-Christians to their way of thinking.

An aspect of Christianity which I find hard to understand is the violence between Catholics and Protestants over small differences in religion. Hindu beliefs, philosophies, and practices vary tremendously, but Hindus have managed to live fairly peacefully alongside each other. So why can't Christians? Even today, some Protestants are reluctant to enter a Catholic church and vice versa. The persecution and hatred of Jewish people throughout the history of Christianity is difficult to explain, though people argue that persecutors such as Adolf Hitler and Joseph Stalin were motivated by politics and were not religious. Christianity, Judaism, and Islam have more things in common with each other than other religions do, but they have also had the most troubles between them.

In general, I have had positive experiences with Christians in this country. I appreciate the amount of charitable work that they do. I like the celebrations of Christian festivals, though I do feel Christmas has become more materialistic than religious. I enjoy listening to the church bells on Sunday mornings and have found pleasure in attending a few services. I do wonder whether the decline in followers is attributable to the incompatibility with science or is because people have difficulty with some aspects of the religion and reject it completely. I feel sad because religion can offer so much in terms of focus, discipline, comfort, guidance, community spirit, inspiration, and peace if it is not followed blindly.

December 2015

Through the Eyes of Others

Margaret Jacobi

Rabbi Margaret Jacobi has been the rabbi of Birmingham Progressive Synagogue since 1994. Before becoming a rabbi, she studied medicine at Birmingham University and then started a career in medical research, earning a PhD in physiology and working for two years in St Louis, Missouri, USA. She studied for the rabbinate at the Reconstructionist Rabbinical College (a liberal American branch of Judaism) in Philadelphia and Leo Baeck College in London.

Margaret has been active in interfaith dialogue since she was a rabbinic student, when she was inspired by a week-long Jewish–Christian– Muslim (JCM) conference in Germany. She is a past chair of the Birmingham Council of Christians and Jews and a member of the Birmingham Faith Leaders' Group, and she values the opportunities for interfaith dialogue which Birmingham offers.

She has also maintained her interest in medicine and has published papers on Jewish medical ethics, most recently 'The Challenge of Genetic Research' in Aspects of Liberal Jewish Thought. *She has a PhD in Talmud and is the honorary Progressive Jewish Chaplain at Birmingham University.*

Margaret is married to David and has two teenage children. To relax, she enjoys playing the violin, listening to music and walking in the countryside with her family.

Introduction

In 1994 I started work as the rabbi of Birmingham Progressive Synagogue. Not long afterwards, I received a letter from a Christian minister whose church was down the road from our synagogue and who wanted to meet. That was how I got to know Richard Tetlow.

At our first meeting, Richard spoke of his regret for the Church's history of anti-Judaism and his hope that we and the members of our synagogue and church could get to know and learn about each other. Thus began a personal friendship and an enduring relationship between our synagogue and Richard's church—the Church of St John and St Peter, Ladywood. For some ten years, our synagogue and church met two or three times a year to discuss topics as diverse as suffering, the Messiah, and bringing up children. Deep friendships were formed between our members. Aided by Richard's inspiration, the Ladywood Interfaith Education Project began in 1997 and continues to inspire hundreds of children in Christianity, Judaism, Buddhism, and Islam. Members of each faith teach in their own place of worship, and so the children learn about the holiness of worship and of different faiths working together.

The practice of Christian principles

Richard's friendship was probably the first of many I have formed with Christians in Birmingham. They have included Catholics, evangelicals, liberals, and more traditional Anglicans and Methodists. I have learnt about the variety of Christian beliefs and practices.

Some Christians defend traditional doctrines such as the bodily resurrection of Jesus; others are more questioning. In my experience, what seems to unify Christians, whatever their doctrine, is the example and inspiration they find in the life of Jesus. This leads to engagement with the world and, especially, to reaching out to the poor. Christian principles are put into practice in this outreach—I think Christians would say 'ministry'—to the poor. I have seen it at the local level when churches are located in the poorest neighbourhoods and their ministers live there, available at all hours. The Church is there for all, whatever their religion or belief. If the Church of England has any value as a national church, this must be it: putting Christian principles of love into practice for anyone in need. However, being available places a strain on ministers and their families, and the art of finding a balance is something they must struggle with.

These principles are put into practice, too, in concern for global poverty. If you enter a church, you are likely to see something about its partnership with a developing country. It has been my privilege to work alongside Christians of all denominations—as, for example, in the heady days of the Jubilee Debt Campaign, when we formed a human chain around Birmingham city centre at the G8 Summit in 1998. Their commitment has been remarkable and inspiring.

The Church and its theology

Christian theology still provides much to challenge a Jew. There are aspects which I don't grasp, despite attempts by Christians to explain them to me, such as the Trinity and the resurrection. This is no obstacle to dialogue—rather, it adds another intriguing dimension, and some of my most fruitful dialogue has been about what I couldn't understand. More problematic are the beliefs of some Christians about other religions and more particularly Judaism. I find it difficult to understand the Christian concept of salvation, let alone why, for some Christians, the only way to salvation is through Jesus. I realise that adherents to some other religions, too, see themselves as the only path to God. I also realise that not every Christian holds this belief, only those from certain strands of Christianity.

However, this has never been the case for Judaism. Everyone has his or her own path to God, and it is deeds, not beliefs, which determine whether someone has a place in the 'world to come'. When I first came across the idea within Christianity that as a nonbeliever I would be damned, I felt personally hurt. It does not trouble me now—I do not believe in damnation in any case, and what Christians may believe does not affect what I believe will become of my soul. Nevertheless, I find it disturbing that kind and good people should hold this belief about people of other faiths, as if God were concerned with our beliefs rather than with how we live our lives. Equally, I believe there are many paths to God. The exemplary lives of so many non-Christian—and indeed nonreligious—people demonstrates the truth of this for me.

As well as general beliefs about non-Christians, Christianity has in the past held very particular beliefs about Jews. Anti-Judaism is deeply entrenched in the New Testament. As a new movement struggling to distinguish itself from its sibling, early Christianity was sometimes virulent in its accusations against Judaism. Despite arising from Judaism and basing itself on the life and death of a Jew, Christianity positioned Jews as antagonists who ultimately were accused of being the killers of Jesus.

It was not all one-way in the beginning; anti-Christian polemics can also be found in Jewish literature from the early centuries of Christianity. However, they were not central to Jewish teaching and had very little practical effect. The effect of Christian anti-Jewish teaching, on the other hand, was devastating. For centuries, Jews were persecuted, exiled, and slaughtered in the name of Jesus. This pervasive anti-Judaism created a climate in which the Holocaust was possible, because the Jews were already seen by the majority of inhabitants of Europe as demonic and less than human.

Over the last half century, there has been a recognition of the problematic nature of what the Gospels say about the Jews. Many Christian ministers will now temper their Easter readings with introductions which point out the problems and put the Gospels in the context of their time. The training of ministers often includes teaching about Judaism, which helps them to be aware of the effects of Christian teachings.

Yet still, the effect of the Gospels and their interpretation is pervasive. I continue to hear casual remarks which reflect the bias of the Gospels and the subsequent history of anti-Judaism, such as, 'Jesus wished to heal on the Sabbath, but the rabbis/Pharisees/Jews opposed him,' or, much more often, 'The Jewish god is an angry god, but the Christian god is a god of love.' This is not the place to argue against these statements in detail. Suffice it to say that the first statement does not reflect the historic reality of Jesus's time and the second is a simplistic statement which ignores the fact that the two commandments about love which Jesus said were most important (love God and love your neighbour) are both from the Hebrew Bible (Deuteronomy 6:5 and Leviticus 19:18 respectively).

The theology of the Church towards the Jews has changed in response to the Holocaust, most notably in the Catholic Church, beginning with its document *Nostra Aetate* in 1965. However, preaching in its churches and the media does not always reflect these changes and sometimes still reflects centuries of anti-Judaism. It may not seem blatantly anti-Semitic, but Jews are depicted throughout the New Testament as opponents of Jesus who refuse to recognise him, even though his disciples and those who follow him are also Jews. Such depictions of Judaism are corrosive and need to be addressed.

Jewish–Christian relations in Great Britain at the present time cannot ignore the subject of Israel and Palestine. Sometimes, it seems as if all the positive work that has been done in interfaith relations over the past fifty years will unravel over this question. Some denominations of Christianity have been highly critical of Israel and have joined with moves for boycott, divestment and sanctions. Anti-Israel protest has sometimes dominated whilst human rights abuses elsewhere, notably in the Arab world, have gone unremarked. I have vivid memories of a Church of England minister flourishing his keffiyeh (Palestinian scarf) and proclaiming that the Palestinians symbolise the victims of oppression everywhere. I wrote to ask him whether that meant that Israel—and hence Jews—represented oppressors everywhere, and if so what that said about the demonisation of Jews, but I never received a reply.

That is what I find so disturbing about the present moves to criticise Israel. It is not that Jews, inside and outside Israel alike, are uncritical of the state. Many find the policies of successive governments unacceptable and ally themselves with human rights organisations in Israel that work with Palestinians. Yet many Jews find the singling out of Israel puzzling and disturbing, especially when it approaches the denial of the state of Israel to exist. Why single out Jews? And why should Jews, alone of all religions and peoples, be denied a home of their own? It feels as if there is an underlying and unconscious anti-Semitism in this unremitting focus. Attempts at so-called 'theologies of the land' have imposed judgements from the outside and have failed to understand what the land of Israel means to the Jewish people as our ancient homeland, a refuge from persecution, and a place we can live freely as Jews.

Yet the situation offers an opportunity, too. When Jews and Christians have attempted to address what is so often the 'elephant in the room', greater understanding on both sides has resulted. There is hope that all the work on Jewish–Christian relations can provide a framework and a basis of trust so that when difficult issues arise, they can be discussed and worked out together. For example, the Council of Christians and Jews brings Jews and Christians together to discuss difficult issues; and following the publication by the Methodist Church of a consultation document on Israel and Palestine, discussion took place at a local level in Birmingham and elsewhere between Jews and Christians.

The present-day impact of the Church

From the vantage point of a liberal Jewish woman, I find that the Christian Church seems something of a paradox. In many ways, it is a beacon for progress. The work done at a local level is inspiring, particularly the care extended by parish churches to those in need. In Birmingham, the commitment of Christians to campaigning for a better world has made a powerful impact. It has brought together people of different faiths who share that commitment and who have forged strong partnerships and friendships. At a national level, it has been heartening in recent months to hear the bishops speak out about increasing poverty and inequality.

Yet as an outsider looking at the Church of England, I continue to be puzzled and frustrated by its attitude to women and people in same-sex relationships. Its acceptance of women to positions of responsibility has been painfully slow, though the recent ordaining of the first woman bishop is an enormous step forward. The Anglican Church at an official level continues to deny the love of two people committed to each other just because those two people happen to be of the same sex, justifying the stance by quoting out of context from the book of Leviticus. By opposing legislation first for civil partnerships and then for same-sex marriage, the Church of England has appeared reactionary, when it is in so many ways a force for good.

Finally, though, it is a tribute to the honesty, openness, and faith of Christians I have met that I have been able to have conversations with them about all these subjects. Interfaith dialogue with Christians and work beside them has enriched my faith and the life of my congregation. It is not every faith which would be open to a critique such as I have written, and it is only because I have had that experience that I feel able to write as I have. I thank Richard Tetlow for giving me this precious opportunity, and I thank all the Christians I have worked with, especially in Birmingham, for the privilege of having done so.

December 2015

Christians and Christianity: A Sikh Perception

Pyara Singh Bhogal

I was born in Hoshiar in the Indian Punjab in 1953. In 1961, I moved to Handsworth, Birmingham, to join my dad, who was a carpenter. I spent my childhood and youth at school in Birmingham. I stayed here to train as a doctor, and I have worked for forty-four years largely as a diabetes specialist in podiatric medicine, becoming head of that department in the Heart of Birmingham Hospital. I still work part-time as a podiatric surgeon.

In 1991 I joined the Council of Sikh Gurdwaras, of which I am now assistant secretary general, and became the chair of its health education committee, organising voluntary clinics for the Sikh community, particularly for diabetes. I managed school visits to the Ramgarhia Gurdwara, Graham Street, which I attend and of which I am assistant secretary. When I realised my lack of professionalism, I undertook the Tourist Faith Guiding course run by Ruth Tetlow. This taught me essential skills in communication, knowledge of different faiths, and not least an increased attitude of respect towards their members.

I joined the chaplaincy team at the Queen Elizabeth Hospital as the Sikh advisor. I experienced the last ten to twenty years of increased interfaith activity, communication, and understanding between people of different faiths, as I'd felt that there was a habit developing of inward-looking selfishness amongst individuals and faith groups. This has changed very much for the better. Our school and hospital visits are much improved as compared to what they used to be.

I see the major world faiths now as all equal under God—different, of course, but equal. Perceptions, however, can unfortunately suggest inequality. I am fortunate to have three sons by my wife and to still appreciate hockey and badminton.

Comparisons

I'm going to approach this subject by making some comparisons between the Christian and Sikh faiths. The first difference that strikes me is that Christianity grew up two thousand years ago, and the Sikh faith just five hundred. I used to think the Christian faith was created by Jesus. Anyway, I know now it wasn't. The Sikh faith was created by the first guru himself, Guru Nanak, who lived from 1469 to 1539 in India's Punjab. I understand that Christianity developed in memory of Jesus through a number of followers, all with their different ideas, stories, and reported memories.

Why did Jesus not create Christianity himself? Perhaps he was happy being a Jew, except that Jewish leaders were pushed around by the Romans. I think he wanted to try to improve the ways of both.

Christians in time had to fight to survive against the Romans; same for the Sikhs in India. Much later in Africa, Christians unfortunately chose to fight to assert themselves during colonial times. I wish our prime minister would apologise for Britain's complicity in the Indian Hindu attack on our most holy shrine, Shri Harmandir Sahib (the Golden Temple), in 1984 and its genocidal aftermath. He stands for what is seen in India as the British Christian country. Sikhs would see such apology as Christians supporting justice and truth.

I understand that Jesus gave his own life to save this world, so he was called Saviour of the World and friend of needy people. Sikhs back in India have different names for him that I like: Jisu, Masaih (messenger), Prabu (Lord), and Maalik (owner). This shows our unity. Christians have followed Jesus's life in seeking a religion of peace, love, and harmony. Sikhs like the principle of the equality of all people before God that Jesus taught. Christians are lucky not to have an old caste system, and they are getting over sex discrimination. I wish Christians were against alcohol, but in my experience, the majority are against drugs. Sikhs are against all four of these things, plus smoking. Christianity shows the path of excellent living and in principle promotes love among humanity and is welcoming to the public. To be honest, my experience of Christians in Birmingham is that they are helpful and show compassion, charity, and a sense of justice. These are all important to Sikhs.

Jesus is obviously a marvellous personal example for everyone, including Sikhs, to follow as a spiritual leader. He taught his Lord's Prayer and said that people could pray directly to God, who loves them all. Guru Nanak was similar. He taught prayer, but as chanting and meditation, and especially to see God in the faces of all humanity. Jesus usually taught in parables. Are these stories less direct yet more subtle than assumed? After ten gurus altogether, all teachers, the last human guru, Guru Gobind Singh, began a new way forward in a brotherhood called the Khalsa. That was created in 1699 in the month of Vaisakhi, which is the Sikhs' New Year. I understand he was like Wesley, who founded Methodism as a Christian reform movement.

Christianity seems to me less organised than the Sikh faith despite the Pope being in charge of the Catholics. Sikhs' authority in procedures and policies comes from Akaal'Takht in the Harmandir Sahib, which is like the Vatican but with no one person in charge. Jesus's birth is remembered at Christmas, a festival we enjoy too, like many others, such as Vaisakhi and Diwali, the Festival of Light, which are also celebrated annually.

It seems to me that Christians are required to follow Christianity with blind faith as a condition for achieving salvation, though good deeds are important to them. By contrast, the Sikh faith is that salvation is achieved just by such good deeds. Guru Nanak Dev Ji said that before they become good Sikhs, Christians, Muslims, Hindus, or Jews, human beings must first become good human beings. Some things Christians do like us: they believe in hard work and give to charity, 5 per cent, I think. The end of salvation for Christians would appear to me the same as it is for Sikhs: heaven or hell now and/or in the afterlife.

I was taught Christians must be submissive to God, like Muslims. Unlike the Sikhs, they do not believe in reincarnation. The cross of Jesus crosses me out. That's not the same for Sikhs. Since the Khalsa, we see people as created not just to fit in but to stand out of the crowds and to be of a faith other than Islam and Hinduism. It's often easy to tell Sikhs from Christians, the latter of whom, I think, are taught to be more meek and mild, especially Christian women, though that's changing. As far as I know, Christians have nothing like our five K's of shorts, unshorn hair, kirpan (Shri Sahib), bangle, and comb. I notice some Christians do wear a cross—and with pride. So they should.

I know that Jesus travelled around his country of Palestine to meet people, especially those who needed his help and healing power. He was very popular with the crowds, who were mostly poor country people—a real loving man of the people. Guru Nanak also travelled extensively and even met the Pope in Rome. Like Jesus showed in telling the story of the Good Samaritan, he mixed with people of different faiths. That's a great thing in common for Christians and Sikhs. On every journey, Guru Nanak was accompanied by Bhai Bala-ji, a Hindu, and Bhai Mardana-ji, a Muslim. The story goes that he was asked by them who was the most good—that is the best—the Muslim or the Hindu? He replied that the question was irrelevant. Our duty is to be a good Christian, a good Sikh, or a good Muslim. I think Jesus would have said the same.

Teaching is obviously important for both our faiths. I went to Christian primary school in Handsworth, Birmingham, in the sixties. I was in the church choir. There was no gurdwara near us then. I thought nothing of it, but I don't think parents now would encourage their Christian kids to go to a Sikh school. I remember we sang 'Onward Christian Soldiers' and 'When the Saints Go Marching In'. They were good to sing. I learned at home that Sikhs had to be soldiers and saints, like Christians: soldiers to protect and saints to meditate. I sense, though, that this is no longer an ambition for Christians. I think that the Sikh faith is more straightforward and clear.

My perception is that Christianity is 'believing in Jesus Christ' as the Son of God who is 'the third person of the Trinity'. Somehow,

Christians seem to think God is three in one. When Christians say that Jesus is God or that 'Son of God' means the same as God, as a Sikh, that seems to me confusing and mistaken. For Sikhs, the distinction is important. They take to heart that the tenth master guru, Gobind Singh, said that he was 'the son of God', but anyone who says "I am (the) God himself" will not get salvation. As far as I know, Jesus never called himself God. We can call God Ram, Allah, Waheguru, or even Christ according to preference. He is seen as the one supreme eternal reality—without time, sex, or form, and not accessible through deities. Christians would go along with all that, I imagine.

The mother will teach the child that 'God is one', because that's our fundamental code. I was taught that Christians see God as beyond words—indescribable, transcendent, and immanent too. Isn't all that why the man Jesus can't really be God? Sikhs have no problem with Jesus's demonstration of his message to humanity and being God's spiritual revelation. To Sikhs, the gurus are too. But that is not to say that Jesus or the ten gurus were God.

When I heard that Christianity and Judaism have a jealous God, I was very surprised. We see God as Creator, without fear or animosity, self-illuminated, unborn, outside the order of birth and death. In our scriptures, God is completely merciful and without a trace of vengeance or anger. The important point is that there are many different paths but one final destination, which is to be with God. When you make the connection with God, you will not be able to express that to anyone else. That will be spiritual union. Through meditation, we discover that he was true and merciful when time began and that he is now and he will be forever and ever. I think Christians agree with all that. Christians I know pray 'Lord, have mercy'; Sikhs pray 'Merciful, merciful, merciful; my God is merciful', which comes from the Sikh holy scripture, Shri Guru Granth Sahib (SGGS) 724, Rag 5, dating back to 1604.

So there seem to be contradictions or just different opinions in the Bible that don't exist in the Guru Granth Sahib. My understanding of the Bible is that it was written over a long period of time—nearly a thousand years—by all sorts of people and that the stories about Jesus were written by four men called the Gospel writers some time after Jesus was killed. Other followers travelled as disciples and missionaries and wrote letters to spread Jesus's message of love for all. I don't think any of them knew Jesus, and even if they did, it would be hard to prove they could remember what he said or what he meant.

The Shri Guru Granth Sahib is not history and is not meant to be, because it is about moral and spiritual truths, so we have no problem in believing it literally, as the writings are just true to life and experience. To the Sikh faith, they are the truth, just as to Christians, Jesus himself is 'the Truth'. The GGS never makes a mistake, because it is not that kind of record—not history, but 'living', more like poetry and music. GGS is so respected that it is called a Perpetual Guru, the Perfect Guru, or the Word Guru.

I'm offended by Christians not treating the Bible itself better than they seem to. I remember seeing it actually on the floor during services. Why is it not respected more? Could be because it's a storybook, not chiefly a history book, and when people find that out, some lose their old respect for it instead of giving it a new respect in a different way. I can't imagine there is much real factual history in it at all, and I've picked up that it has factual contradictions. As a kid, I was taught five things about the Bible that have stayed with me. It is basic (B) and it gives instructions (I) for us before (B) leaving (L) earth (E). That spells B-I-B-L-E. It does not seem to have anything like the same status as the GGS.

I am not sure just what faith means to Christians, except faith in Jesus as the Son of God, which we've referred to already. To me as a Sikh, that's a bit heady; I'm not sure what it means. For Sikhs, faith is love—that is, love of God who is the Creator. I'm sure Christians go for this too. Faith for us means that you will do something actively for God. If you love God, you will not have any doubts or questions about God, and by doing good deeds, you will meet God.

I find two things difficult about Christianity and Christians. Firstly, Christianity can be exclusive, which is a pity. Their Communion of bread and wine in church shuts out those who are not Christians. Sikhs have something similar, but the *kara parshad* (a sweet) is offered to everyone; so is the meal called *langar*, which is served free to all comers to the gurdwara. This signifies Sikhs' equality. From my church experience, despite Christians being kind to me personally, I don't remember Christians as a community being quite so hospitable. I admit, though, that at times, Sikhs have also been guilty of arrogance.

The chief problem I have with Christianity is illustrated on a church noticeboard near where I live declaring 'Only One Way'. That is not right, and it offends the Sikh principle of the equality of all people, as I've mentioned, and which, after all, Jesus himself stood for. Sikhs believe there are different ways to God. I don't like Christians being superior like this, especially when they are not superior in principle or practice. Only God is superior. However, all faiths have found themselves up against violent discrimination at some time in their history, with severe indirect consequences, especially when in a minority situation. Mutual understanding, respect, and equality between Christians and Sikhs and all the faiths in the name of our one God is my priority.

By the way, Christians don't belong to Christianism or 'Christism', just like Sikhs don't belong to Sikhism but to the Sikh faith; otherwise, we would both be ideologies.

February 2017

A Muslim Perception of Christianity

Muhammad Amin-Evans

Muhammad Amin-Evans was born in inner-city postwar Birmingham and, a little later, underwent an education which included what was then called Religious Instruction. RI was an exclusively Christian study of Christianity with heavy overtones of missionary righteousness. Although the complexity of colour had appeared in the cinema, religion for children was a far simpler choice of black or white. However, when he reached the age of twelve, Muhammad found that some light and colour flooded through the shutters in the form of books by Christmas Humphreys and Karl Marx in the Handsworth public library, and he began to laugh.

Having developed into a very strict monotheist, rejecting Christian dogmas and apologies, Muhammad, at the age of forty-two, unexpectedly became a Muslim and entered a Shi'ite seminary, emerging with the degrees Shahadat Al-Alimiyyah and MA in Arabic and Islamic studies, to become a sermonising sheikh and prayer leader. While undertaking a variety of religious duties—including teaching at Al-Mahdi Institute and the Islamic College for Advanced Studies in Birmingham—he earned a degree in humanities and religious studies from that wonderful establishment the Open University. He often leads Friday prayers in Derby, makes regular broadcasts on Islamic TV, and reads when not sleeping. A key element in his teaching is that 'British values' include the rights of assembly, radicalism, and nonconformity.

His present contribution to this book (is it a bonbon or a bitter pill?) is the product of a long life spent observing religions in text and in action—from within and without—and should be swallowed with the cordial understanding that too much sweetness makes pimples on the body seem normal. They should not be ignored.

Behind dialogue

> It is the step from dialogue between people who each believe, at the back of their minds and usually without saying it aloud, that theirs is really the one and only true or fully true faith, to dialogue between people who accept the genuine religious equality of the other, so that they can then benefit freely from one another's distinctive spiritual insights and be free to join together in facing the massive social and economic and political problems of the world.
> John Hick[4]

It has been observed that theology comes into existence when one religion encounters another religion and tries to explain its beliefs. However, the explanation is also an argument to convince the other of the correctness of a belief. With this in mind, a simplistic definition of interfaith dialogue might be an arena for theology without confrontation, but this denies the fundamental truths that language is argument and that those involved in the process of dialogue have a variety of beliefs which they wish others to also believe. The anecdotal evidence presented concentrates upon examples of 'Christian' behaviour and seeks to substantiate Hick's observation of dialogue, while further demonstrating that interfaith dialogue as constructed by Western Christianity may be either a poor man's theology or a substitute for religion but is often a subcategory of ecumenism acting as a vehicle for soft evangelism.

There has been some criticism of Malaysia, a majority Muslim state, from Christians and 'liberal' Muslims for forbidding Christians the use of the name Allah for God.[5] While a majority of Muslims find the Malaysian actions 'heavy-handed', their rulings are based upon fact and grounded in suspicion. Allah has a very specific, precise, and exclusive meaning, and they believe that Christians, other than Unitarians, use the name Allah to deceive Muslims and undermine the state religion of Islam, and are at the very least lexically inaccurate.

Although many of the critics accuse the Malaysian government of something akin to paranoia and restricting religious freedom, there is evidence that their suspicions are not unfounded. A. C. Bouquet, in his still readily available *Comparative Religion*, notes that Tao (pronounced 'Dow') 'is the official rendering of Logos in the Protestant Chinese version of St John's Gospel' in a chapter which concludes by praising Christian missionary activity in China and Japan with wishes for further successes.[6] *Logos* to the Muslim means 'the way of living', not the 'Word of God'. If this were the only example of loose translation and an isolated historical comment, it might be ignored. However, recent Web advice from evangelical groups to their female members is to avoid confrontation, wear Islamic dress, celebrate Islamic festivals, make friends with Muslim women, and use the name Allah instead of God in order to make Muslim families more susceptible to the Gospel 'message'. Of course, the majority of Christians do not use conscious deception or consider women to be spiritual 'weak links', but all peoples are judged to some extent by what is done in their name.

The actions and conversations related, of people who defined themselves as Christians who believe in dialogue between faiths, are analysed to reveal their 'unwitting testimony'[7] so that the Christian gaze which lies hidden within and beyond dialogue, which Hick described as at the back of the mind, may be exposed. As Jean-Paul Sartre observed, 'Insofar as I am the object of values which come to qualify me without my being able to act on this qualification or even to know it, I am enslaved.'[8] Although the gaze may mislead its slaves, it is not necessarily a bad thing, since most humans have and need a gaze for each social role. However, some of those regarded as Christians by Muslims are not considered Christians, let alone 'good' Christians, by some other Christians, whether or not the former live according to Christian principles. It is their gaze which most strictly delimits Christianity's diverse voices and apparently grants some, like Bouquet, the right to judge the correctness of denominations and the validity of any faith.

The strength of the Christian gaze is indicated by the ease with which Christian narratives are wholeheartedly accepted as detached or truthful and occasionally to the absurd extent of welcoming the false statements of known liars. A lay Arab Christian who holds an interfaith post with his church was reported by a group of Christians to have said that the word *love* is not used in the Qur'an. What he neglected to tell them was that the word he referred to was *'ishq*, which is used to mean carnal love and was not associated with religion until long after the Qur'an was recorded. He also neglected to mention that two words which still mean *love*, *'hubb'* and *'wudd'*, appear frequently in the Qur'an. Is the Christian gaze, then, always truly Christian in spirit; or may it be informed by a remnant of the cultural chauvinism that believed in a moral and scientific superiority or of an assumption that other races and their followers are incapable of truth; or is it a remnant of early Christian theological responses and heresy-ographic assaults upon other faiths which freely employed the principle of the ends justifying the means? Whatever the causes, structural as opposed to spiritual Christianity has annoyed writers for Imperial Rome, Saladin, Voltaire, Thomas Carlyle, Crazy Horse, Karl Popper, and Richard Dawkins in various ways. Surely a thinking Christian must ask if these men were all wrong.

A repeated contradictory response to emic descriptions of faith is 'But you _____s believe _____', which reveals an unwitting message of assumed superiority that is certain to offend if we substitute the implicit 'you people' for the name of followers of a religion. An example of the heedless preference for a Christian's explanation was given by a group of Christians visiting an Islamic institute where several Islamic scholars had answered all questions tendered. The ordained leader of the visitors rose to thank the hosts and then announced with great excitement that at their next meeting, attendees would learn all about Islam from a guest, Bishop Kenneth Cragg. Might not Dr Cragg be embarrassed by such a claim for his knowledge, especially if voiced within earshot of Muslim scholars? The gaze's unwitting testimony is almost invisible to those who are subject to its power, and it affects actions, speech, and writing with ingenuous ease.

The described Christian gaze upholds the assumption of an innate right or privilege for Christians to say who should represent other faiths. Those misled in this way have been overheard saying of untypical Muslims, such as a young woman in a short and revealing dress, someone bowing to a shrine, and someone lighting devotional candles, that they are Muslims whom Christians can 'work' with. However, what purpose and what work? Are these men and women who by their words and deeds have rejected the Islam of the majority of Muslims seen as 'weak links' to be befriended? Muslims value modesty and do not bow in worship before anyone or anything except their Creator. Thus, the observer of Christian self-deceptions is led to question the intention of accepting rebellious, subversive, heretical, or ignorant Muslims who have not lost faith but who question parts of it and accepting them as 'useful friends'. This is, at best, not respect for another's faith but the judgemental toleration of another's perceived error or lack of capacity. Christians who define what Muslims were, are, and should be based upon received, partial, remote, or selective observation need to critically reflect upon what they are saying.

We are all tempted to assume that someone who does not accept our particular belief has either not read or understood what our primary texts say. As someone who was introduced to religious studies in school at a time when the phrase meant biblical studies, and being obviously white and British, I find it somewhat piquing to be told, 'You probably don't know this, Amin, but the Bible says ...' However, sometimes a particular knowledge of someone else's dogma may be assumed.

One of the criticisms Muslims have of Christianity's beliefs and practices is of those who do not directly originate from revealed text or divine example. At an interfaith meeting in Worcester Cathedral, I was asked, 'Why do Muslims pray on Fridays?' I answered, and added, 'Might I ask why Christians pray on Sundays?' A retired Anglican bishop leapt to his feet, rudely screaming that I was being facetious and should know that it was to mark the day of resurrection. However, how did

Sunday become the day of worship, and why should anyone know that, and particularly a Muslim? His anger inspired my curiosity.

Further research revealed that the practice of churching on Sunday began in the Roman churches to deter the 'faithful' from screaming at the circus on their day of rest. This was a big problem in Christian Rome, as Augustine describes in his *Confessions*. Saturday remained the Sabbath for a while but was eventually abandoned, except by some denominations who have revived the Saturday Sabbath. However, the superior rights assumed by Christians means that 'the Lord's Day' is imposed, as if commanded by God, upon friends, neighbours, and strangers alike. Brass bands rattle windows before breakfast or congregations of churches travel from far and wide to disturb their neighbours with electronically amplified music from Friday to Sunday night. Is the anger of a bishop or the disruption of peace 'God's work' or proof that 'Jesus loves me', as I am told?

At a community carnival, a Baptist minister asserted the triple Divinity and responded to questions with, 'Ah, that's the mystery!' Our conversation had begun with his questioning why I had become a Muslim and actually concluded with my saying, 'Ah, that was one mystery too many for me.' I walk away when anyone uses mysteries to defend dogma in defiance of observed phenomena and sound reason.

One great fallacy created by European Christians and perpetuated by academic religious studies is that Africa, India, Japan, and the Americas have various religions whereas Europe is Christian. David Cameron, Britain's prime minister from 2010 to 2016, repeatedly asserted that Britain is a Christian country, despite evidence to the contrary. Encouraged by this posture, some Christians have renewed the ancient claim to a right of authority over all matters religious, and having proven the case to the government's satisfaction, have further claimed that they are best suited to control public funds intended for interfaith projects. However, this further claim denies a liberty to many citizens. Those citizens who believe in ancient indigenous faiths and those of Christian denominations 'othered' by the majority Christian churches should also be considered as the religions of Europe and entitled to undiminished liberties. When the rights by birth of large numbers of British Muslim, Hindu, Sikh, Jewish, Buddhist, humanist, and agnostic European citizens are added to the mix, it must be asked why so many scholars of religious studies have ignored critical voices and demographics, and supported the divisive political fantasy of fortress Christendom.

Citizens, the majority of whom obediently pay taxes, must have equal liberties protected by law without preference. If one faith is permitted preference or exception, the citizenship of all becomes a sham. It is paradoxical to uphold the customary religious privileges of Christianity, for which other faiths should pay, and issue ill-informed attacks upon the principle of Jizya, the tax introduced upon non-Muslims exempt from paying the zakat, which they have always paid, to the shared public purse. The reasoned arguments of Thomas Jefferson,[9] James Madison, and John Leland for religious freedom, citizenship for all, and just taxation fuelled the American Revolutionary War, but they were all accused of being non-Christians in their lifetimes and carry little weight with today's Christians and Christian governments. However, it might be asked what—other than dubious, dehumanised, and inappropriate business theories—does carry weight with the custodians of Christian Europe. Beliefs that have led to the ethical and egalitarian principles of Enlightened reform are being submerged beneath a surge of calls for citizenship to be linked with wealth or particular religious and ethnic identities.

My Muslim gaze suggests that the messages we, including our elected representatives, receive from Christianity today are somewhat different from the message the first disciples heard. Muslims are acutely aware of differences between early Christian teaching and its later crusading imperialism and artful evangelism. In the early church, men's and women's rights to be different were recognised, but they are now told that they must mingle, even if it is against their beliefs, even when both may prefer to be separate, so that the secular gods of pseudo-Christian modernism may be satisfied. While change may be inevitable, the degradation of religious liberty caused by unrestricted liberalism is avoidable. In a nation declared Christian by politicians bereft of honesty, values, and virtue, the moral pillars that spiritual Christianity shares with other faiths have been eroded by the cultured despisers of religion: TV comedians, egoistic bombards, and those desiring to conform to the absurdities of hypothetical modernity. Meanwhile, lost souls seek psychological and spiritual counselling as they recover from exposure to pole dancing, payday loans, and material excesses.

A Christian reader might respond to my anecdotes by asserting that such behaviour is not unique to Christianity and that such incidents may be common to all power structures. However, the brief for this essay was to present what a British Muslim perceives of Christianity, and a distinction was briefly made between Christianity as a spiritual practice and structural Christianity. I could have flooded the page with the good that Christians do in the world, but praise conceals problems, breeds complacency, and thereby halts reform. The common utility of religions is that they offer people the opportunity to raise themselves above common errors by following the divine moral guidance of the path they have chosen, and if and when they waver, they leave themselves open to just criticism. Moreover, since religious 'truths' are offered to the whole of humanity, it is the right and duty of any human to ask those who make the offer what the offer truly consists of and if it is being honestly made.

February 2016

A Buddhist Perception of Christianity

Sinhavacin Walsh

I was born in south-west London in 1951. Though my parents never attended any church, except for family occasions, and were effectively nonbelievers (my grandfather was an active atheist), I was baptised as a child in the Church of England, simply because it was the usual thing. My primary school was attached to the local Anglican church, and we had regular visits from the curate, but I can't remember what he taught us. I attended Sunday school for a while at a nearby church (Baptist?); I think we were taught the Ten Commandments, amongst other things, but mostly I remember such activities as painting a picture of the baby Jesus at Christmas. For a while, when I was about nine or ten, I took myself to evensong at my nearest Anglican church, mainly because I liked the hymns.

In my late twenties, I was living a good, comfortable life, but I became aware of a lack of deeper meaning. Since Anglicanism was all I knew, I connected with my local church, and after a while I was elected to the Parish Church Council and was confirmed. I enjoyed my involvement in the church and suppressed my doubts about the metaphysics. Then in my mid-thirties, I happened to discover Buddhism and found that it made sense to me in ways that Christianity never had. In 1999, I was ordained in the Triratna Buddhist Order. I have had little contact with Christianity since then, which shows how separately different faiths and their members can be even in a small section of a big city.

God and responsibility

The request to write this contribution, which is only one Buddhist's view of Christianity as he remembers and understands it from his earlier years, prompted me to read the Sermon on the Mount for the first time in many years—at least since my discovery of Buddhism. The picture of Jesus that emerged for me was mixed in an interesting way. There is much to admire here: keep conscientiously to the path and serve as an example to others (Matthew 5:13–16); resolve your anger against others (Matthew 5:21–26); do not respond to violence with violence, but with compassion (Matthew 5:38–42); love your enemies (Matthew 5:44); don't rush to judgement (Matthew 7:1–5); do to others as you would wish them to do to you (the golden rule, Matthew 7:12).

As day-to-day ethical precepts, these are things that a Buddhist might put into slightly different words, but the moral guidance would often be much the same. I do reject the rationale, though, that Jesus gives for much of this: in most cases, we are told that the rewards (or punishments) come in the next life. A Buddhist sees good reason to behave ethically without any need to appeal to heaven or hell as places other than here and now.

There are other clauses in the Sermon on the Mount that I am more doubtful about. While I can see that it is not good to be overconcerned with food or clothing, or (by implication) the wider material aspects of life (Matthew 6:25–34), it seems to me, as someone who does not believe in Providence, that taken to the extreme, this could become a teaching of personal and social irresponsibility and be used as an excuse for neglecting the welfare of others or that of the world. This depends on practical circumstances. I admire the Franciscan practice of poverty, just as I do the almost identical precepts of Theravada Buddhist monks; but on the whole, they lived or live in places where the climate is gentle, food is (mostly) easy to come by, and the laity can be relied on to take care of the needs that the monks cannot themselves fulfil. Living such a life now on the streets of Birmingham in winter would be another matter entirely. In saying this, I do not belittle the aspiration.

I hope that nobody would now follow the highly sexist teaching on divorce (Matthew 5:31–32), though I suspect this might still be responsible for the view of fundamentalist Catholics. While I would agree that adultery should be avoided (by both sexes), I am baffled by Jesus's statement (Matthew 5:28) that 'if a man looks at a woman lustfully, he has already committed adultery with her in his heart'. This strikes me as psychologically absurd; men (and women) cannot control their emotional and physical impulses, at least not without lengthy training. What matters is what we do about those impulses. And the following two verses (Matthew 5:29–30) 'if your eye should cause you to sin, tear it out' and 'if your hand should cause you to sin, cut it off'—seem to me to be similarly spiritually disastrous. We should be encouraged to control ourselves when it seems possible, not destroy ourselves (and I don't think I am reading this over literally). All this is tantamount to saying that it is sinful to have human reactions. I can see nothing remotely helpful in this. It is our minds that cause us to sin.

My interpretation of what I understand of Christian views of sin is that sin is a transgression, either wilful or negligent, of arbitrary rules made by a person in a position of power, and is something which attracts punishment from such a person. In Buddhism, by contrast, we refer to unethical behaviour as being 'unskilful', in that if I knew or understood better, or were better trained, I would have the skill to behave differently, to the benefit of myself and others. This, like much in Buddhism, is essentially practical: it is something that can be learned, investigated, and practised, and when it reaches a level of proficiency, it just works.

The big problem, of course, is God. Buddhism is explicitly nontheistic, in that there is no place for a Creator, no transcendental personal being to intervene in the world. Since the time I discovered Buddhism, the word *God* has become meaningless to me, and I don't know now what people mean when they say it. I understand that progressive Christians are in a process of rethinking all this, but so far as I know, this new thinking is not the official position of any of the main Christian churches and is not reflected in the Christian liturgies. The result of this is that when I attend Christian services, as I sometimes do when invited, the words said and sung often have their positive emotional ring, but on a rational level are to me still pretty meaningless, since the idea of a God that can be talked or sung to corresponds to nothing I see in the actual world.

My perception, from my contacts with ordinary people over the years, is that the vast majority of non-observing British people, who until the mid-twentieth century would have automatically called themselves Christian, feel the same way, if they give it any consideration at all. I am thinking of people from my own English background, and therefore consciously excluding recently arrived British Muslims, et al. I can see the possibility here of a growing problem for interfaith dialogue. It seems to me, based on my fairly limited experience, that believing Jews and Muslims tend to hold quite strongly to a personal creator God. The more Christianity moves from that, the more difficult the dialogue might become for everyone.

From the Buddhist point of view, there is a much more serious problem with the traditional idea of an omnipotent God, connected with the standard theodicy problem as to how a beneficent God can allow evil and suffering in the world—but it takes a slightly different line. To illustrate it clearly, I have to adopt a rather naive position. As far as I recall, in many prayers, people ask for God's guidance, his protection, relief from suffering, and so on, and thank him for his 'gifts', material and spiritual. But if God is in control of everything that happens in the world in this way, then everything that I might do is ultimately his responsibility, not mine. So why is it 'my sin'? In any case, I only need to repent or atone for it - how deeply or sincerely? - and God will forgive, and then I can forget all about it.

Notoriously, this idea reached ridiculous lengths in the late medieval period, when you could buy 'indulgences' which guaranteed you God's forgiveness for sins you had not yet committed. Perhaps modern Christians will say that they do not actually think like that; but this mechanistic—almost commercial—view is implied in the liturgy, which repeatedly undermines the idea of personal responsibility by unloading it onto God, with whom it is wise to curry favour. What this unloading can lead to is a tendency to think that we do not need to care for the poor, or the old, or the sick, because God is or should be doing it; we do not need to care for the planet, because God is doing it. And if he isn't stopping us from making stupid decisions, then he still has it in hand.

The Buddhist position is that we live as we do as a result of the conditions surrounding us and our individual and collective histories; so, while we are not completely free agents—if I wanted to fly, I would have had to have been born a bird—it is up to us to make the internal and external changes that will improve our lives. It is very much a matter of taking personal responsibility for fixing our problems in whatever way we can. It seems to me that Christianity, at least in its more naive forms, can actually discourage such responsibility, appearing to write everything off as 'God's will'. I am aware that in fact their faith has motivated many Christians to be very active in the world, both for better and for worse; but I wonder how they reconcile this activity with their notion of God as being in any way in control of the world.

Another aspect of this question is that of suffering and blame. Many people in this world suffer terribly—caught up in cruel wars (non-combatants as well as combatants), infected by appalling diseases that cripple or kill, or starved because there is not enough food or it is not being justly distributed. Yet if we are so fortunate as to live long, prosperous, and healthy lives, we must ourselves still suffer the pains of disappointment and loss, at the very least, as well as having the awareness of the greater sufferings of others and the precariousness of our own good fortune. Where is God in all this? The failure of God to intervene to alleviate suffering is particularly acute in avoidable cases such as wars and genocides, which result from mere greed, hate, and ignorance. If God cannot prevent such atrocities, what is he good for? How could he have looked the other way when Hitler was building Auschwitz?

The question is not just an abstract one. The idea that somebody must be in control, and therefore must be to blame, is deeply embedded in the way many people approach the world. I have seen it particularly in ex-Christians, whose immediate response to any misfortune is to look for somebody to blame. Since it can't be God, either because he is good or because they don't believe in him anymore, then it must be their spouse, or their next-door neighbour, or the government. Some politicians do this all the time.

I see what is to me a related incoherence in Christianity regarding predetermination or predestination. Has God decided in advance what our fate is to be, and are we mere puppets? If we have free will, how far does it reach? If we can choose to oppose successfully the will of God, then how can his almighty power be limited by our puny actions? If the only free choice that we can make is to love God and be obedient, then it is a Hobson's choice.

It seems to me that a main thrust of Jesus's teaching was to the downtrodden, teaching a way of life and thought that might reduce their suffering. If that is so, then it is quite inappropriate for it to become incorporated into an established or state religion. In the way Christianity developed as an institution, it took on all the problems of power structures, with institutionalisation dominating the teachings of Jesus as its priority. Actually, I think it is a mistake for any religion to be incorporated into a state, as the concerns of religion and those of political power have very little in common, and the loser is always religion, where power can corrupt to a disastrous degree. (This has happened to Buddhism as well—for example, Zen's enthusiastic and shameful support for Japanese imperialism and warfare in the first half of the twentieth century.)

I have to acknowledge the great contribution of Christianity to European art, and particularly music. My life would be greatly impoverished without music from the Western Christian tradition, and I accept that this has been a fruit of the Christian institutions that I have been criticising. I still feel deeply moved by all sorts, from the motets of Victoria and Tallis, through Bach, to Elgar, Messiaen, and Britten. Interestingly, many of those are Catholics. I wonder if the intensity of the Catholic faith might perhaps inspire some artists to a level of spiritual creativity that transcends the ostensible content of their work, endowing it with universal appeal.

In some ways, I do regret the decline of Christianity in the West. The church used to be a valuable focus for communities—a source of social cohesion and care and moral direction. I suspect that this decline has contributed to many of the problems that we experience in modern society. In Britain, the more recent political assault on the welfare state and the NHS has made this all the worse, as for well over a century church work served as a partially adequate substitute for state activity. God has disappeared in our secular age, squeezed out by the pincer movement of scientific reductionism and economic materialism. All that now motivates many of us is insatiable greed for more personal wealth, the pursuit of consumerism, and a deliberate lack of concern for others, individually or collectively.

Since God is dead and the political consensus approves of all this, there is no impetus to behave differently. If we no longer think in terms of heaven or hell, and if we have rejected eternalism in favour of nihilism (I see both as errors), there is nothing to strive for or care about except ourselves. If we cannot find a way to reintroduce some spiritually healthy element into our thinking and our lives, we could be heading towards a new spiritual dark age. We seem to be rapidly retreating in the direction of Hobbes's 'war of all against all' that a stronger Church might have been able to prevent.

December 2016

1   The Bhagavad Gita, Commentary and Translation, ed. Nick Sutton (Oxford Centre for Hindu Studies, January 2010).

2   Alan Brant, in 'Aceh, survivors and aid workers mourn the dead, then focus on the living', Daily Telegraph Baptist Press, 7 Jan. 2005.

3   At the time of writing, this is changing because of the appalling situation with the Islamic State and other extremist groups in the Middle East, which has included terrible persecution of Christians.

4   John Hick, international professor of philosophy and religion.

5   Sophie Brown, 'Malaysian court to Christians: You can't say "Allah"', CNN, 24 June 2014.

6   A. C. Bouquet, Comparative Religion, 3rd edition (Penguin Books, 1950).

7   A. Marwick, Introduction to History: Issues and Methods (Open University, 2005).

8   P. Sartre, 'The Look': Being and Nothingness (New York: Philosophical Library, 1956).

9   Denise. A. Spellberg, Thomas Jefferson's Qur'an: Islam and the Founders (New York: Knopf, 2013).

CHAPTER 2

Five Christian Responses
to the Perceptions

Josephine Mason   Maureen Foxall

Ruth Tetlow   Andrew Smith

Peter Rookes

Josephine Mason

In 1994, I was ordained as an Anglican priest and served in the parish of St John and St Peter, Ladywood, in inner-city Birmingham. I came into ministry later in life from a background as a professional musician. At that time, I was very involved in education, and this interest pervaded my work as a priest. In 1997, I asked permission to observe religious education (RE) teaching in various local primary schools to see just how the essence of different faiths was taught. My very first encounter was life-changing for me and for others. Out of my initial experience, the seeds of the Ladywood Interfaith Education Project (LIEP) were sown. It is from the lived experience of working as a Christian leader in the LIEP, rather than simply as an individual Christian, that I write this response to the perceptions.

Editorial comment. In response to the five perceptions of Christianity, Jo Mason has chosen to offer more about her own work than have the other four respondents. The Ladywood Interfaith Education Project is worth describing here to introduce her responses, because it illustrates her passion for interfaith dialogue and education that fosters and accepts the unity under God of all people, along with the recognition of each faith's specific traditions, beliefs, and ways of life.

Educating for interfaith awareness, interfaith relationships and the Ladywood Interfaith Education Project

Dialogue in action: the Ladywood Interfaith Education Project (LIEP)

An excited seven-year old Sikh girl on a visit to St John's Church through the LIEP: Will you tell me how to pray and when you pray, and then I will tell you how I pray and when I pray.

My first relevant interfaith experience came when I visited a class exploring Islam. The children were six years old. They sat on the floor in the classroom around a prayer mat with a very rich and complex design. The only Muslim child in the class was begging to show how he would pray, but he was not allowed, which I supposed may have been school policy at the time.

The children were asked to copy the design of the mat with coloured pencils onto a sheet of A4 paper. I tried myself and produced only a very poor image. The teacher was warm and encouraging, but the task was complicated, and I wondered what the children had felt and understood from that lesson. There was obviously much good intention, but there was no sense of a *living* faith and no sense of the *whole* child being engaged in the enterprise.

I came away thinking, *Surely we can do better than this.* Could we not find a different way to convey something of the truth, the excitement, and the spirituality of different religions? I reflected on the geographical proximity of different faith groups around St John's Church—could we somehow use our sacred buildings and the commitment and knowledge of our members for the benefit of local children? From that initial spark, and in collaboration with my friend Marian Collihole, a recently retired primary schoolteacher and a long-time member of St John's Church, we began to grow the LIEP. It now teaches well over thirty-five hundred primary schoolchildren annually from across the city, with increasing numbers of children with special needs and secondary school pupils.

LIEP demonstrates a shared commitment between four faiths: Buddhist, Christian, Jewish, and Muslim. These were selected because of the relative physical proximity of their sacred buildings, so that visiting classes could walk easily from one venue to another. Because of the work of my colleague Richard Tetlow, then the vicar of St John's, the church already had active relationships with different local faith communities, which provided a sound basis for relationships of trust in the emerging education project. Member schools selected sections of the RE syllabus which might best be explored in sessions with LIEP teachers in the different religious buildings.

The purpose was to go much further than simply having straightforward visits to a place of worship. The themes we were asked to explore ranged widely and included celebrations and festivals; food as a symbol; beauty and suffering; being honest and fair; sacred spaces; signs and symbols; giving and forgiving; and art and faith. Our sessions were to include music, drama, dance, dialogue, pottery, textile, cookery, and other methods where appropriate and available. Classes might visit two places of worship in one day in order to draw comparisons, so the presentation had to be clear and precise, and true to the practice and teachings of each individual faith.

Early shared academic planning was a key time in the development of the LIEP for the growth of trusting and creative relationships between the teachers from the different faith groups. Because the children were the prime concern in the LIEP, differences of theological thinking were readily respected and accepted. We had the following agreed-upon fundamental aims:

1. To convey clearly the doctrines, practices, and spirituality of the Buddhist, Christian, Jewish, and Muslim faiths.

2. To avoid proselytising or any attempt to indoctrinate.

3. To encourage a clear understanding of the similarities and differences between the four participant faiths, avoiding meaningless syncretism.

4. To develop respect for people of different faiths based on such understanding.

A pilot scheme involving just two schools grew rapidly to involve fifteen schools, many of which now send several classes each year to participate in the project. The sessions are delivered by a professional volunteer teaching staff of thirteen largely early-retired teachers and leaders of the different faith groups, with the vital input of regular visiting artists, who provide workshops.

As leaders and teachers working in the LIEP, we are challenged to embrace and celebrate our differences and similarities. It encourages us to be as clear and as critical as we can be about the tenets and teachings of our own faiths, and it helps us to continually question ourselves and hopefully not to stand still. Our project is absolutely rooted in our respect for one another and the spiritual friendships we have discovered together. The commonality of purpose is based upon our shared passion that young people at such an impressionable age might gradually grow in respect and understanding and learn how to handle any uncomfortable feelings of aggression or rejection in relation to the expressions of faith which they encounter.

The LIEP is an example of interfaith dialogue in action—a practical demonstration of different faiths working together towards a common goal.

My response to the perceptions

I write the following comments on selected aspects of the perceptions on behalf of the Christians involved in the LIEP team, choosing those areas which speak fundamentally to its vision.

Both 'A Hindu View of Christianity' and 'A Buddhist Perception of Christianity' speak movingly of the confidence to explore the religious journey afresh with adult eyes. Jyoti Patel says in her autobiographical introduction, 'My religious beliefs initially came from my parents and my community, and then as I grew older it became important for me to discover them for myself.' Sinhavacin traces his movement from Christianity to his Buddhist ordination and looks back to view the Sermon on the Mount from a Buddhist point of view. The development of spiritual and intellectual confidence in relation to faith and belief lies at the heart of LIEP practice. Whether this confidence might at some point in later life involve exploring new paths or whether it may enable an increase in joy in one's current commitment, the LIEP tries to encourage questioning and exploration of each faith at a time when the children are young and impressionable so that they do not later fear to encounter change and difference.

Sinhavacin also speaks of the abiding inspiration in his life of European Christian music and art. It is beautiful to read this witness as an example of how we may benefit from the best in each other's religious practice. At however lowly a level, the art and music sessions in the children's visits lie at the heart of our aims—namely to engage the whole child in personal spiritual exploration. Many children who find it hard to contribute verbally come to life in the art workshops, and many who are anxious or hyperactive are able to enjoy short meditations and movement to music.

The quotation from John Hick opening Muhammad Amin-Evans's 'A Muslim Perception of Christianity' is a timely and always necessary reminder that underlying our love for, and commitment to, our own faith, we have regularly to question whether we hide, consciously or unconsciously, a sense that in the end we have a priority of the truth. John Hick speaks of people growing to accept 'the genuine religious equality of the other, so that they can then benefit freely from one another's distinctive spiritual insights'. Working daily with young children and increasingly with teenagers, LIEP teachers regularly encounter the huge danger of consciously or unconsciously believing we each have a priority of the truth. Were such a conviction to be present in our work, it would be immensely destructive to the intentions of the project.

What we try to offer to the children is not the sense that any one of our religions is 'the best', but rather the best practice and spirituality in each of the four participating faiths. We might note here Pyara Singh Bhogal's comment that on every journey, Guru Nanak was accompanied by a Hindu and a Muslim. The story goes that he was asked by them who is the 'most good'—the Muslim or the Hindu. He replied that the question was irrelevant. Our duty is to be a good Christian, a good Sikh, or a good Muslim. Pyara Singh Bhogal concludes the story with, 'I think Jesus would have said the same.' Writing as a Christian, but as a member of LIEP, and responding to Muhammad Amin-Evans's discussion of this sense of possessing all of the truth, I feel this is an immense temptation for anyone of any faith, since underlying this attitude must surely be the ever-present human desire for power over the 'other'.

Margaret Jacobi, too, comments that she finds it difficult to understand why, for some Christians, the only way to salvation is through Jesus. Her Jewish perception that 'everyone has his or her own path to God' is one which many Christians would share, and for Christian teachers in the LIEP, this is a necessary underlying conviction. Many children will come to our sessions already taught within the family that theirs is the one true religion. It is very important for us as teachers to make no attempt to deny that but rather to gently open up beliefs which the child may not yet have encountered or had the chance to explore.

Margaret Jacobi comments on another issue interesting to me and LIEP Christian teachers. She remarks that as an outsider looking at the Church of England, she is puzzled and frustrated, along with an increasing number of Christians, by its official attitude towards women. In St John's Church, there is a stained-glass window that shows three women approaching Jesus's tomb with ointments for his body. They are met by an angel reporting, 'He is not here, he is risen as he said.' The text continues, 'Go … tell …' This striking window is an excellent way of introducing the children on a Christian visit to this first mission statement to women and their responsibility to be the first to share the news of the resurrection. And this in turn enables us to explore the hope that the Christian Church might increasingly be a place of general acceptance and inclusion for all, regardless of gender, race, or sexual orientation.

Pyara Singh Bhogal also highlights issues of equality— 'Sikhs like the principle of the equality of all people before God that Jesus taught'—but he rejects the practice of sharing Holy Communion, saying that it is discriminatory against the noninitiated. Indeed, unless the situation is sensitively handled by Christians, this could well become the perception.

It is interesting as a Christian working in the LIEP for me to read Sinhavacin's analysis of some sections of the Sermon on the Mount. He feels that the injunction not to be overly worried about food and drink and the material aspects of life taken to the extreme could well lead to social irresponsibility and neglect of the welfare of others. This sort of interpretation prompts me to remember that in LIEP visits, we do try to apply texts in a way appropriate to our situations, all the while knowing that not one interpretation may apply to all. An example arises during the topic of 'How do the beliefs of Christians influence their actions?' We frequently prepare a 'Fair Trade' stall and explore the principles of fair trading, the implication being that it would be better for us all to include more fairly traded goods in our weekly shop. However, as I know from my visiting in Ladywood, many of the local children do not come from homes where there is a well-stocked fridge or cupboard. Indeed, in their homes it is hard to make the food go around the family. These differences have to be sensitively addressed and explored.

The children are thus encouraged to look carefully into the texts we explore and be prepared to accept that there may be more than one interpretation. Consequently, I finish with a story quoted earlier. A commonly requested theme by schools is entitled 'Religions in Our Neighbourhood'. As a part of our input into this theme, children interview various congregation members about their role in the Church and what it means to them. A small group had prepared questions about prayer. The teacher asked a little Sikh girl to speak first, as she had been 'longing to ask her question all week'. The little girl said, 'Will you tell me how you pray and when you pray, and then I will tell you how I pray and when I pray.' She was very quiet and gentle, very excited and enthusiastic. Her desire to share and her generosity of spirit were completely natural. What a wonderful gift! As adults in the LIEP, we are constantly learning from the children. May such an innocent attitude be brought to mind whenever we discover in ourselves the desire to assert religious superiority!

In conclusion, a Hindu writing captures something of the beauty of the interfaith sharing of which we in LIEP are privileged to be a part: 'Expand your vision so that it can embrace all fellow beings and link them to yourself by Love. Rise above narrow creeds, cults, communal leanings and national ambitions. Merge your life in the infinity of God!' I believe that much of our perception of one another's faith might well be elevated and deepened by this overarching spiritual vision.

May 2016

Maureen Foxall

I have had an ecumenical life. It began as a Catholic in my teenage years and in being married to Colin and having our two boys, and then it became United Reformed, Methodist, and Anglican, for the children and diversity in worship. We became involved with the Birmingham Council of Faiths (BCF). It was here that we met Richard Tetlow, who in 1994 was chair. Seeing Christianity from a variety of perspectives had the effect of strengthening our own faith. I gave birth to our daughter, Sally, and trained as a local Methodist preacher. We enjoyed the Iona and Corrymeela communities in Scotland and Ireland for their reconciliation work.

Colin and I continued to attend BCF meetings and a women's interfaith group. After working at a Redditch college serving people with learning disabilities, I took a degree in applied theology at Queens Foundation, Birmingham. By that time, my experience had deepened in making bridges for me and family between different Christian denominations and different faiths. I had also become increasingly attracted to the Progressive Christianity Network, which is inclusive and open to diversity. I was challenged when I was at Queens, living and working alongside Christians who did not share these perspectives. This was another learning curve for me and helped me to open up to diversity in a different way.

After graduating, I volunteered as a mental health chaplain, which helped lead to my appointment as one of the chaplains at Queen Elizabeth Hospital, Birmingham. I thoroughly enjoy the diversity in this position, as I offer pastoral care for people of all faiths and none, sometimes when *they are at the most vulnerable moments. I also enjoy and am enriched by the relationships I have built in our multifaith team. Although in some ways the path to where I am now was painful, I am very fulfilled and can see that chaplaincy is a natural choice in my life.*

My responses to the perceptions

Robert Burns wrote, 'O would some power the gift to give us, to see ourselves as others see us.' I feel very honoured to have been asked by Richard Tetlow to write this response. My being able to hear and reflect on these perceptions of Christianity from people of other faiths is a wonderful opportunity for development and growth. My offering below is personal, and I am not speaking on behalf of any denomination or profession. I am taking each faith contribution in turn.

Buddhist

Sinhavacin writes that he admires the majority of the Sermon on the Mount and can relate much of it to Buddhism. He is challenged, however, by the invitation to embrace extreme poverty and says that to do so could lead to social irresponsibility and the neglect of others in the world. I strongly agree with Sinhavacin's point that Jesus had a bias towards the downtrodden in society and that it was inappropriate for Christianity to be incorporated as the state religion of the Roman Empire, when Christianity stopped being countercultural and changed from being the religion of the excluded, poor, and powerless into the faith of the elite and powerful.

However, I firmly disagree with Sinhavacin's point that the concerns of religion and of political power have very little in common. I feel it negates a further point he makes when he writes that the church used to be a source of social cohesion. Is this not part of politics? There is much prophetic wisdom for the Jewish people in the books of the Old Testament, including economics, healthy community relationships, and living with good governance. This helped to inspire Jesus the Jew to preach about the values of the kingdom of God.

Sikh

I share the sadness felt by Pyara Singh Bhogal over the fact that Communion is exclusive and in the light of the problems that this has caused and still causes within the Christian faith. I thank all my Sikh friends for the hospitality, warmth of friendship, and openness that they have shown me. As a Christian, I recognise that it is primarily their different beliefs about the Eucharist that stops different denominations from sharing it. Although Communion is the act of remembrance of the Last Supper which should unite Christians, in reality it divides us probably more than anything else. I am not surprised therefore that this exclusiveness challenges and confuses people from other faiths, especially Sikhs, who give such inclusive and generous hospitality when they offer all visitors complete meals.

Today, many churches have food banks in which food parcels are given to some of the most vulnerable people in our society from all faiths and backgrounds. I believe that this is a sign of liberation for the poor, which I see as an alternative form of Communion for today's world.

Hindu

Jyoti Patel critiques some of the traditional beliefs of Christianity and mentions that they seem out of date, as they conflict with our scientific knowledge. In my view, this has the benefit of leading people to question the literal understanding of scripture and some Christian dogma. Jyoti describes how she has encountered the phrase 'loss of faith' and how she thinks this experience is looked upon negatively by many Christians. This is also my painful experience, as I met such criticism from fellow Christians and evangelical ministers when I first started to express more progressive views within the church community. Jyoti describes how in Hinduism, enquiry and freedom of thought are encouraged without fear of condemnation and are a personal responsibility.

Whilst I agree that doubt is part of the faith journey on which we may travel to become mature Christians, I am also aware that when giving pastoral care, we have a responsibility to honour others' faith and not undermine their beliefs, which may be giving them strength, especially at vulnerable times. Often this will mean that we have to keep in check our own personal viewpoint. I agree, however, with Jyoti that it is a weakness within some churches to condemn and disapprove of people who doubt. I feel that it is through this deep questioning that we grow to a more mature and deeper faith that will stand up to the complexities in life. Surely, just as in Hinduism, this should be part of our Christian personal responsibility.

I agree with Jyoti Patel's view that some Christian charitable groups seek to manipulate tragic situations by proselytising vulnerable people caught up in major disasters. This point is very relevant to my role as a hospital chaplain, as I often meet people at vulnerable points in their lives. We hospital chaplains have to take great care in choosing chaplaincy volunteers to make sure they realise that they are not allowed to try to convert patients. It is not only disrespectful; it can also be harmful to the spiritual well-being of the patient. A volunteer's job is to try to care for everyone.

Muslim

Muhammad Amin-Evans criticises what he sees as remnants of colonialism in superior Christian attitudes and assumptions. He is a well-educated academic and, not surprisingly, is frustrated that his voice and opinion is not more powerful within general society, where media-driven populist opinions drive political decisions. I feel sympathetic towards this view, especially in this year of 2016, when Brexit and Trump won the populist votes.

I discern that Amin-Evans is a purist. Within all faiths, there are purists who feel that it is religion's role in society to offer guidance to help people face and overcome the temptations of a world they see as sinful, especially when public opinion changes and grows more liberal. For example, some people see homosexuality and its acceptance in society as sinful. Within most faiths, however, we also find those who feel that God is leading them to reform religion to make it more relevant to the changing society of their day. The differences between these two groups of people cause heated debates and schisms within religions. So much disagreement across many Christian denominations must look very confusing to an onlooker; but so it might for a Christian onlooker to another faith too.

Whilst Sheikh Amin-Evans recognises that there are good points within the Christian faith, he hungers for the Church to reform. He writes, 'I could have flooded the page with the good that Christians do in the world, but praise conceals problems, breeds complacency, and thereby halts reform.' I discern that he is a purist, because he is not complimentary to the young Muslim woman in Western-style clothing and calls her a 'weak link'. I wonder whether he would listen to the opinions of a younger generation within his own faith. It seems to me that Amin-Evans is expressing himself heatedly. I feel that I could have listened to him more easily if he would have written with less fervour.

Jewish

Margaret Jacobi knows that there is a wide spectrum of beliefs, interpretations, and understandings in Christianity. She recognises that Bible literalism is not a view held by all Christians and that many religious leaders include contextual considerations within their teachings. She then describes some severe problems which occur when the context and culture in which scripture is written are not taken into consideration, such as the readings about the crucifixion of Jesus on Good Friday. This reminded me of my mother, who was a child in Austria in the 1930s. She had seen the rise of the Nazis and told me that her own father had 'disappeared' in 1938 for speaking out against them. When the Russians came into Vienna, her family, living on the outskirts of the city, had to flee to the Salzburg end of the country where the Allies were. In her later life, she would often attend church but would never attend the Catholic Mass on Good Friday afternoon. She said she hated the reading, adding that she felt as if the Jews were being blamed for Jesus's crucifixion. Tragically, they were. Her experience has become mine in my relationships with Jewish people.

Another problematic text when taken literally is John 14:6: 'I am the way, and the truth, and the life. No one comes to the Father except through me.' It has led some Christians to believe that the only way to salvation is through Jesus. Margaret says that she finds this concept difficult to understand, but I think she should question the text and not necessarily take the passage literally, even though John gives other evidence of being anti-Semitic. I support her wholeheartedly when she emphasises that in Judaism, the manner in which one lives rather than the minutiae of dogma is more important. I believe that it is the way of life that Jesus exemplified that leads us to God. Many of us have experienced that it is in 'walking on the way' that we meet God—in the most unexpected places.

Finally, I especially like Margaret's perspective of the impact of the Church today. I agree with her that it is a paradox: how can the Church be both a beacon for progress and frustrating with so much traditionalism? As a liberal woman, I too feel frustrated by many of the gender issues and believe that if the church synods could get their priorities more in line with facing the severe challenges of our day rather than protecting its traditions, it could offer so much more to today's world. There is much fear in today's world that could badly affect the way we relate to each other. I believe that as people of faith, we need to show how to hold out our hands to others in friendship and trust, rather than holding them up in fear, so that we can walk the Way together and find God in our midst.

December 2016

Ruth Tetlow

Ruth Tetlow (MA, PGCE, MPhil, interreligious relations) has been coordinator of the Faith Encounter Programme in the West Midlands since 2007 and is also a senior advisor to the Birmingham Council of Faiths. She has pioneered the development of the Faith Guiding course. She trained as a teacher and has taught in Kenya and Bulgaria, as well as in the

UK. She has taught geography to A level and English as a foreign/second language. She is very concerned about combating climate change and is convenor of Footsteps: Faiths for a Low-Carbon Future, a recent initiative in Birmingham. She is a trustee of Grassroots, an interfaith programme in Luton, and of the national Jubilee Debt Campaign. She is a passionate campaigner for a range of social justice issues, based on a progressive approach to Christianity.

She has three adult children and three grandchildren whom she loves visiting in Banbury and Berlin, respectively. She has been very happily married to Richard for forty-six years and enjoys gardening, walking, and spending time in Porthmadog, Snowdonia, especially with the family.

Reflecting on the experience of faith guiding

Like many Christians, I came to interfaith dialogue in the 1980s. through the twin fields of ecumenism and mission. I worked at the British Council of Churches in the 1970s and as a tutor at the United College of the Ascension (a liberal Anglican/Methodist mission college) from 1999 to 2006. I came to see mission as 'missio Dei'—that is, participating in the mission of God in the world by seeking ways of bringing all people to fullness of life. I saw interfaith dialogue as part of a mission of reconciliation (Reconciling Mission, ed. K. Kim (ISPCK, 2005)) and developed my own five points about The Essence of Interfaith Dialogue. These are:

1. Commitment to your own faith and to the search for truth.

2. Openness—being willing to listen and speak both sensitively and honestly, and admitting you don't know all the answers.

3. Being prepared to face the possibility that both you and the other may be changed by 'God'. Conversion is from unbelief to 'God' and is an unending process.

4. Being prepared to take risks—doing and seeing strange things, not knowing how you may feel—and having confidence in a loving God.

5. Bearing in heart and mind the suffering of humanity and of creation, as the context you share with the other.

In this spirit, I took an MPhil in interreligious relations at the University of Birmingham and wrote a dissertation on 'The Missing Dimension: Women and Interfaith Encounter in Birmingham'.

In 2007, I was part of a small group that set up the Faith Encounter Programme, an interfaith charity based in Birmingham, with the aim of using education to build understanding between people of different faiths. I have worked as its coordinator ever since and have developed the successful Faith Guiding course, accredited by the Institute of Tourist Guiding. Through taking groups of Christians to visit places of worship of other faiths during the preceding twenty years, I am aware of how influential such visits can be to people's perceptions of other faiths, and how this influence can be negative if the visit is hosted inappropriately or is ill-prepared. The major places of worship in the city receive several thousand visitors per year. About two-thirds of such visits are made by groups of children and young people. Even in Birmingham, this may be the only experience they will ever have of certain faiths. Most visitors reported a very hospitable reception, but I can well remember being told by a host that, as a visiting Christian group, we were destined to go to hell after our deaths, and on other occasions finding the door locked and no one to receive us.

We set up a twelve-week evening course to train people of all faiths to give high-quality educational tours with professional skill and sensitivity to the backgrounds of their visitors. The course has now taken place eight times in Birmingham and five times elsewhere, training well over a hundred people of nine different faiths. Highlights of the course are the four visits to places of worship of different faiths. It comprises three parts:

1. Faith interpretation, where people work in small groups with an experienced tutor of their own faith to learn how to express the essentials of their own faith in a way that outsiders can understand.

2. Guiding skills, where the whole group (usually including people of five or six different faiths) learns and practises presentation skills with a professional blue badge guide.

3. Understanding other faiths, where the whole group practises listening to each other, discovering much common ground between them, and learning how to deal with difficult questions that may arise in a visit.

From this background, it was fascinating to read the five perceptions of Christianity. I was interested to see if they demonstrated some of the principles we teach in the Faith Guiding course, such as not making false comparisons between aspects of different faiths and interpreting specialist words that would not be familiar to people of different backgrounds. Was there an effort both to appreciate areas of common ground and to honestly address areas of difference? Clearly the task was different, so there were bound to be differences of approach.

I found interesting references to the distinction between Christian beliefs and a Christian way of life, and some contradictions were pointed out, understandably. On the whole, the Abrahamic faiths share an emphasis on belief in God, while the Dharmic faiths tend to emphasise the way of life of their devotees, but I observe that more and more Christians are finding a way-of-life approach more satisfying than a set of beliefs, some of which they find incredible. Is this perhaps partly due to the influence of meeting people from other faiths?

Muhammad Amin-Evans's 'A Muslim Perception of Christianity' takes a different approach from the other contributions, surprisingly not dealing with the major differences of doctrine between Christianity and Islam but focussing on offensive words and behaviour he has encountered in Christians. He illustrates some of the insensitive and ignorant behaviour we try to counter in the Faith Guiding course—for example, presuming to express what others believe. It is one of the basic principles of dialogue to speak only for yourself.

Margaret Jacobi's piece is based on personal friendship, similar to that which develops during the Faith Guiding course, and on mutual respect, independent of doctrinal agreement. She points out that Jewish people tend to place more emphasis on way of life than Christians do, while appreciating the dedication of many Christians to caring for the poor. She feels bound to mention the offensive anti-Judaism still perpetrated by many Christians, not least from the pulpit, but she doesn't allow it to undermine her respectful interfaith friendships.

Sinhavacin, the Buddhist contributor, comes from a Christian background and struggles theologically with the concept of 'God', especially in face of the suffering of humanity. In so doing, he manages to address key issues at the heart of both Buddhism and Christianity, which our faith guides are also encouraged to address, depending on the level of knowledge of their visitors. In Birmingham, at least, we should now be mature enough to go to the heart of the matter and hopefully be able to learn from each other, as I began to advocate in my five points for dialogue.

Sikh dharam is very much a way of life, so Pyara Singh Bhogal is puzzled at Christian emphasis on 'blind faith' to achieve salvation. What he has seen of Christianity seems to be full of contradictions, whether in attitudes towards the Bible or beliefs about the person of Jesus—was he Son of God, and what does that mean? Pyara finds exclusive attitudes in Christianity which contrast with the openness of Sikh gurdwaras towards everyone, to receive not only *langar* but also *parshad*, the blessed food. However, in the end, his piece is a plea for understanding, respect, and equality, seeing these as more important than disagreements.

Finally, Jyoti Patel, who is familiar with the Faith Guiding course, also refers to her impression that Christians focus on beliefs more than Hindus usually do. She is conscious of her partial understanding, as we all should be, and saddened at the common Christian misunderstanding of Hindu use of images of God in their devotions to the one 'God'. She is understandably critical, even angry, at the hypocrisy and double standards Christians are sometimes guilty of in using charitable work as a cloak for evangelism. It's a necessary reminder that we should not judge a religion as a whole by the reprehensible actions of a few of its followers, a principle that often features in the Faith Guiding course.

Seeing ourselves as others see us is always a valuable experience. We can learn much from their different perspective, even when it comes to the things we hold most dear. I remember vividly reading the Qur'an in a Christian study group years ago and learning to see the life of Jesus/Isa in a whole new way. No faith has a monopoly on the truth about the meaning of life, and cultural influences mean that diversity within religions can be almost as great as between different religions. Being able to hear criticism takes confidence, not the 'I know best' sort, but the sort that trusts in the purposes of a just and unimaginable God, the source not just of personal salvation but also of the whole universe. This project helps us to see ourselves as others see us and so to expand our horizons towards that God.

November 2017

Andrew Smith

I've been engaged in working with people of different faiths since 1993 from my home city of Birmingham. I'm currently the director of interfaith relations for the bishop of Birmingham, a post I've held since 2011. Prior to this, I worked for Scripture Union, pioneering a work that brought together Christian and Muslim teenagers for youth-focussed dialogue and friendship building. In 2009, I founded the charity The Feast to take on this work; the charity now works in four locations in the UK and in Lebanon. I was a founding member of the national Christian–Muslim Forum and was instrumental in writing their 'Guidelines for Ethical Witness'. I'm a member of the Church of England's national Presence and Engagement Task Group that resources churches in multi-faith parishes, and a member of the advisory forum of KAICIID (King Abdullah's (as of Saudi Arabia) International Centre for inter faith).

My master's thesis was on 'The Role of Young People in Christian–Muslim Dialogue', and my Th D looked at how having Muslim friends affected the faith of Christian teenagers. I have written a number of articles on interfaith work and regularly speak on this issue across the UK and overseas. I'm married to Sarah, who works in education, and we have two teenage sons. We worship at St Christopher's Church in Springfield, Birmingham. And if I'm not busy doing interfaith work, I'm probably having a meal with friends or building my model railway. I write this as an evangelical Christian who has been involved in the interfaith scene in Birmingham since the mid-1990s. Many of the contributors are friends, as is Richard, whose courage in inviting these reflections is to be applauded. It is a very generous and vulnerable thing to ask people to reflect on what you hold to be most dear.

Response to the perceptions

It was with great interest that I read these articles. If I'm honest, what I really wanted was to hear lots of positive comments about Christians and the Christian faith, to make me feel good and to vindicate the way that I and others have tried to explain and witness to our faith. There are many positive comments in these articles that, in the main, refer to the person of Jesus and to the deep and real relationships formed with Christians. The experience of encountering Christianity as a child also comes up as a base from which to reflect positively on some aspects of the Christian faith. As someone committed to educating children in different faiths and to including young people in active dialogue, I was encouraged by these comments. It's a timely reminder that building cohesive societies is not just a task for adults but also needs to include people of all ages.

Too often in dialogue, we like to focus on theological conundrums, social ills, or controversial topics, yet what was apparent here was that exploring the teachings and example of Jesus was of interest to the writers and a point of connection rather than division. Too often there has been a call for Christian engagement with other faiths to move from Christo-centric to a theocentric model, yet what we read here is a greater appreciation for a Christo-centric approach than we might have thought. This can give Christians a great confidence to turn to Jesus more rather than less in our discussions with friends of other faiths.

However, having highlighted these positive comments, I also have to acknowledge that some things that were said about the Christian faith and the behaviour of Christians was hard to hear and painful at times. This doesn't make these comments wrong, but it is always a challenge to hear negative messages. As I said at the start, I know many of these writers, so I read these as the thoughtful words of friends rather than as abstract criticisms. I wonder how I would have felt if I didn't know them, or how you felt as you read them?

There was clearly incomprehension at some Christian beliefs, particularly the Trinity, and also objections to some Christian teaching, particularly in relation to exclusivity and some of Jesus's moral teachings. When we read these, I believe it should do two things for us as Christians: firstly, cause us to seriously consider these comments and look at what their questions teach us about the doctrines we may have taken at face value; and secondly, move us to rethink the way we articulate these things, and consider whether the incomprehension or objection is the result of our clumsy speech or the actual concept. We also need to be able to disagree, graciously, with our interlocutors. I won't be giving up my belief in the Trinity, but I will agree to look again at why I believe in it and how I can live in the light of that teaching and talk about it in new and relevant ways.

There was also strong criticism of the way some Christians have behaved, and many of the concerns raised I share. For example, as an evangelical, although I am comfortable with the notion of people sharing their faith (whichever faith that happens to be) and inviting people to join that faith if they wish to, I do oppose—and often speak out against—coercive or manipulative proselytising that exploits people's vulnerabilities. However, I don't think it is reasonable to object to people's right to share their faith or to convert because of bad practice by others. With regards to acts of evil committed by people in the name of Christianity either historically or today, I think we should condemn this and work to make reparation where appropriate. Whether I can, with any legitimacy, apologise for those acts is something I would want to continue to reflect on.

Overall, it's been interesting and informative to read these, and I want to thank the authors for their honesty and thoughtful words. I hope this will lead to deeper understanding and stronger friendships between people of different faiths. I also hope it will inspire people from different faiths to attempt something similar in the future.

September 2016

Peter Rookes

Most of the experiences on which this contribution is based were joint experiences of my wife, Jean, and me, and are based on our shared beliefs and values. I have, therefore, used the pronouns we, our, and us, and I dedicate this piece to her, from whom I've learnt and to whom I owe so much. My responses are naturally affected by Jean's very recent death.

Over the years, we have increasingly appreciated the importance of faith to people at critical times in their lives, even when they don't practise their faith at other times. As chief nursing officer for Central Birmingham for ten years, hospital chaplaincy was part of my responsibility, and with our chaplaincy coordinators, we developed support to patients and their families from both ordained and nonordained chaplains and volunteers of different faiths.

In 1992, Jean and I worked for two years at what is now the University of Maldives, which provided the opportunity to learn from very diligent Muslims in a totally Muslim country. In addition to our other responsibilities, we organised workshops for the local Maldivian nurses and the newly arrived Hindu and Christian nurses from South India to work in the recently opened national hospital. This presented many faith-related and intercultural challenges.

Following this revelatory experience, we worked for the Anglican Church in Papua New Guinea (PNG) for eight years, Jean as national coordinator of the Village Health Volunteer programme and I as national health secretary. This led to our research of Christian health services in twenty-two developing countries, for which I was awarded a PhD by the University of Birmingham.

For the last ten years, we have been third-sector liaison officers, and more recently secretary, for Birmingham Council of Faiths, and faith advisors for Birmingham Scouts and West Midlands Police.

My response to the perceptions

Many of the challenges posed in these perceptions from people of different faiths are familiar and challenging to many Christians, including us, influenced by where we are on the wide spectrum of beliefs between Catholics, Protestants, Evangelicals, and Pentecostals, for example, as well as those on the margins of Christianity, such as Mormons and Seventh-Day Adventists.

As a result of our experience in the UK and overseas, we have found it difficult to settle in any one denomination because there are parts of different denominational beliefs and practice and different faiths which resonate with us and others which we find more of a challenge. Our Christian view is therefore something of an amalgam. Much of what we now believe as Christians comes down to two points: firstly, whether we regard the Bible as a literal record, as do Evangelical Christians, and secondly, what we accept on the basis of our faith.

For Jean and me, some of the theological issues which divide Christians—and separate Christians from people of other faiths— are far less important than the example set by Jesus in loving God; loving our neighbour; and demonstrating a preference for the poor and otherwise vulnerable people by practical action rather than just words, as promoted by James, the brother of Jesus.

The perceptions raise some particular challenges. Rabbi Margaret suggests that Christians regard the 'Jewish God [as] an angry God but the Christian God [as] a God of love'. In reality, Jews and Christians worship the same God, and the Ten Commandments given by God to Moses remain central to Christianity. The first four of these are about honouring, obeying, and loving God, whilst the following six are about our attitudes towards others. Jesus made it clear that he was not rescinding the commandments but endorsing that all of the commandments are underpinned by the commandments of loving God and loving our neighbour. Several passages in the Gospels refer to reaching out to people of other faiths and/or ethnicities, such as the much-quoted parable of the Good Samaritan and the story of Jesus reaching out to the Samaritan woman at the well. We believe such reaching out is mandatory for Christians.

Two other challenges are the tension between self-determination and predestination, and whether God is omnipotent or God is good. The first of these is exemplified by Jesus when he was tempted by Satan during his time in the wilderness. He had the choice, as we do, of succumbing or not to the temptations offered to him. God clearly gives us free will to choose—otherwise, as pointed out by Sinhavacin, the Buddhist, we are not responsible for our actions. On the other hand, Jean and I have felt so many times in our lives that God has a plan for us and was nudging us in a particular direction, but it was our decision whether we followed the direction in which we were being guided. We have been able to call on God's help, through prayer, to guide us towards the right course of action and aid us in pursuing the course of action we had chosen.

The question 'Why doesn't God intervene to stop bad things happening?' is, perhaps, more challenging. The challenge is related to the previous point: excepting some natural disasters and some diseases, many of the 'bad' things which happen to us are the result of our own or someone else's actions. Thus, for example, if an individual exercises self-will by breaking the commandment not to steal or not to commit adultery, this will have unfortunate consequences for someone else. It was a great challenge to our faith when Jean—a teacher and a passionate Christian who had spent her life serving others—was diagnosed with cancer. After we got over our anger with God, calm reflection presented us with two choices: complete abdication of our faith or seeking God's help in the challenge ahead and making the most of the time left to us. It was clear that as Jean was approaching the end of her life, the second option was the only way forward. This was regularly reinforced by the many friends from different faiths who visited her at home and in hospital to pray with her and help her to face her inevitable decline and death.

We take the point about the lack of opportunity for questioning in most churches. The traditional Sunday service in most denominations is for the congregation to sit in rows facing the priest or minister, who spends approximately twenty minutes preaching on some aspect of the earlier biblical readings. Neither the seating arrangement nor the method of delivery lends itself to questioning or discussion. Often we have thought, *Hang on a minute, there is another point of view on that…..* This may no longer be an appropriate model for contemporary congregations, particularly for younger members who have been taught to question and not accept statements on face value. This may, at least in part, account for declining numbers in congregations. Methodist churches traditionally allocate their congregations to house groups, and other churches establish study groups, particularly during Lent, when there is more opportunity to explore, discuss, and challenge issues. Additionally, the hierarchical nature and administrative structures within which some churches operate can constrain churches from being more creative and innovative.

We recognise the experience of Pyara Singh Bhogal, the Sikh, but contest that the Christian view of forgiveness is that, having repented of a sin, we are forgiven and can then forget about it. It is expected that having recognised the sin, repented, and been forgiven, we examine what led to the sin and make every effort not to repeat it. Jesus said, when forgiving the adulteress, 'Go and sin no more.' In return for being forgiven by God, we are expected to forgive others, as we pray in the Lord's Prayer: 'Our Father ….'

The perceptions have identified a range of Jesus's practices that promoted justice, love, charity, compassion, and assistance to the poor and needy, which have become models for Christian aspirations to serve people in need, including the homeless, refugees, and people experiencing difficulty in feeding their families. Some churches take this aspiration very seriously, but others observe it more in intent than in action. Some often have a concern for global issues, such as the effects of globalisation, climate change, immigration, and poverty. Many pursue eco-friendly initiatives or partner with their denominational church in a developing country, with which they work together on a development programme to improve the environment and lives of some of the most vulnerable people, embracing the ethos of Jesus's love and preference for the poor and needy.

However, it is debatable whether Jesus promoted peace and harmony, as his challenge to the authorities on behalf of the poor and marginalised created great tensions. It can be argued that a search for justice almost inevitably leads to disharmony, as it challenges the status quo. There is disagreement, for example, amongst Christians themselves about the role of women in the church, and of homosexuality, and about the questions of justice and priority these issues raise. Christians continue to be at the forefront of campaigns for justice, such as the abolition of slavery (both historical and contemporary), prison reform, and eradicating developing countries' debt. Others have been guilty, directly or indirectly, of sustaining modern slavery and inequality, by exploiting cheap labour, for example, to maintain their own standards of living.

Jyoti Patel sees Christian missionaries as a difficulty. Matthew's Gospel reports Jesus as saying to his disciples, 'Go and make disciples of all nations.' Christians have called this the Great Commission, and it has motivated Christian missionaries through the centuries to take the

Good News to people across the world in the sincere belief that the former were offering the latter salvation. The dichotomy continued between those missionaries whose intention was to 'save souls' and the political and religious colonists who saw the spread of Christianity as part of the inculcation of their own culture on others. From the beginning of the twentieth century, a spectrum of views developed between those Christians who continue to feel mandated to seek converts by any means because of their belief that the only way to God is through Jesus Christ, and those who believe that perhaps there are other valid paths to God. This difference is manifested between Christians who provide voluntary service and humanitarian aid as a means of serving others and those who do so as a means of seeking converts, as we observed in our own research of Christian health services in developing countries.

This variance of views is also manifested in attitudes towards people of other faiths. Anti-Semitism and Islamophobia are evidence of hostile attitudes at one end of the spectrum, whilst at the other end, Christians enthusiastically work with people of other faiths on joint projects and in promoting cooperative relationships through local and national interfaith organisations. In other words, some of the faith contributors observed there is a difference between a superior attitude towards people of other faiths and respecting them as different from but equal to themselves.

Our own life's journey together showed a similar variety of views. Our experiences both at home and overseas have been both a manifestation and a reinforcement of our Christian faith. Our association and relationships with people of other faiths increased our awareness of the parallel paths we were following and the extent to which we are all able to work with and learn from each other.

March 2017

CHAPTER 3

A Review of the Dialogues, Perceptions and Responses

A review of the dialogues

Aims of the dialogues; dialogue with the faith contributors; dialogue with the Christian contributors; general comment

A review of the perceptions and responses

Recognition of God; appreciation of Jesus; knowledge of the Bible; views of the Christian Church: appreciation, misgivings, problems, profound problems; mutual learning

Final comment

Preamble

It is commonly assumed that there are difficulties, articulated or not, between Christianity and the other major world faiths. These vary between the faiths, among which I am making no distinction here according to size or influence, Abrahamic faiths or otherwise, in Birmingham or elsewhere. My experience is that similar difficulties with Christianity in Britain are currently experienced by the non-Christian and the non-churchgoing population. This chapter explores what these difficulties might be. It begins with discussion of the dialogues between the faith contributors and me, including a discussion of their experiences and priorities. The dialogues suggest that the contributors believe that Christianity is too valuable to be wasted, as it can unfortunately appear to be. I agree.

All ten contributors have either lived or worked in Birmingham and know Birmingham's interfaith life. All ten have personal and professional experience in interfaith activity and thought in Birmingham and are personal friends/colleagues. All five faith contributors have different professions; all five Christian contributors were or are engaged in some way with education, formal and informal, of children and adults: the Ladywood Interfaith Education Project (for schoolchildren); the Faith Encounter Programme, focussed on teaching adults about faith guiding in their place of worship; the Birmingham Council of Faiths; faith advisory work for the Anglican bishop of Birmingham; and the interfaith chaplaincy at the Queen Elizabeth Hospital.

A review of the dialogues

Aims

To give a ready context for this review, I include what have broadly been my aims. The overall purpose of creating all ten writings has been to discern not just the features of a tide of perceptions and responses about Christianity but also what they leave behind on the beach to promote Christian response and the common good. Aims developed after the Perceptions and Responses are to be found in Introduction 1. These were my original aims three/four years ago, before the Perceptions and Responses were completed and I wrote this review:

- to throw light on the effects of Christianity on the everyday lives of British people of whatever faith, religious or otherwise— and, in reverse, the effects of the social and theological context on present-day Christianity;
- to focus on the possibilities of goodwill and partnership of body, mind, and spirit between people of different faiths;
- to discover in response what theological reflection and action might be taken in the name of God and loving our neighbour to improve relationships between Christians and people of different faith.

Dialogue with the faith contributors
See Introduction II, Dialogue

It was with great care that I presumed to select a member of each faith from amongst people I had known, mostly personally, in Birmingham over the past twenty-five years, all between young and old. After the initial invitation, explanation and discussion, the dialogues developed in discussing first, second and sometimes third and fourth drafts. In one case, the first draft was made on the spot. I asked, 'How did you first come across Christianity?' The reply was, 'There was no gurdwara nearby in those days, so I became a choirboy in the local church.' I continued, 'Please write that down.'

In first asking the five to describe their perceptions of Christianity and Christians, I did wonder what problems with process and content they might register for themselves and for me and what our dialogue would be like. I asked myself what I would personally make of their perceptions. If there were a problem- not the greatest potential problem in the world compared with others - what might the practical implications add up to in the light of my stated Christian obligation to love everyone, as all are made in God's image? Would the river 'Jordan be chilly and wide'? What would that love mean? Personal probing dialogue was going to be essential, for the five and for me. I did not share the three above issues, because they were my issues and not to have any influence on the very focussed task of the five.

In practice, if a problem did arise in the dialogue between any two of us, we sought to explore whether or not it was divisive and deep-rooted, and how we would address it. Most significant, in retrospect, was that our dialogue felt to me like holy ground. This meant 'shoes off', like at the mosque. Here were five people telling me—and thereby you now, the reader, whom they do not know— their intimate story in relation to their own faith and to Christianity, a faith that had had a dominant effect on all their lives. Qur'an 49:13 was offered as inspiration. It quotes God as saying, 'Oh, Mankind, we created you ... that you may know each other.'

My suggestion to the five was that possible subheadings might include the practice of Christian principles, the Church and its theology, including God and Jesus and the present-day impact of the church. My own role was to try to make encouraging recommendations about the many drafts created through our personal dialogue meetings. So that the five's own points of view would come through strongly, I aimed to ascertain the priorities of the writers themselves as to what *they* wanted to say about Christianity in relation to their understanding of their own faith. Duplication amongst the five was always likely; that was part of the exploration but could not have precisely the same origin.

It was a determined undertaking. All the 'courageous five' might well have wondered 'Who am I to express any opinion about another's faith? How far can I push any deep feelings I may have about the Church and Christian politics? And how far can I run the risk of seeming to the reader, as well as to myself, both ignorant and presumptuous? And what about the editor?' All that was a danger, but one they all accepted and overcame in their different and honest ways by their considerate manner of writing.

The faith contributors, both in their dialogue with me and in their writing, have shown interest, trust and belief in the venture. Whilst others of the same faith in Birmingham or members of another branch of their faith - never mind elsewhere in the country - might well perceive Christianity and Christians in an entirely different light, they have had the courage to make their own personal and honest observations. They have all wanted to say positive things, however differently. They knew they risked at times seeming ignorant, offensive and off-track according to the interpretation and knowledge of others. Upstanding parties sometimes have to pay a price for their different aspirations, backgrounds and faiths. Shared honesty has been a major marker and merit. It has been a function of this book to provide a safe place to take risks, test out possible costs, propose ways forward and hope that others will be constructive in any criticism.

We have all needed one another's trust to try to make the venture work. The faith contributors would agree that a trusting relationship increased their willingness to participate. As editor, I have been dependent on all five, as well as on the five respondents. We were all partners in the same venture. At the two lunch meetings that I have hosted so far, each faith contributor presented his or her script to the others, demonstrating a capacity for listening and dialogue in conversation as well as in writing. We are the book together, despite my having the major role. We have no pretence of superiority. We have simply aimed to have confidence in our own experiences translated into perceptions, to be ourselves, and to respond as fully, patiently and honestly as we can to what is a stimulating and urgent situation. This concerns partnership between the faiths. This, in turn, urges the need for peaceful relationships between and among them. There was a job to be done.

The personal dialogue and friendship that evolved during this enterprise has made me realise that my task has been to listen, take note and respond in whatever way I could, as a model for you listening readers—and how fortunate I was. None of us is fully in another's shoes, but it is satisfying even exciting to try those shoes on. Confidence in interfaith dialogue with its essential listening and learning is a recurrent theme of the writers. This dialogue has fostered 'writing friends' from five other faiths, people whom I trust all the more, now that we have built mutual bonds even if we meet little again. Our minds have been matured by the undertaking, our perceptions stretched and God-honoured—or 'generously acknowledged', as the Buddhist contributor said, using a different theological language that we others respected. The whole process of meeting, talking and listening offers a way forward to address questions and attitudes that elsewhere, and at other times, have given rise amongst people to disunity, distrust, animosity and violence, as well as satisfaction, pleasure and hope. Our joint hope is that the future produces more and more national examples of the interfaith dialogue that some of us have applauded and watched developing over the last twenty-five years. Birmingham is only one example.

I describe all this background to demonstrate the possibility of sharing of deep truths about our faith. It is *not* impossible. It is to be desired, and it can be immensely enlivening. I believe it is actually about meeting God through one another. In some ways, it may be easier across interfaith boundaries that are often assumed to be fixed than it may be across intra-faith boundaries within Christianity and within other faiths. There can be sheer inspiration from freshness, detachment and purposefulness, lacking in tired, age-old Christian debate. Our dialogues felt as though we were dealing together with the heart of Christianity and that of the different faiths as concerns Christianity. It *was* actually exciting! Confidence in perception generated more confidence in further exploration, even though, naturally, there was probably a lot that was not said. 'Heart speaks unto heart', quoted Pope Benedict on visiting Britain in 2010, quoting 16th century, St Francis de Sales.

Whilst no one was in a didactic role with the other, and although our knowledge of one another's faith varied, we inevitably sought to find out about the others. It was not, though, entirely mutual, because we had different roles. For my part, it was satisfying, for example, to listen to our Hindu writer asserting that she as a Hindu believes in one God and that what Christians have long called 'idols' are simply expressions and symbols of God. She likewise understands that for most Christians the cross and the bread and wine are symbols of God through Jesus. I learnt about a Buddhist view of God and how a rational mind saw Jesus's miracles, recognising that Buddhist views can vary as much as Christian views. Sometimes I did assert another view of Christianity from what was assumed to be the truth, such as that Christians believe that Satan is the root of evil and that at death they might go to hell as God's punishment. Not my beliefs!

These interfaith dialogues have been the highlight of my interfaith life. To share in such profound discussions was a great mutual privilege. I really felt we were gathered, two of us at a time, together in God's name. I'm sure all five enjoyed being able to talk about their own givens. Most people enjoy being heard. Speaking one's religious views is not a very common experience unless one is a minister or leader in a place of worship. We shared ourselves as profoundly as we saw fit, keeping firmly to our different roles of enabler and perceiver. I hope and think the religious views were a blessing to all of us.

In my extensive phases of dialogue with all the five faith writers, none of them presumed to pronounce what Christianity might or should do about their perceptions. It is generally an agreed-upon rule in interfaith circles that people do not talk about another's faith in their presence except in specific situations, or indeed out of their presence. That then was not the explicit agenda. The inference from some perceptions might have been why Christians do not succeed in doing more about something— anti-Semitism, Israel and Palestine, the Christian superior gaze being powerful cases in point. Perception here to me implied criticism, which implied necessity for action. Action, however, at that point, let alone conversion, was neither the explicit agenda nor the implicit agenda. I listened, seeking to enable, neither of the two of us becoming antagonists or protagonists. We appreciated one another in our different roles. While trust was basic, it had to be allowed to grow of its own accord.

The whole process, though, was about potential response and transformation. This was a new task for all involved. Christianity is—and was—an active context for those brought up and/or living in Britain with their eyes and ears open. Discussion about it in the context of one's own different faith was bound to create some change in mind and attitude one way or other. At root, the dialogues were an inclusive activity about God and in the Buddhist case, 'no God' - though that is still about the spiritual reality which I myself would call God. Yet it was crucial that a different Buddhist and Muslim understanding of that very word *God* was given.

Translation can lead to frustrating crude assumptions. Inspired by the different faiths, there is now in British society more change and more questioning. In my limited experience, this includes more questions about God and different views about Christianity than what was spoken about in Christian schools a generation or two ago. The perceptions, though, were that, in general, Christianity was averse to change. In this respect, public discussion about faith was considered by the five to be controlled by traditional dogma and authority rather than the love of God shown in the liberating way of life of Jesus, the latter being already admired and respected by all the writers.

The development from my dialogue to discussion with all five together was limited by practical factors. This has been frustrating, because specific powerful views, such as about the Christian gaze and understanding of God, have so far been left unexplored. All faith writers spoke to their own perceptions in the two combined meetings, but time and work agendas did not allow further investigation to continue as hoped. There is always the future.

Dialogue with the Christian respondents

The chief difference between the perceptions and the responses to them is that the respondents chose essentially to be constructive about ways forward, not just to make comments. That was to be expected. Their brief from me was to base their comments on their own direct experience of the interfaith work in which they had been and mostly still are professionally engaged. Their own work ranks among the most progressive and inspiring in Birmingham.

Naturally and rightly, they have wished to impart their knowledge and experience by their comments because they are deeply concerned both with the future of Christianity and that of future interfaith relationships. Just to read their bios and work context gives a strong notion of the importance of their comments in the light of the quality of their own ground-breaking work in Birmingham, described at the beginning of each of their articles.

The respondents knew no more about my agenda or even my plans and early writing than did the faith contributors, even as the project developed. Nor did they have any knowledge of each other's commentaries or the overall context, apart from the broad title. I was seeking their honest spontaneity and wanted them—indeed asked them—simply to comment on the five perceptions as they listened to the written words. I was in dialogue with the faith contributors, but the Christian respondents, on this agenda, were not. That was a conscious decision on my part for the sake of the activity, which was to respond to the writing, not to the personality and dialogue. Rather like the television programme 'The voice' in which the judges do not see the singer.

This was later commented on at our joint meeting once the draft of the book was nearly completed. It was felt to be to their loss. I underestimated their task, although I knew each of them well in one way or another. The respondents had to write, in a way out of the blue, about the perceptions of people whom they mostly knew, even well in some cases. Remember, we all live and work in Birmingham and will continue to meet or come across one another. Our differences in person and inter faith work enhanced the dialogue when so often they create difficulties. Their task with the perceptions was different from mine. I literally had to listen and carefully but keenly probe deep experiences and opinions in dialogue with them; they had to pay attention to what they read and respond accordingly with no dialogue with the faith contributors. One big issue for the respondents was directness and openness—their own with themselves and in what they wanted to say in response. That was their personal responsibility.

The following questions arose at the time:

- What is to be done if someone I know well and like expresses a critical view about something precious to me? Do I, metaphorically or actually, shut down? How much do I say and not say?
- Do I take such perceptions of Christianity personally? Why is that? Am I allowed to consider an adverse perception rude, offensive, startling and just wrong? Is the potential for self-knowledge one of the very reasons we are engaged in inter faith relationships?
- Do I really write from my own mature experience of Christianity and inter faith life and activity, or as an apologist for Christianity otherwise wanting to sit on the fence?
- What's the difference between disagreeing strongly and simply acknowledging that I see things differently?
- Do I sometimes feel and think 'I'm right, you're wrong' when the issue has perhaps become more one of my power and authority, or my religion's, over someone else rather than truth?

My own exchanges with the respondents were often friendly testing challenges. One of their number very honestly admitted it was a 'challenge to hear negative messages but [he was learning to] see them as thoughtful words from people [he knows] rather than abstract criticism.'. Some respondents' prior knowledge of the faith contributors had the potential to hinder. There was the possibility of my asking personal questions about why someone was responding in this or that particular way.

Interfaith relationships are a great gift of our modern age: they assist human spiritual growth by offering opportunity to learn with unsparing honesty about ourselves, our own faith, and the two combined together. It is interesting that the respondents did not generally take up the Christian sense of superiority attributed them in some of the perceptions. There was, though, a generosity which, for example, led one respondent to look hard at the doctrines we may have taken at face value and consider whether the problem is clumsy speech or the actual concept. Such awareness is not easy to come by, but it can be learned from listening to others' perceptions.

In reading/listening to a variety of views, respondents have been reminded of differences within Christianity and indeed of its changes within their own life-span. The varying views about paths to God illustrated this. Mutual acceptance is the way forward with differences of people and faiths. Within this bond, there is room for disagreement and even correction. This was freshly emphasized for one respondent in relation to Christians' prime understanding of God as a God of love rather than one of anger. The fact of differences between people is as potent as the fact of differences between faiths. Put both together, and the mixture has potential for human growth and for grief. We have all perhaps learned from the project as much about ourselves and those involved on the combined journey as we have about other faiths. Not for the only time, potential relationships were the prime beneficiary.

General comment

All ten contributors have shown strong and natural intent to uphold their own faith. No syncretism here, and no need, although we can always learn from one another! It is not generally a major interfaith bogey or agenda any more. Inter faith relationships are about being ourselves and enabling every participant to be likewise—discovering, learning and living with both similarities and differences. Freedom to choose perceptions and responses may be our freedom, it may not and it may depend on the subject/s. Readers will have their own perceptions and conclusions. I seek briefly to comment from my own insider's knowledge of the united faith journey.

None of the ten writers has known where his or her stories and opinions would lead. No more had I when I asked for them. I had not been clear of my own agenda for the book, except that I knew it would be interesting and important to me and others to hear what people of different faiths might say about Christianity with no pretence of representation. That was the initial job. I wished to follow the contributors' lead and respond personally where I could. I greatly appreciate their trust. I have developed the book's agenda throughout the whole experience as I have explained in Introduction I

I have treated the five perceptions as both distinct and integrated. All ten writings reveal to me two broad dimensions in their understanding: one social, about the world context of globalisation and the other theological, about Christianity in its relatively new Western world of interfaith relationships. The writings throw up the central issues that arise from our changed and changing modern world about the future of Christianity and the contribution of the Church in Britain to the modern-day national and world context and

Christian relationships with the different faiths. In this way, the writers unwittingly responded to hopes later worded in Introduction 1.

There are several significant subjects discernible within the social and theological dimensions of the five perceptions of Christianity. These are God, the Trinity, Jesus, the Bible and positive and negative roots and comments; difficulties of apparent decline, loss of focus, status and confidence in the Christian Church; and Christianity's veiled but persistent tradition of power and empire. They are all grist to the mill of improving Christianity's interfaith relationships.

A review of the perceptions and responses

Recognition of God

God and the issue of God, especially in connection with Jesus, features strongly in the perceptions. In different ways, the Christian perception of God is generally considered by the faith contributors to be confused and contradictory. To different degrees, in some cases by implication, the writers are 'puzzled', as Rabbi Margaret Jacobi generously puts it. She, Jyoti Patel, and Pyara Singh Bhogal ask how God can be both immanent *and* transcendent; jealous, cruel, *and* merciful; creator of heaven *and* of hell; both God of anger *and* God of love. Peter Rookes is keen to insist that God to Christians is primarily the God of love and not anger. There is an implied recognition of powerful human projection. Sinhavacin wonders how and why evil is allowed if God has ultimate responsibility, which is the theodicy problem. Where lies responsibility for sin if God is all-powerful and all-forgiving? Why should people care if God is ultimately in charge of everything, including the destiny of us and Planet Earth? Why is there so much suffering for some and not for others?

Prayers particularly do not make sense to Sinhavacin. This God talk is incoherent, meaningless, and unrelated to what he sees 'in the actual world'. He suggests that our blaming of society and others, stems from people blaming neither God nor themselves, and that this results in consumerism, carelessness and greed. Sheikh Amin has difficulty with Christians assuming their idea of God fits with that of Islam, and so is emphatic that the meaning of the word *Allah* is not the same as the meaning of the word *God*.

Translation is indeed a persistent issue for the whole subject. Hindu belief is that God is omnipotent and omnipresent, and therefore unlimited in form (*sakar*) or in no form (*nirakar*). God with a form provides a focus for some Hindus to build a loving relationship, whilst other Hindus are more drawn to an abstract God who has no need of form. Either is acceptable.

Appreciation of Jesus

Jesus, the man, is greatly admired in himself. His loving inclusive way of life has been an inspiration for centuries and still is for the writers, whether this way is called Christian or not. Jesus himself gathers much appreciation for his moral teaching, personal freedom and quality of life. The Christian writers themselves are united behind Jesus. Singled out by Pyara Singh Bhogal is Jesus's teaching of the equality of all people before God—not easy in the caste-ridden society known to him personally.

Muhammad Amin-Evans admires Jesus's sense of peace and harmony. One Christian respondent, Andrew Smith, appreciates being reminded to include young Christians in interfaith discussion and that reference is often made to Jesus. He is grateful for this Christian understanding of God as likely to give confidence to Christians in their turning to Jesus as well as to God. Another, Peter Rookes, appreciates focus on Jesus as demonstrating love in action but was open to suggestion that such love led Jesus to strongly criticise the Jewish leadership, and this hardly promoted peace.

It is only when Jesus is called 'divine' that problems begin. Pyara Singh Bhogal cannot see how the *man* Jesus can be on a level with *God*; be human and also divine and therefore superior to any other person. The ten Sikh gurus—or saints—certainly are not. Jesus to Pyara is a great spiritual leader for everyone, including Sikhs, to follow, seeking unity and peace and treating all as equal, whatever their background. Jyoti Patel is confused by the potential difference between 'God the Son' and the 'Son of God' and why and how Jesus was exalted to *divinity*, itself a questionable term. Rabbi Jacobi is confused by the bodily resurrection of Jesus and the notion of salvation only through Jesus.

It is logical that puzzlement about Jesus leads to a sense of incomprehension of the Trinity, as was noted by one Christian respondent. The Trinity, as perceived, is the fundamental issue between our members of the five faiths and Christianity. Naturally, tentative questions are asked and tentative comments made. It was not easy for the writers to comment confidently about the faith of others. The tone of enquiry was therefore respectful and even self-accusatory, as in Rabbi Jacobi's statement that she does not grasp either the Trinity or the resurrection despite her own theological training and seeking of Christian explanation. 'Christianity is so complicated,' Pyara Singh Bhogal, sighing, said to me. The five certainly had differing perceptions of Christianity. These are further explored in Chapter 5, 'Challenges to Christianity'.

Knowledge of the Bible

The variety of Christian beliefs was apparent but not examined, as might well be the case with different Christian congregations, especially among those not theologically minded. The faith contributors make little mention of the Bible, even as the Christian Holy Book and sourcebook on Jesus. Nor is much mention made of biblical criticism, its Jewish basis, both the Hebrew Bible—the Old Testament—and the New Testament, or its role as subordinate to Jesus himself. There is generally an absence of analysis of the meaning of words and of the nature of the Bible and its authority. Such omission may be an issue of time, space and priorities or possibly of understanding and communication. Perhaps that is some indication of the limited scriptural criticism apparent in their own faiths.

The Bible does, though, come in for individual criticism. How hurtful and demoralising for a friend to be told by potential friends, neither of whom are Christian, that all 'nonbelievers' will be damned, as the Bible is assumed to say. The Bible, rather than the Church, is felt to bear some responsibility for much of the confusion in the lack of Christian clarity as to its nature. John Spong's latest book, *Biblical Literalism: A Gentile Heresy*, is invaluable on this subject. Several contributors, in their apparent ignorance of biblical criticism, are impatient about what they see as the Bible's confusion of story and factual history. They have no problem with Jesus being alive in memory and a living inspiration, but it is asked, 'How can anyone prove what Jesus said about anybody, let alone his fellow Jews?' We are assured that by contrast, for example, the Guru Granth Sahib, which is the Sikh holy book and the eleventh guru, is not history but actually alive like art and music, invaluable stories certainly but not 'real factual history'. It is interesting that personal experience is accepted as a counterbalance to the authority of the Bible, both Old and New Testaments, although the fact that the Bible and even revelation is very much written from personal experience is seemingly ignored. Unfortunately, that is often ignored by Christians too.

Views of the Christian Church

Appreciation

Appreciation is expressed of Christian generosity and concern for the poor, especially from those ministering to the inner city, and also for liberal openness to others, such as humanists. One writer considers the Church 'a beacon for progress'. Good, generous, pastoral, educational, and community work and campaigning about the danger of climate change at home and abroad is frequently noted, based on the writers' historical and local knowledge and experience.

Generous tribute is paid to the wide inspiration and scale of Christian music and art that achieves the transcendent and universal. Approval of Christianity gives the impression of being a common factor that feels to me more than just casual. Difficulties only arise for the five—as we have noted—when Jesus is called divine by whatever meaning. Youth work, choir, Christian schooling, and Christian festivals are valued.

Misgivings

Views are mixed. There is a sense to me of 'yes, but ...' and 'if only'. Regret is expressed about the apparent decline of the Church in the face of its great value in terms of buildings and congregations, its moral and spiritual framework and homeland. The rabbi regrets what she considers reactionary unloving attitudes to gay people and women that are still prevalent. She sighs at the common failure of Christians to recognise the roots of Jesus the Jew and his teaching of the supremacy of love—which, after all, stems originally from the Hebrew Bible and Judaism, not Jesus or Christianity. The Hindu writer praises the inspirational guidance of the Spirit, provided it is not followed blindly. She even gives advice that Christians should not be apologetic but rather still be confident even if they reject some of the old traditional thinking. She laments Christian intolerance of Hindu icons of God, especially when they are called idols, when Christians themselves value their own symbols and mythology by appearing to worship wooden crosses and Christian statues.

Discrepancy is observed between early Christian teaching and crusading imperialism and between spiritual practice and structural Christianity. The Buddhist writer admires Jesus's teaching to and for the poor and the Church's valuable focus for communities and social cohesion, care, and moral direction, but he believes such values and practice fit uncomfortably within the state power of the established Church. He regrets, too, any present-day loss of such focus and the nihilism and self-positioning which replaces what he sees as the dying of God and essential 'eternalism'.

Problems

Christianity is considered to be less straightforward than Sikhism and confusing in its variety of practice and belief. Its apparent exclusive theology and exclusive behaviour belies its assertions about generosity and loving your neighbour. For example, the community meal for Christians, celebrating and remembering Jesus Christ, which is the Holy Communion of bread and wine, debars those not baptised

Christians; whereas the *langar*, which is at least comparable, is the Sikh meal freely offered to all comers, as is the *kara parshad*. One respondent particularly notes and laments this too because Christians may sing 'All are welcome,' but all are not welcome, for some put up notices saying there is 'Only One Way' (to God and to Christianity), a policy that offends equality of all, whether or not they are different churches.

Christianity is seen to set unrealistic and misguided aims. Sinhavacin claims that some of Jesus's own words about our physical needs and about sparrows and lilies looking after themselves have left Christianity apparently confused in itself, irresponsible, contradictory, or hypocritical. It is, for example, unreal of Jesus apparently to oppose a man looking lustfully at a woman and deny his physical evolutionary needs—needs actually created by God. His human spiritual credit resides in his acceptance and control of such feelings. Such narrow thinking leads easily either to hypocrisy—saying one thing and practising another—or to unnecessary feelings of guilt or speculation about punishment and reward in any next life. Then who is going to pluck out one's own eye if it causes one to sin?

Some respondents comment on the need for greater recognition of metaphor by Bible writers. Reference is made to a strong wish for apology from the British government for its known connection with the Golden Temple massacre. Such honesty has always to be heard with whatever consternation or even initial disbelief if healing is ever to be found. And forgiveness, understandably, is easier said than done.

Profound problems

It is clear to me from their five perceptions that our perceivers *do* have something against Christians, however veiled the criticism might be. Here lies forceful indication of the degree of waste that befalls Christianity, which I proposed at the start. I name it in this way because such honesty is a purpose and raison d'être of this book. I cannot measure the scale and degree of angst and problem.

The elephant in the room seems to me to be primarily about a sense of assumed—in both ways, however generously conveyed in different degree, way, and word—Christian superiority, arrogance, exclusiveness, and hypocrisy. Beliefs of whatever kind have contributed to Christian behaviour that is contradictory to what Jesus taught through his way of life. Hypocrisy easily arises from confused theological priorities—the right brain not knowing what the left brain is doing or thinking, consciously and otherwise. It reveals a tragic history, as Jesus actually saved his most harsh criticisms for hypocrisy, 'the yeast of the Pharisees', those who say one thing and do another. Naturally, members of all faiths may at times be hypocrites too, and the faith contributors did look at the failings of their own faith, as well as seeing such failings in others. Perhaps the honesty and openness fed awareness in both sides, as it often does.

Sheikh Amin is critical of those Christians who let down Jesus and the faith they bear in the name of Jesus by what he calls their 'unwitting testimony' and 'gaze'. This is an unusual and instructive observation of a conveyed attitude of demeanour and speech that betrays an inner sense of rightness and superiority over other religions, whom the Christians have indeed 'othered' in disrespect and even untruth. For example, to him—and to me—it is common to hear from unknowing Christians that Jesus brought love into the world when it was falling apart with wickedness, and moreover that love is not mentioned in the Qur'an. It is almost shockingly untrue what the modern Christian hymn appears to say of Jesus: 'A new commandment I give unto you, that you love one another'; it does add 'as I have loved you', if it is heard. Margaret Jacobi makes the same point, illustrating it with the truth that Jesus was quoting the Jewish commandment when extolling love as the greatest commandment, as quoted before from Leviticus 19:18 and Deuteronomy 6:5.

Sheikh Amin's crucial point revolves around translation: *ishq*, which is carnal love, yes, is not in the Qur'an, but *hub* and *wudd*, other Arabic terms for love, certainly are. He calls this cultural chauvinism, relating it to moral and scientific superiority and particularly to an attitude of knowing best, even about the other's faith in content and representatives. Being well versed in Christian scholarship himself, he deplores Christian use of the so-called 'mystery' (of God) to defend contrived dogma. He accepts that other faiths have similar problems but defends his criticism as from an academic who seeks to ward off the religious hypocrisy and complacency to which Christian gaze is heir for the sake of truth and equal liberties and rights. To those who offer truths to humanity, he asserts that it is necessary to ask of what they consist and whether the offer is being honestly made.

Jyoti Patel comments on the behaviour of some Christian missionaries she has met in Africa whose aim is conversion—conversion above all other human costs. She provides many an example with comment: disaster victims used as good candidates for conversion, not in Britain but by Christian missionaries in Indonesia and Zambia, particularly from Muslim to Christian; knowledge of the spread of Christianity by forceful means and imposition of belief of being the only true religion; underpinning by arrogance and ignorance of others;

the threat of such attitudes to world peace; and justification through personal salvation by whatever means. Pyara Singh Bhogal derides British state support for the Indian government in the massacre of Sikhs at the Golden Temple in 1984, which he remembers starkly as a remnant of Britain's imperial power.

Rabbi Jacobi is admirably forthright in naming the 'devastating' anti-Semitism 'entrenched' in the Bible—as she knows, for example, in John 8:44—setting a basis for two millennia of persecution, exile, and slaughter in the name of Jesus. Sinhavacin warns of an encroaching 'fear of a new spiritual dark age' and 'war of all against all' kindled by the growth of Islamophobia on British streets, a resurgence of anti-Semitism, and general fear, suspicion, and even hatred of foreigners in post-Brexit Britain. That is strong, but we must indeed be wary of small beginnings and outlandish behaviour becoming the norm.

Racism is the most terrible truth with which Britain, and particularly Christian Britain, has still to cope, for it is not yet dead. The themes of this book are diametrically opposed to such barriers between people. I consider this condition of Britain to be disturbing, disgraceful, and profoundly anti-Christian. It is exemplified by some Jewish people feeling driven back from supposedly Christian Britain to a newly welcoming—though also Christian—Germany, which their recent ancestors quit from Nazism in the 1930s. First-hand indirect experience and inherited memory of the Jewish Holocaust produced quiet and powerful openness about originally hideously traumatic experiences of universal significance. The fact that such prejudice exists in other parts of Europe and the United States of America is no excuse. Britain could be a good example of faith harmony, not another bad one. We should both fear and welcome prejudice being brought to the light.

Mutual learning

There is constructive intent and goodwill behind all these positive, critical, and at times confused 'profound problems'. The faith contributors and I recognise the project is about how, together, the faiths may be beneficial to one another in the name of God and loving-kindness. Suggestions therefore are freed to arise with determination and goodwill from potential buried and concealed anger and frustration. As Pyara Singh Bhogal declares, the wish is for all to have respect, equality, and mutual understanding in the name of one God. To this end, he is convinced of the universality of prayer— that it is prayer whether in church or temple. Sinhavacin advocates belief in rebirth, spiritually guided teaching, learning and discipline as aspects of truth, progress, relationships, and improved standards of living. Jyoti Patel says that questioning of religious truths is essential for learning and a sense of responsibility.

Rabbi Margaret pleads for directed learning for Christian clergy, especially in training in connection with Bible-based anti-Semitism and the danger of the unravelling of fifty years of interfaith work against anti-Semitism. She suggests gentle but firm tempering of Easter readings as, for example, with the reference to doors being locked by the (Jewish) disciples in 'fear of the Jews' in the Gospel according to John 20:19. She recommends too the necessity and value of initiatives to share problems, sometimes more easily begun at the invitation of Christians, but now with increased confidence by those of different faiths. She specifically recommends the benefit to her and her Jewish congregation of shared meals and mutual discussion on topics of mutual importance. Examples for her—such as suffering, the Messiah, children, and interfaith discussion itself—occurred regularly in when she and I were rabbi and vicar in Ladywood between what we called 'her Anglican church and our synagogue'. Amin-Evans would uphold such discussion with his respectful confidence that Christians can and will cope and learn from home truths. Peter Rookes is keen to press recognition and mutual benefit of the sheer variety of views within Christianity and between different faiths, no less than it is between personal relationships.

Final comment

I have aimed to stick to what the five faith writers themselves have said and to select what I feel they would wish me to say from their point of view. I may sometimes have gotten it wrong. Overall, my own reaction is one of great satisfaction and pleasure with the whole project and appreciation of the richness of the six faiths and the combined gift of five of them to one another along with their similarities and differences. The perceptions and responses open up the fundamental importance in interfaith activity of personal relationships and dialogue for the sake of creating love, understanding and mutual relationships.

I have five specific comments:

I accept the varying considerate criticism of Christianity as contained herein because I trust and know it to be honest and well-meant. Good enough prior relationships are vital as a setting for criticism. Christianity has much in every generation to learn if its inherent qualities are not to be wasted.

I enjoyed particular comments, such as Rabbi Jacobi's assertion that everyone has his or her own path to God, including non-religious people—not just those of different faiths. Pyara Singh Bhogal notes that love is universal and above faith, and that we are all to have faith in God out of love, not from guilt of sin or reward, but for love. I'm reminded by the tone of some of the perceptions that behind the head questions is the heart with its different questions -despite the reality of all coming from the same brain. There is something of God to be learned from all the perceptions if we choose to pay heed. The heart needs the head but without the heart the head is dead. We do have both after all!

I noted the lack of knowledge of basic Christianity that Christian respondents felt lay in the faith writers. Understandably, there was a lack of knowledge about Christianity and the Bible in its modern progressive light but I too missed questions about the authenticity and authority of the Bible and definition of its truths. I do, though, ask whose responsibility that is and has been. The power of child-learning was apparent. Frequently teaching had been of the old school, oblivious to modern biblical criticism, whether concerning the metaphorical nature and poetic imagery of much of the Bible or some modern Christian ease with evolution and scientific discovery.

Once issues of biblical criticism are recognised in dialogue, an oppressive veil of criticism is lifted and like-mindedness across the faiths discovered and appreciated. Issues of scriptural authority, for example, are important to Islam and Christianity alike—more so perhaps than the other faiths, but within Christianity there is a generally acceptable variety of authentic scriptural interpretation not realised by most of the writers, as, regrettably, it is not by some Christians. Generalisations about majority or minority Christian views are confounded by the variety of 'Christianities' and perceptions of it.

I have talked with people of different faith to Christianity who, conversely, have *not* had the same experience or perception of Christian arrogance as our faith writers. Questions, investigation and magnanimity or rejection may all be appropriate. Such variety of perceptions is evidence of the extraordinary nature of people and our perceptions; potentially too of the richness of any honest faith, once discussed and explained with mutual integrity. It is easy to live in the blind or forgetful alley that 'ours' is not only the one true faith but also the only true version of that faith. Likewise, with our perceptions of that faith, ours and theirs. Agreement and disagreement may be irrelevant if we just listen and learn whatever our faith, hard or soft. Conflict, friendship or reconciliation become a choice.

In conclusion, there are human preconditions that in essence are more important than all these five, namely generous openness, humility and hope. Without these three, comparable to St Paul's 'faith, hope and love' in his epistle to the Corinthians, it is unrealistic to expect worthwhile journeys in good mutual relationship. Without them, peace, justice and harmony may be straws in the wind and inter faith relationships blown onto the rocks.

PART III

CHAPTER 4

My personal journey;
reflections on my interfaith journey;
a Christian context: God, Jesus and love;
a Christian theology for inter faith Britain

Preamble

Theologian Sally McFague[1] has insisted that 'anyone writing a theology today must identify the social context from which they write …. It's one of the most heartening academic developments of our time.' To give some clue as to what I stand for and who I am to author and edit this book, I now, for my part, share my own life experience in its social and Christian context and how it has fostered my more recent inter faith journey. I indicate why all this matters to me. It is meant to lead to ways forward for Christian and inter faith Britain - both components of Britain at the cross-roads - through exploring potential theological bridges within Christianity and between Christianity and different faiths. I see it as constructive reflection not confessional.

The proverb's advice, 'Physician heal thyself', quoted from Greek and by Luke of Jesus, 4.23, encourages essential awareness for someone with my privileged background and foreground. I aim to give a basis for showing that a universal theology which respects differences and similarities between and among faiths is, to me, entirely compatible with a treasuring of the different world faiths and the genius and truths of the Christianity that originates from Jesus. Each has its own eternal light. God, in my understanding, is in, with and behind them all. A universal theology expansive enough to embrace every faith may indicate the foundation of life in British society for which many are urgently searching.

The author's personal journey

My personal journey began in the middle of World War II with the Holocaust raging as I learned from later films - whose films and aftermath had their effect on me as a young man and as much, though differently, throughout my life. I was born into a large, non-church-going, loving but troubled professional family near Newcastle and became a curly- haired choir boy in Harrogate, north Yorkshire. I've continued to sing wherever, to believe in God - in my understanding - and to be a constant church-goer. I have always enjoyed relationships both personal and professional with people from different walks of life. That is my image of myself, my identity even. Throughout, I've had more than my fair share of love and happiness. I do realise how fortunate I am to know and to have always known my roots and my identity. Absence of such knowledge can be a powerful source of anxiety and trouble for some whatever their Faith. Very much due to my cushioned position in the family of 3/6, early childhood had few negatives for me. They even spread into positive veins through scouting, rugby and a mixed open-hearted grammar school. I knew then that some kids were left out. It was still the time of post-war belief in service to society.

My worldly independence began with miles of European hitch-hiking - and catching TB for my gap year! From happily attempting teaching at a posh Prep School in Broadstairs, I went to Cambridge University – blooming marvellous Trinity College too and read History. I revelled in its mixed fruits. Great privilege surrounded me. Unrecognised classism and racism were probably rife. I knew I was ignorant but played my part. I learned increasingly about difference and enjoyed it all. Time would tell.

Cambridge had inspiring add-ons for me. It took me from Coventry to work on rebuilding bombed-out Dresden and to live in a Borstal for a week. Concurrently into my life came the college mission in Camberwell and Cambridge House Settlement in inner-city South London. A friend thought they would suit me; they did. I visited regularly and, in an odd way, felt equally at home, acquiring a lifetime passport to door-knocking. I was encouraged to note and experience inequalities of human lives and society, strengths, weaknesses, kindnesses and injustices. Two vacation jobs in South Africa and the United States, in 1965 and 1966, fostered my independence even more in a new setting for me of disturbing black and white tensions. My guts were stirred up for life. I chose 'slavery' for my history dissertation.

The University Settlement movement caught my imagination. I moved to living in Pembroke House, a small settlement in Walworth, inner Southwark, South London and had an inadequate go at teaching nearby in a good large comprehensive school for a year. I was inspired by two leaders/ clergy friends, Eric James and John Austin, both vicars. I finished up feeling more drawn to the kids than to my subjects. On top of everything, in 1970, Ruth, who had been a fellow Cambridge undergraduate, returned from teaching in Kenya and we married for good. After due training, I became a social caseworker and community worker based in Cambridge House Settlement and then in Southwark

Council's new Social Services Department. I was very happy there, except when my red old post office bike was pinched. It became my objective to connect my privilege and others' deprivation and relate my understanding of Christianity to my new daily experiences. I had a job to do. It remains so, as it does for many, to interweave activity, understanding and faith.

After nine years, with mixed feelings but seeking different experience, we moved to Lancaster for me to teach what I had learned something about. I was not a good academic but enjoyed the work and the students. I continued the role I'd begun from Southwark of being external examiner in Pastoral Studies for the Northern Ordination Course based in Manchester. Then, almost quite out of the blue, I had a powerful, savage, inner and outer experience. I simply heard 'you must be ordained'. I sensed I could not turn my back. Ruth generously agreed. Whatever its origin, the experience - which was fierce – boosted my sense of purpose. I had known that five years in Lancaster was a waiting time. We moved with three small children for me to be an ordination candidate at Queens College, Birmingham. Ruth generously agreed

Queens was enjoyable for me but not easy. I underestimated the tutors' lack of street experience. From 1983 to 1988, having stayed in Birmingham, I became curate at the church in the markets, St Martin in the Bull Ring, a marvellous place to work especially under Peter Hall, soon to be bishop of Woolwich. I heard formal and informal talks and discussion from Christians about 'the other faiths'. In first getting to know the city, I went on bus tours organised by Ruth to the places of worship of people of other faiths to see and meet 'them'. I do not recall anyone, myself included, asking of 'them' what they thought or knew about 'us' and Christianity. We

Christians were the norm -to us. They were the outsiders, in a way naturally, as I then shamelessly supposed. Then I filled 3 to 4 months between jobs by going to the West Indies, St Kitts, as a priest. I was very happy in a culture both very different and very similar. I was very chuffed to encourage a Kittitian in Ladywood to be our church warden. British churches had been shockingly uninviting of black Christians in recent memory.

Having moved nearby, in 1989, to become vicar of inner-city, multiracial St John's (and St Peter's, after 2000) Church, Ladywood, an adjacent parish to St Martin's in the city centre, I realised I could do something to change that norm. I became aware of how many came wanting to be of some use to 'them' in an area labelled in 1995 as the poorest health area in the country. But they were the alternative 'them', keen outsiders, not always appreciated. Inequality of background was too apparent.

My real interfaith enthusiasm began when my Anglican parochial outlook and realisation of anti-Semitism in the New Testament led me to become friendly with the new Progressive Jewish rabbi, Dr Margaret Jacobi - her Perceptions are in chapter 1 - and the local Burmese Buddhist senior monk of the local pagoda, whose perfect English I could barely understand, nor he mine, which was less perfect. New relationships quickly grew to include Muslim and, later, Sikh and Hindu leaders through the Birmingham Council of Faiths. I was discovering how ripe Birmingham was and is for such friendships.

I therefore involved our church in making positive new steps in three specific directions: initiating a Buddhist–Christian meditation group, sharing lunch and dialogue once or twice annually between members of our Ladywood inner-city church and the Progressive Jewish synagogue and supporting the Ladywood Interfaith Education

Project (LIEP) for schoolchildren.[2] For two to three years, I also convened a stimulating Men of Faith group of six guys from different faiths. I became an active member of the Birmingham Council of Faiths and served as its chair in 1994.

In the meantime, also as vicar, I led the restoration and redevelopment of our 1854, large Victorian Gothic church - it had lovely space and acoustic potential. The church had a rotten leaking roof but somehow raised £941,000 from below scratch and architectural and artistic talent to release a truly beautiful setting for worship, artistic and musical pursuits and children's interfaith activity which Ladywood people could be proud of. It included a Jewish gift from our very friendly local synagogue of a stained-glass window featuring Psalm 133, 'How good and blessed it is to dwell together in harmony.'

That all took ten years, with five years beforehand of pre-thought and four more for me to enjoy making it work alongside everyone else. We had an attitude of outreach, outside the Church. I chose to spend time on visiting as my chief priority and on good inter faith relationships rather than on other essential church structures like synods. Except with the Jews and in non-public discussion, I did not pursue as many congregational and theological worship issues as I might have done. The church's redevelopment and its funding from zero funds took time! We made a few new symbolic progressive steps through regular evensong discussions, changing a prayer about God's children to one about God's 'people' and inviting congregations to join in saying the Nicene Creed as 'the faith of the Church', if they wished. But I chose other priorities. It does though, when we moved away even only three miles, still feel hauntingly cruel, counter-intuitive, counter-Christian and hypocritical - all that! - to have broken off most of my relationships in practice with the Ladywood local and church friends I loved. I honestly did not see much choice but making such a break belies what I advocate in this book about relationships, an institutional practice I strongly question.

My challenge in retirement in 2008 from being vicar after nearly twenty years was how, in our new retirement home in nearby Moseley/Balsall Heath, to make connection in *theological principle* as well as practice with my new priority of creating inter faith relationships. Retirement has given me freedom and space to develop many of what were then radical but, in certain spheres, common-place Christian ideas I inherited during my student days of the 1960s. Already I had, as any vicar might, spent almost the second quarter of my life in a general way, enjoying relationships with people of different culture, that is Caribbean and African, and also those of different faith. Now Ruth and I have found more day-to-day inter faith possibilities - involving Islam in particular - than those available twenty to thirty years ago in Ladywood.

I am now involved in two inter faith areas and convene the Moseley inter faith group and also the Birmingham branch of the Progressive Christianity Network (PCN), Britain. This is a branch of a national movement that, since 2003, has mercifully opened alternative doors to the vast storehouse of differing priorities and authentic interpretations of scripture, Christian theology and Christian attitude and integrity. Such an approach is very relevant to inter faith relationships and theology. My two arms of work, inter faith and progressive Christianity, co-ordinate wondrously. Four/five years back I came to realise that relationships between Christianity and members of Birmingham's different world faiths, trying to connect principles and practice, asking others what they think and listening to their replies and pondering on 'progressive faith' as a whole, would be a focussed and worthwhile subject to write about. As far as I knew, no one else had taken the particular approach of asking particular individuals of other faiths what *they* thought about Christianity and Christians.[3] I have more recently deepened the subject by adding essential thinking about why and how we have perceptions and what hope, through reflection, they offer for our one world.

Reflections on my interfaith journey

I have been very fortunate in my opportunities. Looking back to my childhood, I jumped my first hurdle of gender through having three sisters (and two brothers for balance) and a literary professional mother and went to a mixed school, I jumped my first class and poverty hurdles through Cambridge and inner-city Southwark, my ecumenical hurdle in Lancaster - I was for a time Chair of the local Council of Churches - and my first race hurdles in Southwark and Ladywood and my disability hurdles in Ladywood, although still finding others' obesity 'challenging' to me and my skinniness. All these prepared me to leap what may be my last hurdle, inter faith. Older age might just take over.

In my experience of relationships with members of other major world faiths in Britain, who are now our Birmingham neighbours, Christians and Christianity on the whole do not thoroughly address the fundamental theological and psychological issues involved. This is no doubt done in some academic circles, but within the churches and specifically within Christian worship, liturgy and most church life, it often is not. When it is, whether in academia or some progressive churches of inclusive mindset, it tends to be at the level of observation, visitation and meeting. Discussion topics are usually limited to comfortable similarities and differences. Questions come from 'our'

Christian vantage point: how do *we* see other faiths, and what can *we* teach and learn about *them*?

I suggest our first tribal identity has to be left behind just as it was healthy and liberating to leave behind our childhood. 'When I was child I thought as a child ......now I am grown-up I discard childish things' wrote St Paul to the Corinthians, 1.13.11. Childhood tribal loyalties have their place but can be childish and misleading when resulting in division and misunderstanding in the face of significant public ignorance and deathly splashes of ideological extremism. Responsibility goes two ways between one faith and another, but British Christians, in religious faith and historical terms, still have the responsibility – at least, out of the major cities - of being hosts. Their task is to use their power to empower others, literally to enable others. In well-seasoned communities, different faiths take a lead, but more often initiating relationships is seen as Christians prime responsibility.

It can take many years, even generations, for newcomers to feel sufficiently at home and be made - enabled - to feel at home and feel confident enough to take initiative to reach out to others. That depends on the context from which they have come. Horrific traumas from the holocaust caused Jewish people to be unable to open up for fifty years and more. Our largest local mosque, understandably enough, looks to itself. Most of its women wear the full-face cover of the niqab when in public. (While I respect the right of every woman to wear what she chooses I do confess that I prefer to see the female human face). The enduring British Empire, however idealistic its missionaries, provided few exceptions to the normal class, social and racial divisions. One exception, Bede Griffiths, a British Benedictine monk, 1906–1993, lived a village life as a Christian Buddhist in South

India and had the confidence and humility to sit alongside others of different faith rather than over or against them. Such exceptions are thankfully much less rare in recent years; the word for SPG young missionaries now is 'dialogue', for God is acknowledged as already 'there'. Visitors to Ladywood were also no less free to discover this.

An unthinking and dogmatic media and public assume there are difficulties in relationships between Christians and those of different faiths. We might benefit if we ask why, to what degree and what is our own attitude and part in any such relationships and their improvement. My feeling is that the problem of relationships between Christians and members of the different world faiths is little more than it is with families, not primarily a matter of similarities and differences, although, yes, it can be. Human differences of opinion and being can be experienced as denial or enhancement of personal and community identity. A whole range of reactions may arise on both sides, whether in fear and threat from difference, essential and strong disagreement, savage argument, active injustice or amused contradiction. Knowledge and evidence are crucial to discussion and argument depending on our situations, our personalities and our 'them'. Fake-news and post-truth are totally non-acceptable, as I shall probably repeat.

Identity politics is very understandable for sense of home and security. Indigenous people covet this, but, so do immigrants whether for their past life or their future in Britain or wherever. I know some people indigenous to Britain who have less sense of identity in Britain than some immigrants because of past family history and uncertain circumstances. Refugees often just have to be pull up their roots for they may be left entirely without safe homeland. How does anyone – this is 2018 – go back home safely to Syria and Yemen? Adaptability and encouragement are vital for everyone. New amiable multi-faith culturalism may give more sense of identity to some people than absent bombed out homes. Staff of your local city hospital could be an inspiring example of the strength of new identities. I was recently treated by hijab-wearing young Muslim woman severely contorted in her physical disability, arms included. She is an audiologist! People naturally vary. Separate development whether of place or faith has no walled future. The internet is seeing to that. And the human spirit. British Brexiteers have had to realise this has to be faced. The conscious seeking of alternative identity such as through employment, sport, the arts, natural environment and scientific facilities, especially education is becoming essential. Mosques, churches, synagogues, gurdwaras and temples with their membership and traditions may come to have increasing significance in facilitating 'identity' through initial confidence then reaching out to others of different faith. My local parish church in Moseley has welcomed Muslim faithful to its Christmas and Easter services for the last 3 years. Nearly half the 200 or so congregation on Christmas Eve, 2017, was Muslim. I received the bread and wine of Communion standing at the altar next to a Muslim lady in a hijab who asked simply for a blessing[4b.]

The possible relevance of all these factors is not to be ignored in religious or in interfaith discourse and relationships. I simply comment that human beings - some or even most, maybe - have the potential to live amiably with both similarity and difference in whatever aspect of life. I have experienced that on my international visits as well as in Britain. However, when we fail, family and community hostility develop rapidly. This is most likely when the bounds of ethical normality, healthy expectations and justice are breached always to someone's disadvantage. Rivalry and personal power can be all-consuming at whatever human level, the church and other places of worship not excluded. Think of any group you belong to. 'Yesterday' in a mixed faith group I enabled a lady I had never met to say: '*I never realized what power I sometimes have*'. Genuine difference of opinion plays its part but so does the human psyche and the context.

Any suspicion by those of different faith of hangovers of arrogance, superiority and exclusiveness in British Christians however unintended, can provoke mirrored aggression and arrogance especially in those aware of their inferior economic and day-to-day resources alongside their lack of freedom. Franz Fanon taught me this, in theory, in the sixties in books like *Black Faces, White Masks*.[5] Fifty years on, 'Tetralogue: I'm Right, You're Wrong,'[6] is a cleverly named text. Both superiority and inferiority suggest exclusivity. At their worst, they can provoke tragic vicious circles of supremacy that create fear, suspicion, distrust and compound aggression. Apparently, it was customary for Christians in the 1st- 6th centuries to hound non-Christians by every 'social, legal, financial and physical method to destroy Classical Greek and Roman teaching and arts[6b]. The barbarism of IS or ISIS, the warmongering Islamic State has been nothing. Bigoted history became integrated into an inherited reality of twenty-first-century British Christianity when it prolongs theological and imperial hangovers from the British Empire. (See Fanon again). Any possible personal evidence and awareness of this tension in ourselves is worth consideration.

Such circles can be visible in the tendency across some Christian denominations and groups practising unofficial sectarianism which announce that 'we have the real message', not just as Christians, but as *we*, our denomination, our group. Whatever the cause, in relation to Christian ideals it demonstrates contradiction, possessiveness, selfishness and a shaky identity. Nor does it work, particularly within the wider society. Voiced or unvoiced, it is unlikely to produce genuine friendship and creative human relationships. The practice of supposed love and exclusivity, particularly when it concerns subterranean attempts by Christians - or by people of any faith - to convert others to their own faith, can produce confusion, distrust of motivation and integrity, disrespect, breakdowns in relationships and ultimately undesirable separate development. Old-style missionary idealism can be high even idealistic but undue elements of personal and spiritual power can be traceable and in today's terms possibly 'abusive'. A foundation missionary text, Matthew 28.19, requires thorough examination in the light of modern scholarship. What, to you, is the meaning of these words of Matthew and supposedly of Jesus if he could have recognized them as his 'teaching them to obey everything I have commanded you'?

I know much considerate, imaginative and constructive work in Birmingham to be admired but there are reported situations that I know of that are not good. Lack of honesty and integrity augurs ill for faithful community harmony, justice and peace between the religions. Above all, this depends on the quality of relationships, the friendships, that can cope with difference, whether vis-à-vis dress, language, friendship, marriage, family or any manner of social connection.

An important qualification has to be made. There is a world of difference between that unequal situation and the highly legitimate situation of followers of a particular faith preferring their faith and recommending it to others on honest and mutual terms, even certain that their faith is the truest to God. The reality is that others may believe likewise in respect to their own faith. Personal responsibility for right judgement is essential. It is, though, a complicated business. Hard and fast generalisations hinder personal well-being and honest relationships. Providing that it is recognised and respected and the other listened to, such loyalty to one's own seems to me wholly acceptable, even if generosity to the other is also desirable.

A Christian Context: God, Jesus and love

What is this Christianity? Millions of words must have been written about it. I seek only to define it for the sake of clarity within the context of my central question as to how best the British Church is to respond to its present national situation and particularly inter faith relationships outlined already. My experience is that the British Church, Christianity and Christians like myself fall short of its God-given potential. Of what is it falling short, with the consequent effects also mentioned already?

Aware of possible presumption, I offer my own experience and understanding of Christianity as it relates to our subject. I have to be clear about how I see the Christianity that has, in whatever interpretation, contributed to the perceptions on which this book is founded. Despite our 'faith perceptions' having have their own integrity and even a touch of ignorance, there remains a reality - call it truth - sought after by our contributors including myself. While I have defined it already as the faith upheld by Christians who are churchgoers, confidence in Christianity being much more than this is crucial for all those engaged in inter faith endeavours. Then while some define Christianity as based on when we die and Jesus's death and 'resurrection' that is neither my belief nor are heaven and hell after death my reality which is here and now in this world as I experience it.

Christianity is a faith in God. Customary public access to Christianity has been through the institutional Church. I have sometimes, in this context, used the two names interchangeably. I do, though, treasure awareness and further hope of an ever-inspiring, ever-evolving Christianity in people's hearts and minds, outside as well as inside the Church which aims to make sense of being human. In reality, Christianity and the Church vary hugely in practice. Insiders and outsiders may express both according to their own gospel or anti-gospel, with which others, even in their own party, may well differ. Sheer reality - and sense - tells us that 'the gospel' is an interpretation of experiences of revelation which may or may not be of God and is subject to human choice, context and influence. Nevertheless, Christianity has a central rational core. In current gambling terms, it is not 'a beta game' nor is it 'all a superstitious fabrication', though I have conjured that view with a good friend who holds it. Rowan Williams helps, through his interpretations, to keep our feet on firm ground:

> Christian life is lived in relationship with God through Jesus Christ and, in common with other Christians, seeking to deepen that relationship and to follow the way that Jesus taught. Central to that relationship is knowing we can trust God. Saint Paul says 'if God is for us, who can be against us?' And this is the heart of faith. 'Nothing'—says St Paul in the same passage— 'can separate us from this love.' And to proclaim the Gospel is to proclaim that it is ... possible to be properly human: the Catholic and Christian faith is a 'true humanism' ... the humanizing enterprise will be empty without the definition of humanity given in Jesus.[7]

Rowan Williams above mentions God, Jesus and love. All three are fundamental benchmarks for Christian perceptions of other faiths, other faiths' perceptions of Christianity and interfaith relationships. I now expand what these key elements might mean in our context.

I want to demonstrate that all three are, in practice, connected to my evidence of the reality and experience of my present-day multi-faith context and therefore to this book. They are entwined with its rational purpose, proposals and vision of the future. Otherwise, there exists an irrational disconnection of heart, mind and soul; disconnection from human experience, especially that of receiving and giving love and wrath; disconnection when it comes to the common inability to experience what is assumed to be God in the joyous and suffering mess of life, with the cross of Christ supposedly triumphant; disconnection from our post–digital age of individualism, turbulence, violent terrorism and change. Most beliefs carry the danger of including what is arbitrary, meaningless and dogmatic. For me, for example, in much Christian worship, 'Christ will come again' and from the Nicene Creed. 'He sits at the right hand of God', whether literally or metaphorically. Disconnection is less likely if we test and trust (believe in) our and others' own human experience and way of life based upon real possibilities of good, loving and transformative relationships where God is found.

It is not just the Church that is the body of Christ[8] but also our own body, individual and corporate - and in Christian terms, that of everyone else, especially people of different faiths. It is not just Christians who are the people of God but everyone. Remember Jesus and the Samaritan woman.[9] Were I a Martin Luther or John Wesley in their respective contexts, I imagine I would have more appreciation of the notion of God's judgement and of eternal damnation, but I am not and I don't. Basic is what we mean by God and therefore who we all are as God's people.

God

I cannot honestly write of God without being subjective - who can? - without saying how I understand God myself -who doesn't? Otherwise, what are we discussing together! It is so fundamental but how often it is not done! I know the very word, God, is a turn-off for some people for whom belief in so-called 'God' is therefore a non-starter. Associations with father, paternalism, patronising, then manipulation, gender discrimination, control and fear are easily identified. Fear association can be extraordinarily rampant. Distaste and fear of hierarchy especially of the Church and clergy can follow.

Who knows what is meant by the name! You may say 'what do I, the author, mean, anyway? What on earth is meant by the word or name 'God'? Fair enough! How many times might we hear on the media 'amazing, I can't put it into words'? 'It' could be concerning falling in love, seeing and climbing a favourite big hill, winning the under 11s football trophy or Wimbledon, sky-diving whatever anyone likes or loves or is humbled and empowered by. Whatever faith we are, we have similar challenges with the word and concept of God.

Our own human attempts at understanding God are basic to our human existence. I take it, with body, mind and spirit, that there is more to life than just me, and indeed you. There is something going on up, down over, or out there and in here that is not just personified, personal projection but a thoroughly wonderful, mysterious, ever-present and supreme dimension of life. At least to me and others I know, it feels like this. In this, I trust myself, whatever name I give it.

Some, like me, see God as the chosen name for what or who somehow creates life and sustains it. Some see God out there, transcendent, others in here, immanent. That is Christian tradition.

My experience is both. I derive hope from the persistent evidence of the reality of death, incarnation and resurrection in daily life because I consider that what I choose to call God is somehow at the bottom – and top - of life itself. Incredibly, the sick body is for some reason programmed to get better if possible. Maybe the whole universe is benign. In my understanding nothing can be bigger, literally eternal and omnipresent than this God. From 1000 years ago, in 1078 Anselm wrote of God: 'than which nothing greater can be thought'. A common notion of God is just too small. We need an understanding of life that makes sense to us.

I have heard that 'different faiths don't have the same God as us, do they?' I do not believe that either God or Jesus are or have been in the business of making insoluble problems for human creation; rather the reverse. Within Christianity itself, not least in both congregation and parish, there is considerable variety of understanding and definition of the name *God*; outside of Christianity, maybe more so. That is part of the mystery of God and of us human beings.

For a start, *God is not a Christian*,[10] nor male. In my understanding God has no faith label or sex in whatever sense. 'My ways are not your ways', God says according to the prophet Isaiah (55.8,9). I think I have always realised that, long before I could make any attempt at analysis. I now find in local inter faith discussions that a mysterious God *is* referred to by Christians, Muslims, Sikhs, Jews, Hindus and even Buddhists, but not usually up front; more often, God is taken for granted as totally other than all of us. This seems in practice to be the God who bears any variety of name, attribute and label attached by these faiths, Buddhism excepted. As a young man I was inspired by a book called *God of a Hundred Names*.[11] Islamic tradition has ninety-nine attributes for God, still not considered enough. Hindus have a multitude of gods arising from creation and nature who symbolise and represent the one God. Jews have such respect for God that they generally reject naming God altogether and Sikhs accept any major faith's different name for God.

However, behind such naming - helpful in practice despite inevitably appearing divisive - I sense a common willingness in people to accept, if explained, certain philosophical universal terms that are way beyond daily chat. 'Way beyond' suggests here not geographical location but appropriate indefinable mystery, so I value expressions like *Godhead* and descriptions like *unspeakable, ineffable,* and *transcategorial* - as John Hick[12] loved to say. The best singing teacher I've known, Jeanne Jones, speaks of 'accepting breath not taking it'. That's such a fine metaphor concerning God. My own use of different words depends on the company and my memory.

Significantly these universal terms are ironically a firm and inspiring inter faith basis for faith relationships. They may be considered attitudes, symbols and metaphors for the God-beyond-words, alongside more traditional Christian or another faith's understanding. They might be expressed in countless ways, with or without words, especially in music, experience of nature and science, and, supremely, love. For me, God's universal expression and characteristic is silence. I find it naturally in the mountains but wonderfully too in our local Hamza mosque, packed with five hundred or more worshippers just before prayers. It is strange that this is so because God's presumed silence is a common criticism of God from the psalmists to our own day. Both may be personal experience, but the first is profound, whereas the second to me, is misunderstanding because it may assume that God is unacceptably manipulative.

The anger of God as a concept is not one I relate to; it is too much a personal projection of ourselves. I can relate more to the righteous anger of Jesus with the Jewish leaders as a man. True, the text of Verdi's Requiem, 1874, assumes damnation and eternal fire on the last day of God's wrath. Perhaps that really does still linger in many a mind. For some, right or wrong, it is their perceived reality in feeling and mind, with due effect on prayer and well-being. For me it is horrific church theology except that evil behaviour is a fact of life which I reason around. 'Dies Irae', in Verdi's Requiem though, what a marvellous full-blooded piece to sing as I once did in the Albert Hall as a recording with the London Symphony Orchestra Chorus. As a tenor I have sung many of the religious oratorios, requiems and anthems repertoire along with other singers who understand know more of the meaning of the music than of the words. Again, our view of God is fundamental; our own contexts differ so much but I could easily see why God might be angry, if I thought of God in that personal way.

In a sense, as Karl Barth wrote at length, human beings cannot *by definition* reach God.[13] If God *is* beyond definition, then God is above any literal language of all the faiths, including Christianity. There is a different and mysterious level of my own experience beyond the everyday. A good friend of ours, Professor John Hull, seemed to find this level of experience. He became blind in middle age and struggled to eventually realise his blindness as a gift of God.[14] If the whole world, created and evolving, is the product of a creator I call God; and if it and everyone in it 'belongs' to that creator God; and if everyone is included as God's created beings; and if love, presumably created by or actually *being* God, is the most important element of human existence; and if Jesus is for Christians the supreme demonstration of God's love; then everything and everyone is in some way connected to God by love. These are indeed ifs, but they are all made reasonable and plausible to me by what thereby follows, which is that our life with God and one another, now and in the future, would be meaningful, validated and experienced in reality as a life of love. Potentially and in truth it is just that.

The name given to God by the writer of the book of Exodus, when questioned by Moses, is recorded as saying '*I am who I am*',[15] and the fact that the writer frequently imagines that 'God said', both denote recognition of God as in relationship with the humanity of creation. The writer, who had such insight into God, was claiming a simple profound truth for all existence, and for God, Jesus and all of us: we are what and who we are. I love that! God was imagined by human perception as having the kind of presence that Jesus himself apparently had after death. New life through birth and rebirth, through death and resurrection, rather than - for me, others see it differently - any literal bodily resurrection, is evidence of God's continual energy for creation and for life-giving spirit, from random variability by definition without divine intervention. Some might likewise be willing to see evolution as prime evidence of God viewed as creative Holy Spirit, that name being invaluable in its universal accessibility. I record it because it has creative universal bearing on interfaith relationships and dialogue.

God, then, while being an eternal question, is not - by this understanding - a barrier to inter faith harmony, nor necessarily a barrier to the non-Christian 'none' or person of non-religious faith. That would not be in the nature of God and God's mysterious relationship with everyone. The God problem is more in the unvoiced and unchallenged assumptions that we and others may make which reveal our ignorance, arrogance, fear and prejudice. "Do you believe in God?" 'It depends on what you mean by 'believe' and by 'God,' so please tell me". Such simple discussion can be meteoric. If members of different faiths do not have the same understanding of God to oneself - which is fairly likely even just within Christianity - then logically they are not stopped in theory from recognising the same God, who is beyond category. So much of our identity, motivation, attitude and behaviour and of our understanding - or otherwise - of prayer, worship and scripture, comes from our personal understanding of God. Further exploration of God will happen, always remain imperative. In whatever sense, for me, God is basic, always with us and dependable by definition, whatever world faith we inhabit.

Jesus

Christians pray to follow the way of Jesus as a natural substitute for God, easier to understand, easier to identify with, more flesh and blood, in order to lead what we may hope to be godly lives. I understand Jesus as being human like you and me, and therefore one to whom ordinary human beings may always relate in our own way. On this rests his credibility. The man Jesus who preaches and lives out 'good news to the poor' as prime amongst his social and political ideas which led him to be a martyr to the truth, is someone who, in a powerful, welcome sense is alive to me. I accept that the incarnation, that is God becoming a man, is a basic Christian tradition. It is meaningful to many but not to me. It is much more comprehensible and motivating to me to understand Jesus as representing the mystery of the human incarnation of God in all of us, from conception to death. What a supreme combination of godliness and humanity he was! The varying versions of Christianity that call him divine as well as human, or even equivalent to God, need unpacking of meaning. They tend to puzzle Christians like me, possibly equally qualified and God-loving people of different faiths and even some more orthodox Christians. The Church has often given Jesus that description, originally adopted at the nascent Trinitarian discussions in

Nicaea in 325 CE and finally at Chalcedon in 451 CE, but Jesus himself said nothing about such doctrine and nothing about being God in whatever New Testament account of his life. If *divine* is taken to mean 'Son of God', it is, to my knowledge, a historical label for Jesus only acceptable in the inter faith world, as a potential symbol, or even the face or persona of God for all humanity along with any other name he attracts, be it *prophet, teacher* or *Son of Man*.

Otherwise, Jesus is a rival to God. This is wholly unacceptable to Muslims, Jews and Sikhs and myself and some Christians I know. It could hardly be acceptable to those who think of God as without form and as *no thing* - except with a very limited meaning of the words - that infinite God could literally have a finite son of whatever kind. Nor that Jesus as *Son of God* should be matched with Jesus's rough and powerful contemporary, Augustus Caesar, the first Roman emperor (from 27 BCE. to 14 CE) and with Aeneas, Dido's friend, who were also called 'sons of God' with and without a capital S. The Romans had many gods who had many sons - and daughters. It is no wonder that insiders as well as outsiders to Christianity are baffled by the powerful tentacles of the myths of Greece and Rome, unless they are wise to the powers of metaphor, mythology and symbolism in religion and history. I accept the name Son of God as a figure of speech essential for understanding the Bible and the history of Christianity. For God to become man seems to me a superfluous man-made mystery.

God has left, and constantly leaves, traces, footprints, signs and symbols for us to follow in the manner of Jesus, despite our common human failure to see them. Many people, whoever they are, are naturally attracted to Jesus, enhanced or not by human projection and comfort. He symbolises holiness, and is respected, appreciated and accepted by members of the different world faiths, as he was for the hymn writer, for the man he was, shepherd, brother, friend, prophet, teacher, pastor, holy man - as is sung in the hymn 'How sweet the name of Jesus sounds'[16]. My perception is that Jesus is highly accredited by Christians, Christian sympathisers and those of different faith, religious or otherwise. What is known of his way of life as a real live person is seen to surpass that of all others, not just in his socially divided context but also universally; a way accessible to imagination more readily than many a traditional belief, literally understood story, dubious divinity, mysterious skill or messianic doctrine devised about him by others, during his time or in later centuries.

Jesus devoted himself to the building and restoration of relationships and was indeed God's Jewish humanist. It is clear from our 'Perceptions' that Jesus's life and teaching are in no way a problem for harmonious inter faith relationships. I know personally how Muslims honour Jesus, as they feel exhorted by ninety-three verses in the Qur'an to see him as God's messenger, the Messiah and the penultimate prophet to Mohammed. Nor, in my experience from inner-city London and Birmingham, would Jesus's life and teaching be a problem for many a non-churchgoer and non-Christians. Many would acknowledge that he demonstrated supremely the commandment to love God and to love our neighbour as ourselves and see it as command and duty. It is relevant to our main theme of inter faith relationships to point out that this was not original to Jesus. He was a Jew well versed in Jewish scripture, and this commandment comes from what was recorded as God speaking through the Jewish Torah in the *Hebrew* Bible – that is, the Old Testament - Leviticus 19:18 and Deuteronomy 6:5. How murderously tragic that so many people, including so-called 'Christians' and, most notoriously, German Nazis, failed for centuries to realise this. Repercussions rebound relentlessly and so tragically in modern-day Palestine/Israel and still currently 2017/8.

What Jesus stands for is of universal and eternal importance to life in all its fullness. He is for everyone, yes, but not for all people to be Christian. He did not establish Christianity as a new religion. He was a Jew- an astonishing, shocking reality considering later centuries of so-called Christian pogroms against the Jews! His personal Samaritan contacts were not about converting them to anything or anybody other than God. My crucial tool of exegesis to understanding what Jesus is described as having said and done and who he was, is to ask, 'what does Jesus stand for?'

One example of a famous passage that I hear commonly quoted is in John's Gospel,[17] 'I am the way, the truth, and the life.' The Way of Jesus is explicable as being a metaphor, similar to the way up a mountain - not unlike a holy satnav perhaps for today's unsure traveller - with the mountain being God. Why not, if that helps? Understanding of imaginative metaphor in religious language is crucial. The Way of Jesus is traditionally the Christian way followed by many Christians, myself included. The epistle writer John considers the Way of loving 'brother' - our neighbour - to be as important as loving God.[18] My experience is indeed that this is the Way of Life which Jesus stands for. I say as much to inter faith friends—to their approval. They, ordinary people like most others, as well as those who have become famous in Christianity and other faiths, religious and otherwise, have to discover their way in whatever light they can find. That is the gift of the human journey. This may be what many people believe when they say they believe or 'have faith' in Jesus, rather than that he is a mysterious demonstration of undefined 'divinity'. I can see why history and experience have considered him divine, but it makes no sense to me to see him other than human. But God in Jesus the man, God in Christ the man, yes Christ the man, yes.

Jesus was a supreme demonstration in his time of the crossing of barriers between male and female, weak and powerful, thriving and outcast. A famous story is told by Jesus about the Good Samaritan.[19] He told it in response to being asked 'Who is my neighbour?' and to illustrate what he advocated as God's way, which became his way. Samaritans were an ancient sect who hoped to amalgamate with the Jews but at that time were not accepted but rejected as different. One of them, rather than Jewish passers-by, showed love of neighbour by going to help a man beaten up and left on the roadside.

An important addition: Jesus is recorded by Matthew as saying 'forgive those who persecute you' and 'love your enemies', because anybody can love their friends.[20] That is the most radical thought and command in scripture. It is interesting, though, to note that Jesus is not recorded as having responded to a possible further question, 'Who is my enemy?' It is not very friendly or inclusive of him, though very human, in his parables to distinguish people as either wheat or weeds and as either sheep or goats, with threats of everlasting fire or eternal torture from his heavenly father. Such warning, in the context of his time, conveys recognition of moral righteousness, the eternal question of human freedom, the tension between good and evil and the consequences for the evildoer and the righteous.[20] (My modern psychological reasoning is anachronistic. My anger at evil and punishment of evil are different reactions). Nor is Jesus apparently known for seeking time with his mother and family or reconciliation with the Roman and Jewish authorities. Jesus seems, at least according to Luke, to warn the people of Chorazin and Bethsaida[21] of a fate like that of present-day Syrian massacres, 2011–17. That seems very harsh!

I still like the humanity of Jesus's limitations: families aren't always easy but nor are so-called enemies. I know which I prefer.

Everyone, not just those of faith, may have a problem with how to identify and live or work with one's enemy. We might ask what *enemy* and *evil* mean, and what to do about them both where they arise and through whom. I wonder whether Jesus would have called the Romans and the Jewish authorities and Judas his 'enemies' or 'evil', as gospel tabloid instinct has sometimes presumed to do. The word is common in Christian liturgy but let us say that enemies are maybe no more in British society at present than those you don't get on with. (It has been very different in war zones of this 2010 decade like in Syria from where many Muslim refugees come to Britain.) Then such questions may be about our everyday life, even perhaps at home. And then the question grows into one about where love is and why and how to love, which is just what Jesus taught and died for. Again, these are issues appreciable by all faiths.

Jesus, to me, in his presence with others, is the iconic demonstrator of the loving will and ways of God and the human symbolic version of God's kingdom here now on earth, all the more because of his human limitations. His potentially unifying power in life and death is expressed by Paul in his letter to the Romans describing how the body has many parts that work together. That applies whether the body is ours personally or belongs to the family, the nation or the world of many faiths. Jesus's presence was so powerful that I can quite imagine that it continued after his death to those who had loved him. At a recent funeral I heard it said of the deceased father by his family that 'he lives on in us', whatever that means – a biological fact for offspring not recognized at the time and a potential psychological fact for those affected by the life deceased. And elsewhere from other loving family members, 'She's still alive (to me), you know!' As a father I hope this will be a loving poetic reality as well as true physically. Says this is potential, loving poetic, reality. We may hope to become some atom of the same and not just beloved grandchildren!

According to the Gospels' writers, Jesus himself used the term *Father* more often than the term *God*. The name Jesus had unfortunate school and university hymnody associations for me and still does, while my ordained best man feels that Jesus loves him personally. I do find using the word *God* easier if not used too glibly, as in *God is good* and *God has been good to me* (for what else is to be expected?) For me, I am in some ways what I perceive as very English, more modest than shy, so words like *God* and *Jesus* can sound pretentious to me, even superior, especially if I have to wave my hands about! Temperament makes a difference.

Love

If people feel they cannot get hold of the idea and name of God or Jesus, or vice versa - what and who is this God who we're told loves us? - they often find love itself, at least the idea of it, more accessible, because it can be incredibly simple and democratic, as well as egalitarian and universal. Why we both can and cannot love to whatever degree is the same question in Introduction 2 under 'The Book's Development'. It is a vital question, for the central ethic of this book is about loving our neighbour. Why, again? Because, again, we are all of equal worth before God whatever our apparent inequalities in body and mind. What is our perception of that question for ourselves and others; what freedom does it require which we may not have ever been given?

Those who see themselves as neither religious nor Christian, nor as believing in whatever they mean by God, may consider love with its different overtones easier to handle. The word *Love* likewise, except in special circumstances. Jesus did not apparently use the word *love* in conversation with the Samaritan woman.

With an understanding of St John's Gospel that 'the Word' is Jesus and is God, and that both the Word and God actually existed before the understanding,[22] it is arguable that the qualities of God which led to the conception of God in the sense of a living power of life, also existed before God came to be recognised and named as the one true God. My own view is that it was those qualities themselves that came to be called God. Who knows about 'the beginning'? They have been named in every generation since Plato in the 5-4th centuries BCE described his forms, ideas, or qualities, for example of beauty, rightness and justice. These were an introduction to the name *God*.

What is omitted on that breath is the concept of love which, voiced or unvoiced, seems to me the most basic quality of our whole human existence, developed through evolution out of sexual necessity. The receiving and giving of love is our fundamental and eternal human experience since the dawn of life. Given that love is the greatest element of human life with all its different manifestations, as St Paul described,[23] it is also the most universal. It defies superficial definition, but of all human elements, it is the most far-reaching, formidable, all-embracing and multifaceted, the fundamental characteristic of our shared humanity. It is about what we all do and say to one another. Primarily it is about who and what we are to one another, which embraces what we do and say. To repeat, 'God is love and love is of God,' as John wrote in his Gospel. The beautiful and poetic artist and philosopher, Kahlil Gibran, in 1923 wrote in his famous book 'The Prophet', "When you love you should not say 'God is in my heart' but rather 'I am in the heart of God'". All Synoptic Gospels declare that Jesus's two great commandments are 'to love God and to love our neighbour as ourselves'. From that love of God, 'nothing can separate us', says St Paul.[24] Love is the greatest gift of all, as St Paul ventured further in his first letter to the Corinthians, 13ff, even above faith and hope.

Tragically and sometimes overwhelmingly, love is also prone to loss, directly and indirectly. Suffering in body heart and mind is the reality of human life and death, natural as well as unnatural, simply because all life dies, naturally or unnaturally. One may even have hardly anyone to love. Evil is a tragic product of love's denial, whether expressed in violent extremism, abuse, loss or fear, sheer chance or bad luck, in whatever combination. Considering love's fundamental nature, it is likely that loss of receiving and giving love from babyhood upwards can be a lifelong buried trauma. Many of us probably know on one hand or another that this can lead to intense suffering from overdose, rouse personal reaction, even a selection from the human deadly sins of pride, jealousy and greed. Naturally, the human dynamics accruing from such loss of love are as relevant to one faith as to any other. Yet, love is its own validation in a way that God, for many, is no longer.

Like God, it is never ultimately lost, but remains, waiting patiently in the wings. In one form or other, love therefore wins life hands down, publicly, privately, even commercially, despite, as we know, being vulnerable to the verbiage and vicissitudes of life and spoliation. Positively, cakes, cars, and kettles we are told, are all 'made lovingly'. I would bank on 'Do you love me?' and 'I love you', as asked by Jesus[25] and replied to by Peter, as the best of the hundred top human statements and questions. For love, we would go to the ends of the earth, and we do, whoever we are and of whatever faith, joyfully taking on spouses and babies. It is meaningful salvation, the foundation of human experience. 'O Love That Will Not Let Me Go' is a common hymn for joy and suffering, pain and goodwill, at home and away. I would welcome it being accepted more up front in all our lives and regarded openly as the foundation of our lives and of Christianity and the major world faiths.

As Christianity is founded on love of and for God and humanity, it is appropriate to write of love in the context of the relationships of all Christians and Christianity, including therefore those that are inter faith. Once this insight into our fundamental human purpose and equality before God fully dawned on me, I was one more who felt there was no going back, especially when I realised how highly *all* the major faiths and their members as human beings would naturally also esteem love. It was like my conversion to marrying Ruth and seeking ordination: there was no going back. As noted many times in this script, from what Jesus says according to Matthew's Gospel, 22:36, it is Jesus's commandment, as Jesus recalls from his Jewish scriptures, that *the first and greatest commandment* is to love God, and the second likewise, to love our neighbour as ourselves. It is a question of 'Thy will be done', and if we do or don't heed the commandments, individually and corporately, we take the consequences. That is simply a prime ingredient of the simple order of the universe, potentially sustained on this earth too. It is humanity's duty in return for its gift. Repentance and forgiveness, the ultimate loving of our enemy, love as hospitality, respect, acceptance and due empowerment may be very necessary. From love will flow justice and equity.

It is not to be forgotten by any faith that if we are to respect and love others as God's creation no less than ourselves, we are likewise to love God's creation, nature, our environment and our earthly home. This requires our gratitude and acceptance of our responsibility to be good and thankful stewards in caring for God's creation and passing it on to future generations. This in practice means that however we can, we are to love our work, our home and our streets and their people. This then means that we have to humanise our institutions; health service; schools; businesses, voluntary and statutory, big and small; cities; countryside; and streets in order to bring out the best in one another, patients, students, clients, customers, doctors, teachers, bosses, and executives among all of whom there are now in Britain, people of different religious and non-religious faith, whichever you identify with. Common knowledge is that this dehumanising is a major and costly present-day deficiency of love and care.

Our British constitutional monarchy and Parliament have been constituted on the basis of what Church and State essentially contribute to one another. The inter faiths annual Commonwealth Service in Westminster Abbey in the presence of the Queen is an outstanding example of let us say, inter faith love. Perhaps extraordinarily in today's climate, the day in Parliament starts with prayer.

Two questions relating to love arise regarding the interfaith context. Firstly, what does 'the love of God' mean in the face of the suffering and fearful political and moral challenges not least of our present times? I take it to mean wanting an attitude and habit of mind, heart and body of fostering one another's well-being and, corporately the common good for everyone, and potentially, in the same breath, enabling one another – in religious language - to experience and practice the presence of God. It means to take sides in the battle between the the destruction and enabling of the unprivileged. Secondly, what does it mean to love our neighbour as ourselves? Liking is of a different order. The Samaritan and the beaten-up man he helped symbolize our neighbours, one rejected, powerless and weak, another intensely caring of the alien. This suggests that, through love, everyone potentially has a fundamental unity and oneness in God and with other people. The two commandments go together by their very nature. At a lecture in the series 'Who Is My Neighbour' in St Martins-in-the-Fields, Rowan Williams, the former Archbishop of Canterbury, advised in his typically beautiful language, that one's neighbour

'is likely to be the most improbable person around so our openness to neighbourliness has to be a profound, all-encompassing, all-embracing thing … acting out the truth that is deepest in us. The deepest condition of our humanity is recognition, interaction and the exchange of life. We are … bound up in the life of everybody else around us. Who is God … the one who calls? God's … everlasting, loving intelligent action is focused utterly on you and me, and on every other being that is made. And the meaning of life is that I and you should grow together in our willingness to serve each other … having faith in a universal and given human solidarity.'[26]

Such words urge me to recognise a pre-existing universal faith, maybe called 'the Word', that embraces all the different world faiths. I do not see how they relate to any form of exclusive Christianity. I would like to think such a notion of love appeals to young people as much as anyone else, for they are by nature forward in seeking and finding their identity through love of another. I remember the time! A transcendent beauty of love is that despite human difference, disagreement even antagonism, political, personal and/ or religious, it leads to the practical beauty of human unity.

A Christian theology for inter-faith Britain

Preamble

I include here those people who consider themselves 'without religion' but very much do have their own non-religious faith. Basically, my theology has not depended on doctrinal premises but on my experience of the love -in whatever form- of human beings which, above, I call the love of God. Much of Christian doctrine and tradition does not ring true to me, it does not connect - at least, I don't - to my experience and comprehension of how life works. I've mentioned examples already but here are three more: Jesus 'will come again', Jesus has saved us by the cross again it depends on the will of God -inshallah, God will save us (from being massacred in Ghouta (Syria). Really? I mention these examples because I believe Christianity has to be credible to those thinking and wise people who see its merits but otherwise reject it.

My extended visit to South Africa in 1965 - Mandela's year of being imprisoned while many churches I witnessed advocated apartheid - and the American deep south in 1966, still fiercely divided by race and colour, first led me to feel deep down that Christianity in those situations did not do itself justice. In the one I was treated as priority customer as in the Durban Cleaners and having fallen off Table Mountain taken unconscious to hospital probably by an unknown Cape- coloured man; in the other, in Birmingham, Alabama, white racist Governor Wallace country, three young black men got off the pavement to let me go by. I was about their age.

Such apparently trivial and simple yet strong memories raised two simple touchstone questions for my lifetime - as can happen: why such inequality and what do I and we do about it? This brief chapter emphasizes afresh in more personal terms the previous theological assertions. They are, in my experience, a mixture of the traditional orthodox and the less traditional.

'There is nothing more important than discussion and understanding of God'.[27] That is my experience and it has increasingly become the prime means of my confidence in Christianity and life in general. How far, however, does a different understanding of God affect understanding of Christianity in its priorities, prayers, practices and understanding of different faiths? For me personally, as I said in the different context of Introduction 1, God is the name I accept for what or who creates and sustains creation, humanity and me, and therefore members of all faiths and all faith, and for that which is outside *and* inside us, immanent, present and transcendent, God always with us, always reality, the infinite eternity and source of our reality and person. God is the name I accept for the creation of the mysteries, science and wonders of nature, which are both stunningly beautiful and dangerously fragile, the sun, that huge ball of fire and the diminutive snowdrop that according to the gardening expert, Monty Don, lives for 200 years. God is the name I accept for our own astonishing personal creation, God in the beauty of holiness of music, art and nature, God conveying a sense of the oneness of life. I like the sacred Sikh song 'Mul Mantra', sometimes sung at inter faith gatherings, translated 'We Are One'. Attendees at the Christian Holy Communion declare from the prayer books, 'We are one body because we all share in one bread.' Yes, if 'we' is the human race symbolised in that service but to which all people should be welcome to participate fully; and yes, even if we are not. Perhaps you respond to this.

God immanent, within us, and transcendent, beyond us, experienced as energy, love, creativity and mystery are both in here in me and you and out there for us to reach and yearn for. I had no name for the experience I had that led me to ordination but those five minutes changed my life – and quite rationally because the experience was so powerful. (See my personal life journey in this chapter). Maybe a concept of God out there or up there could disappear, come and go; that is some people's experience, but not mine for it would be impossible by my definition. God in here, in us, logically, can't do that on God's own terms, because God's creation has natural rules. Such an understanding of God means, thankfully, that there is no escape any more than there is from our breath whether we consider ourselves of no faith or the reverse.

I am both theist and non-theist: it depends on my experience of the context and situation of relationships and priority and resultant feelings. For me to understand my own experience is more important than any label, as otherwise I cannot justify my own experience as being valid to anyone other than myself. Both understandings of God motivate me, and both are absolutely essential at times as they were to many of my congregation in Ladywood, that is God as a Being and God as Being itself. Otherwise the one is put up to compete with the other through our having differing experience, background and temperament. This fits my idea of God beyond words, labels, and categories, but is potentially inclusive of them too. Rather mysteriously to me, God is God, just as, in a somewhat miniature but logical way, I am I (or me), and you are always you. Jesus cannot be God and could not become God because he was a man and these two are different categories that are not to confuse or diminish one another. I entirely though accept that God was in Christ: God is in all creation.

Human life therefore to me is about loving God and all humanity, our two most important experiences and relationships. It is not about utopian ambitions any more than is this book. I recently visited, in Berlin, an exhibition commemorating the centenary of the Russian Revolution of 1917. Within weeks of the revolution those who were in opposition were murdered in the name of 'us'; and it continued. As it once was within Christianity of the British 16/17th centuries so has it recently happened within Islam with ISIS in the Middle East and within Buddhism in Myenmar. It is the enduring message of Jesus' teaching and of Christianity that people are to love their enemy. The exhibition castigated naïve utopianism and its history of disastrous consequences. 'Love God and love our neighbour as ourselves' is a precept accepted by the Jewish faith, the Christian faith and virtually all faiths, because at root it is about our human relationships. Great artists, musicians, writers, poets, scientists of religious faith or otherwise, are its witnesses. Despite those I know who have endured strong contrary forces of loss, selfishness, strife, suffering even hatred and segregation, once this ethos is explained I have met no one who disagrees.

For me, the literally overwhelming problem for such love is that it is too much to ask. How can I or anyone else possibly have equal love in practice and even in mind for burning tower -block residents, drowning refugees, ethnic - cleansed Rohingya people, abused children? The list is obviously endless. How are we supposed to choose? I can well pass by homeless people in the street in Birmingham feeling there are now- since the Brexit vote of June, 2016 - just too many to cope with. It was easier when they were rare but I saw just one in Harrogate the other day, my posh home town. I felt creased. I leave the question to you; we have to choose our priorities, whatever faith we hold.

It is in 'the image of God' that we are born, according to the Genesis writer,[28] - does that personify God already? - and in whom we 'live and move and have our being',[29] as Paul says. I cannot separate my experience from my learning to interpret that experience. Nevertheless, my experience is that my experience comes first. With doubting Thomas,[30] there had to be evidence for me to acknowledge and then name. I go further and consider experience to be one type of evidence. I value Simone Weil's insight:[31]'The apparent absence of God in this world is the actual reality of God.' Within this paradoxical framework of God and that kind of experience, I discover my - our - own being and my - our - own presence, what I consider to be God's ultimate gift to us all. It is our natural recognition of mystery. For me, music, nature and mountains are beautiful symbols of the great mystery of life. I can see such pantheism offers warning to the monotheistic faiths that they can be exclusive of other faiths who have less tight boundaries of faith and practice but perhaps more sense of beauty and wonder[31b]. Perhaps not, for variety is endless.

I can only deduce that we are partners with God. Peter exclaims in the Acts of the Apostles,[32] 'I truly understand that God shows no partiality, but in every nation, anyone who fears him and does what is right is acceptable to him.' Love means wishing and trying and failing to enable the very best for everyone, for the very best is symbolised by the word *God*, most succinctly described as 'the ground of our being';[33] we could say 'our guts'. That is an open-ended poetic idea of Paul Tillich, but I cannot find better. There is, in my experience, a power of love in all creation, just as there is a breath of life for each of us to grow and encourage in one another in order to uphold our human purposes. I call that God too, realised in whatever personas and creations.

The God I presume to sense is of universal omnipresence, founded on my human experience of love which, in very different patterns and to very degrees, is the eternal feature of my human existence. It makes sense to me that love was and is created in the first place for all of us by God. I cannot think of a better concept, though I do not see how my understanding of love tallies with my understanding of God as Creator. This, evolution and social Darwinism, demand further discussion. I do not usually ascribe personality or any objective substance to God, nor feel the need for an imaginative story however good it may be, unless it can avoid being misguided into literal reality. I see God as neither Christian, Jewish, Muslim, Hindu nor any other faith, and as belonging to no one although everyone belongs to God. Pluralism of faiths signifies equality in God – not under or before, which I understand less. Prepositions as significant theological indicators have become become fundamental to me. If God is beyond us all, for one faith to be seen as superior to others in its concept of God, is clearly and seriously a logical problem. It makes sense to me that any truth we can all grasp is conditioned by our own circumstances. That is more than to say human beings are all equal - which the history of homo sapiens denies. Unity and equality *before God* is quite different truth to the dangerously utopian, selfish, supposed economic or racial truths espoused by Marx and Hitler. God first, Christianity and all other faiths are means and expressions of God and therefore second. It is within this understanding of God that I aim to follow the way of Jesus in multi-faith Britain.

Also, within my understanding of God, comes prayer. I do pray. It's rather like breathing, sometimes very conscious sometimes not at all conscious; potentially constant communication because from conception we are in God and God is in us. Prayer, that is sensing God, communicating with God, is akin to continuous communication with anyone you love. It is not about trying to deny the forces of nature. Its expressions are infinite. I believe God is continuous, always with us, no less than my body, mind, and soul; so is the potential for prayer. I do not believe I should say 'please God' for that assumes a different understanding of God to my own, but that is theirs. Prayer is dependent on one's concept of God, either up, out, or down, there or not, 'all powerful' or not, depending what that means. Church liturgy tends to dress it up, put it out on the railway line and people sometimes find it down on the sleepers. Formal prayers are an essential backup offered by the Church, invaluable for personal confidence and communal solidarity of persons, the Church itself and society.

Despite their short-term comfort and strength, which can be life-saving, as they were to many people I knew pastorally in Ladywood, prayers can seem for some to be an awful, naive trap which can court tragic disillusionment. 'I prayed hard, nothing happened and she died'. Prayer, unfortunately, can in practice be more about authority, power, unreality and irresponsibility - sometimes unrecognised - than about relationship, faith, hope and love. It is more than strange to me in principle, though less so in pastoral practice, to beseech God privately and publicly for life or death and anything in between. Such action suggests to me acceptance of the kind of Santa Claus God who takes requests and returns them unopened. Such a process seems to me arbitrary, rejecting, disillusioning, cruel and possibly unfaithful to the constant to the God not of magic and superfluous supernaturalism but of constant love. And to exclaim 'Lord, hear our prayer' is superfluous! We don't - usually - ask our breath to take heed of us or our heart to beat, although it can be comforting to do after a stiff climb even just upstairs; likewise, in practice, with God. The best option for addressing God seems to me in terms of a sensing of God-always-with-us.

It is also inevitably within my definition of God that I see the Bible. It is certainly *the* means to Jesus. It is therefore primarily a means to God and regularly an end in itself for study and learning. As is clear from the text and chapter references for which I have frequently mined the Bible, I have great respect and appreciation for much of what is written there about God, no doubt inspired by God, as God inspires all good loving things and people. But since we cannot be literal about God, in my view we cannot be literal about the Bible. God is the prime subject of poetry, science, music, art, love, relationships, speech, creation and nature, indeed of all our existence. The Bible, a vast treasure house of all this, conveys meaning in different measure and context through figures of speech such as metaphor, symbolism and parable. It is essential to realise this or be taught it.

A literal view of the Bible, especially a fundamentalist one, literally does not make sense to me. The context of the writers is all-important. The words become the Word of God only when they convey the wisdom, goodness, love and justice that stand for God, or for Jesus, amidst whatever disharmony. They often do. The story of Adam and Eve is the first in biblical chronology to do just this but that does not make it truth literal. For readers to pronounce 'This is the Word of the Lord' indiscriminately after every pre-gospel Bible reading in church, seems to me actually to cheapen its truly inspired content partly because the congregation are rarely told what that means. Is it literal or metaphorical truth? Or is it neither? I suggest you look up John 8.44! Besides, how could gospel writers possibly have known, word for word, of Jesus's personal conversations? My history degree taught me indirectly that when the Bible is presumed to be 'true' history, then history's discipline asks, 'Who says?' This especially applies to stories of profound wisdom which, taken literally, I consider sentimental superstition, however understandable, as for example a serpent talking to Adam and Eve in the Garden of Eden and a star settling over baby Jesus in Bethlehem. I look forward to imminent discussions about the Qur'an with progressive Muslim friends and, in good time, with those of them who are literalist. Hindus generally love the truths of their stories without need for literalism. Most novel-reading adults are no different!

Literalism is a very harmful aspect of Christianity for it appears to be a deception. I know people it has deceived and disillusioned. That is literally tragic for it confuses spiritual truth with literal truth and what anyone of imagination and discernment can see was intended through the Hebrew language medium of poetic spiritual metaphors, symbolism and parables of Jesus and the gospel writers with dodgy, spiritless and strange assertions in matter-of-fact prose. A vital question is: what do outsiders to religious faith and people of different or non-religious faith make of biblical and liturgical literalism? I think the future will get harder for Christianity in this regard if literalism remains a major problem created by of over-zealous, under-tutored evangelism. It may though be cast as a positive bridge of both sighs and joys between those of traditional orthodoxy and those of progressive Christianity. The question of John Betjeman, 1906-84, poet laureate, at the end of his Christmas poem which asks 'is it true?' that God became 'a Child on earth for me?' has maybe roused many discussions already and they could well continue.

Jesus comes within my understanding of God. He cannot be God and could not become God because he was a man. These two are different categories and we have seen already that God is above category. It is true that some believe God could do as God does and wishes. They and I disagree. God and Jesus are both who they are. Exodus's writer, who had the insight into God sufficient to have God say to Moses 'I am who I am',[34] was projecting a simple profound truth for all existence, for God and all of us: we are what and who we are, whatever Faith we belong to. Jesus likewise. His 'I am' pronouncements according to John's gospel do not necessarily make him part of God or 'God' in human form. They are symbolic words of his own reality; rather God part of him as and all creation He is, for example, following 'I am' - 'the bread of life…that came down from heaven' (6.35,41) and 'the good shepherd' (8.12) and many more testaments. I particularly like the Jewish word *chesed*, pleasing to Buddhist friends and meaning loving kindness. Ally it to Jewish *tsebek* signifying social justice and that's equally powerful. Both words tell us about Jesus.

My post-experience – a word I've coined to describe experience beyond the everyday - is that there is a different and mysterious level to my own experience. It is one in which happy children conspicuously live, revelling in the sheer presence of the other and Life itself. Adults of every faith could do the same if conditions of 21st century become favourable, maybe more so if they do not. Jesus is already such a powerful and essential bridge for all humankind with itself, with the world's faiths and with God! I regret his being labelled 'God' and what is to me the seemingly superfluous and arbitrary belief that 'God became man' because of the serious barriers this creates in principle and practice for many of different and of no religious faith. Open discussion over such issues is vital. I look forward to traditional orthodox Christians openly communicating what they mean by this and about Jesus being to them the divine 'Son of God'. Discussion could well develop, a suspension bridge however lofty, worthy of engineer, Thomas Telford, built between them and Christian outsiders and different interpretations recognised and respected.

It would be rewarding were there discussion of Jesus apropos God and what are first and second order principles and why. Room for manoeuvre could be found; just safe spaces to cultivate our self-awareness. Take one example of a famous passage that I hear commonly quoted, about Jesus's assumed-to-be exclusive claims to be *the Son of God*, namely John's Gospel 14:6: 'I am the way, the truth and the life', by implication for everyone. My experience is indeed that this is what Jesus stands for, and I say as much to interfaith friends. It is the name, Son of God, again and again, which conjures up perceived superiority, dogma and associated images, prejudices, history, undesirable power and exclusiveness and causes problems. For me, personally, I willingly accept the name as metaphor, a figure of speech essential for understanding the Bible, but it requires explanation in comprehensible language. It is a paradox of yes and no. Who visiting a church for the first time is told what and how to distinguish metaphor from literal truth and may well leave confused? (I refer to 'confusions' in chapter 5).

Jesus, to me, is centrally the iconic demonstrator of the loving will and ways of God and of the human symbolic version of God's kingdom here now on earth. Jesus's potentially unifying power is expressed by Paul in his letter to the Romans,[35] describing how the body has many parts that have to work together. This applies whether the body is ours personally or belongs to the family, the nation or the world of many faiths. The human/spiritual qualities which Jesus stands for are, I believe, meaningful and acceptable to everyone. Christianity developed from people knowing the man Jesus in life, death and resurrection and consequently aiming to follow him.

In Jesus we see embodied that love and its experience which reveal my most profound wonder at the mystery of life and death. Symbolically, all people now on a global basis, part of the Body of Christ if they so wish. We could all, symbolically, share his body and blood of the Holy Communion. Love is the direct sunshine onto the dirty windows of our world. No wonder Jesus is seen as the light. It is crucial to remember that the whole theological point about him is that he was, at the least, human. What is the possible alternative? The ultimate words of value 'I love you' and any accompanying dazzling smile, convey more to me of the mystery of life wherever. The presence of Jesus is recorded as having that effect. He demonstrated the imminent God-with-us who at the same time transcends practical realities. Just as love is an instinct so is Jesus (my wife's beautiful idea). Labels can tell us as much about the labeller as about the labelled.

Creeds and hymns are a mixed blessing for inter faith appreciation, positive in principle by stating a case, negative when they present an exclusive God and Jesus actually as God, 'very God of very God' in the Nicene Creed, rather than a human being in God. It is within my understanding of God, of Jesus and of literalism that I see and hear the Creeds especially the Nicene Creed. It does not express my Christian faith and I regret that it seems officially still to do so for 'the Church' in an utterly different context to that in which it was formulated, very usefully, 1700 years ago. Even in that fourth-century gathering at Nicaea with Constantine in 325 CE, I doubt the words were ever meant to be immortal, as they are in danger of being treated today. Rather they are attempted means to God and means are rarely meant to become ends.

Then, as to be expected, likewise with some hymns. There are many that I just cannot sing. Such an opportunity wasted for real integration of mind, body, and spirit! More than just one example is inappropriate, but here is that one, 'How Great Thou Art', by no less a famous figure than John Wesley, in an 18th century very different age. Again, such wasted opportunities considering the modern hymns with profound theology and good music that are available!

*And when I think that God, his Son not sparing, sent him to die,
I scarce can take it in.*

With respect, nor can I, and I don't intend to. Nor do I intend
to delve into 'sacrificial atonement'. Good tune, though – tunes and
meaning provide common conflict not only for singers! Contrast no
less a traditional hymn than 'The Lord Is My Shepherd'- good words
and music for anyone of faith to hear!

Put together, that is my own not very doctrinal faith. It
aims to be seen as a universal theology of relationships and meaning
relevant to members of the world faiths, those of religious and non-
religious faith and those who consider themselves nones. Belief of
this type is more inclusive than an alternative which is doctrinal belief.
I find it helpful to recognise that faith and belief can in connotation
be different. Irrational faith however, is not my cup of tea when it
unnecessarily dresses up profound Mystery in outdated, spuriously
immortalised doctrinal language assumed to be God's words and
which is ultimately conjecture and possibly superstition about past and
future and even present. Many prayers and biblical passages seem to
me to get bogged down in this confusion about faith. I often find this
frustrating, trivial, arbitrary and unnecessary. They have been and can
still of course be means to God and Jesus but if they are prioritised
above 'love God, our neighbour and ourselves' I again jump off any
fence of relativizing and ask 'what is the Church fundamentally about?
Do we make our God too small, just to suit our eyesight?' I thank the
NHS for my daily eyedrops against glaucoma.

We come back to again to God our anchor. I seek the God
who not only loves us but is the 'one' who creates the desire for
ready affirmation and therefore confidence in people to love others
as well as ourselves. Myself, I see a problem of the Church as being

too often a misguided impediment to inclusive relationships and so to the essence of life, despite any best of intentions. Yet I love it dearly, not just Christianity but the Church. It has sustained me throughout my life and for this I am immensely grateful. That is why for the sake of the world in which somehow, for some reason, we find ourselves, I want it to embrace a Christianity which is more appreciated than it clearly is by the majority of the British population of whatever faith, religious or otherwise and particularly by members of different world faiths.

The foregoing discussion about God, Jesus and the notion of love leads me essentially to practical relationships between members of the major faiths. In Ladywood I had some idea of the essence of life for some inner city, non- churchgoing good, ordinary people. I have friends and family too who quietly share their similar essence of life. Perhaps this is it, in just one insight: Shakespeare and his Shylock knew our common humanity: 'I am a Jew. ... If you prick us do we not bleed.'[36] Such is the truth of life that everyone knows. Yet anti-Semitism, a terrible criminal perversion, comes and goes and comes again. At the British Mosques Open Day 2017, in 150 mosques around Britain and specifically in Birmingham,[37] I was part of an open gathering of members of all six major faiths, all in principle avowing their aim and raison d'être to be this truth of our one humanity.

A galaxy of difference in and between different faiths, even disagreement within this overarching framework, is to be seen as another utterly acceptable and wonderful gift of creation itself. Temptation to exert psychological pressure fuelled by power and possessiveness, leading to *I'm right, you're wrong*,[38] is to be understood but mostly resisted. The 21st century has already had endless opportunities to learn this and, often disastrously, not to learn it.

Human relationships, good, loving - that is respectful - ones across the faiths, are paramount for our human survival. Theological and ethical principles and vision have to accompany practice. The aim of loving God and our neighbour as ourselves combines both.

It is a truism that love is inadequate in many situations. Global warming, uncontrolled infection, nuclear disarmament, savage civil wars with weapons Britain itself sells so scandalously, are all overwhelming examples. The Church itself is easily derailed, even by its own doctrines that, however useful a framework and holy tradition they provide, require balancing with the dynamic and creative Holy Spirit of God. Too powerful an example for me has been the notion of original sin, from which Jesus is said somehow to have delivered the world for God by his death. Did God really create us 'sinful'? Jesus's own brave and powerful example of sacrificing himself for what he saw as the truth of God in the face of the violent Roman and Jewish authorities he probably riled against as a boy, is seen by some devout Christians as a symbolic sacrifice and a saving of the whole world, even that Jesus was sent or commissioned by his so-called 'Father', God. I do not see that. Sacrificial action is not exceptional, bloody warfare has always seen it. Yet it is a persistent story throughout Christian and especially Wesleyan hymnody

It is within my understanding of God again that I make this note on the Holy Spirit, the 'go-between God'[39] so determining in interfaith relationships. I understand the Holy Spirit as the unceasing breath of the energy of God, flexible, omnipresent, powerful, the great connector between us all and therefore between all the faiths, the one who, in Christian tradition, leads us into all truth. It is an energy not necessarily distinguished from God, but by tradition the third powerful persona or face of God. I believe the power of the Holy

Spirit is demonstrated in both human incarnation, the mystery of birth, in resurrection and in the mystery of continuous renewal and rebirth as exemplified by Jesus. Both are to be perceived as a wonderful reality and motivation of all life. The Holy Spirit is so powerful a concept because of what is considered its overarching inclusivity. Its very lack of a body, unlike Jesus, empowers everyone's potential, just as in the chorus of voices of different faiths at Pentecost and indeed the large choruses in which I have sung for years. It sets us free to be ourselves with God in a different third way, in addition to the two ways of God and Jesus. Jesus is recorded by Luke, 4:18, as quoting the Jewish prophet Isaiah (in Isaiah 61 - my version): 'The Spirit of the Lord ... is upon me to bring good news to the oppressed ... liberty to the captives ... sight to the blind ... freedom to the oppressed.' Being imageless itself, it guards against exclusive concepts of God in our own image. It is therefore good for inter faith relationships and could be 'publicised' more in inter faith discussion as a third aspect or way of seeing God.

There is a universal ethical context which intermingles with Christianity that has been important to me and relevant to inter faith relationships. A central Judaeo/Christian text, which originates from the Jewish prophet Micah, declares: 'The Lord has told us what is good. What he requires of us is this: to do what is just, to show constant love and to live in humility with our God.'[40] Then it is symbolised by three well-known quotes about our human existence. They are from three wise and authentic Christians, divided by a mere 350 years.

The first is from John Donne:[41] 'No man is an island entire to itself .... Every man is a piece of the continent ... because I am involved in mankind.' The second is from Hans Kung:[42] 'There will be no peace between the nations until there is peace between the religions ... no peace between the religions until there is dialogue between the religions and no dialogue between the religions until there is investigation of the foundation of religions.' The third is from *Nostra Aetate* of 1965, resulting from the Second Vatican Council of 1962 under Pope John XXIII: 'In our time [then!] we recognise the oneness of all peoples and of their origin, for God made the whole human race to live over the face of the earth.' Together with my Christian and inter faith experience of human interdependence, these thinkers have been with me in my questions and confidence in how I see Christian inter faith theological relationships. Then the scientific discovery of DNA (dioxyribonucleic acid!) the bases of which are virtually the same in all people is wonderful, modern, universal context for our history and common humanity.

I have written and edited this book as a challenge to Christians initially based on challenges from five people of different faith. We are all equal people before God and made in the image of God, whatever our faith, with a new commission renewed in our 21st century to act as if we are. This may well mean a distinct potential shift in our personal and theological attitudes to people of different religious faiths. Together, we all have new opportunity - however small - in our new world to seek a transformed world, however local, that reflects the mystery of both human similarity and difference and the wonders and needs of all creation under our eternal God. Christianity has to play its part as best it can through relationships and God-given priorities, but so does every other faith. A Judaeo-Christian model to seek unity between 'us and them' - in our case Christians and members of different faiths - is offered with open arms through the way of Jesus. The faiths are to teach and learn, learn and teach. New habits are required, like non-smoking. Their prime focus is to love God and our neighbour as ourselves alongside the golden rule, remarkably or not, of *all* these faiths: 'to do as you would be done by'.[43]

No one is to be excluded. That includes those of different non-religious faith. Not only is this the challenge for Christian interfaith relationships but also the challenge of the predicament of Christianity in Britain in this century that Christianity in name is only honoured – at least that is by a relevant survey - by about half of its population. Maybe its Church fails largely to honour the other half, as is a common perception. My premise is that the two challenges are fundamentally connected. My predominant response to many locals I knew when I was vicar in Ladywood, which was not a community of different faiths and was mostly non-churchgoing, was respect for their innate moral consciousness (*synderesis*), and faith in life, in their baby, their partner, their parent, their friend, even the 'unnamed God' whom Paul found in Athens.[44] Bob and Christine - I can't remember their actual names - were their epitome: 'We'd like you to baptise our baby.' 'Why?' 'Because we love her so much and want to say thank you for her!' What could I add? Of course situations varied; perceptions do too. I do not think the Church is good at recognising fertile ground which belongs to God already. National and religious opposition to Christian evangelists bringing to say, China or India, their version of God, Jesus and the world is understandable. The pain, suffering, battering, fear and anger that existed in Ladywood needed far more than our church and I could offer. Effective partnership with the church needed so much encouragement. There were many tragic lives, sometimes even collapsing onto our doorstep or once resulting in a guy being shot and killed on the road outside. 'The vicarage' could no way be always helpful.

It is not trivial to consider the worlds of art and music that we did foster there, all symbols of God's Spirit. Central Ladywood was very much of equal black and white numbers. Andy Hamilton, West Indian British jazz sax supremo, lived in the flats and respected the Church greatly, despite not coming regularly. His musical spirit led the way of life with young followers. What did inspire many with a sense of wonder was the stunningly beautiful redevelopment of the church itself. It was not then a multi-faith area. We did though take time to build up a completely black and white congregation to mutual blessing. My insistence on our having a West Indian Kittitian as churchwarden symbolised the church's intent.

It is easier to accept difference when we know one another. That is much of the whole point of the book - to demonstrate perhaps a fresh way forward to listen to and learn from one another not just knowledge but also how to encourage harmonious and just relationships across what are unnecessarily seen as barriers to the fulness of life rather than means to it. We all have body, mind and spirit to integrate together, individually and corporately. The developing British context was simply widened to include British people from overseas and members of different world faiths, building Britain and Birmingham during the last 50-60 years into a magnificent microcosm of the whole world, especially its world faiths. No need for holiday. aeroplane, ship or hardly a bus for Ruth and me to enjoy and benefit from different varieties of the world's faiths and peoples.

The 21st century question seems to me to be how Christianity and Christians contribute in partnership with others of different faiths, religious and otherwise - to find old ways and create new to save one another and our earth home. That is a joint life-long project for us all. Such a challenge stirs me with an inner Christian conviction that has been sharpened since I have become involved with those of different faith. I now simply ask myself, 'What is the Christian priority? What was that of Jesus? What does it mean in practice, as it does in principle, that all people are equal in the mind of God, the Creator of all?' The answer to me is that we are to love God and our neighbour as ourselves, whomever that neighbour is, with our hearts and minds and in whatever ways present themselves with whatever problems are thrown up by the contexts in which we live. My own personal context has to be God and increased attempts at loving relationships with people of different faith, without whom I am no longer me, notably in relation to Church, inside or outside. That context has to be rooted in the context of the world that God has given us all to care for. Obvious, simple? Maybe. Love one another? We do already, well, sometimes. Liking helps, but it is second-class loving. Just let's give it a better go, together!

1   Sally McFague, theologian, *Church Times* interview, 14 Jan. 2016.

2   See chapter 2 on LIEP, started in 1998 by my colleague Jo Mason, and still going strong.

3   Paul Griffiths, *Christianity through Non-Christian Eyes* (Orbis books, 1990) discovered by me in 2017.

4   Micah 6:6–8, Good News Translation

4b See under 'Partnerships in Theological discussion'

5   Frantz Fanon, *Black Skin, White Masks.*, (1952, Rebel books)

6   Timothy Williamson, *I'm right, you're wrong;* (OUP, 2015).

6b Catherine Nixey, *The Darkening Age: Christian Destruction of the Classical World*, Macmillan 2017

7   Rowan Williams, address to the Synod of Bishops in Rome, October 2012.

8   Corinthians 12:12ff.

9   John 4, general.

10 Desmond Tutu, *God Is Not a Christian* (HarperOne, 2011).

11 Barbara Greene and Victor Gollanz, *God of a Hundred Names* (Gollanz196,).

12 John Hick, personal conversations, 2010. Besides becoming a world-famous philosopher of religion, he was, for many, the most personable of mentors.

13 Karl Barth, 1886–1968, foremost Protestant Swiss theologian, whom I do not wish to oversimplify.

14 John Hull, 1934–1985, *Touching the Rock* (London: SPCK, 1990) and *Notes on Blindness* (Curzon Artificial Eye, 2016).

15 Exodus 3:14, general.

16 Hymn: 'How Sweet the Name of Jesus Sounds'.

17 John 14:6, general.

18 1 John 4:20, general.

19 Luke 10.25, general.

20 Matthew 5:43ff, general, and 25:32ff.

21 Luke 10:13ff, general.

22 John 1.

23 1 Corinthians 13:13, general.

24 Romans 8:35ff.

25 John 21:15ff.

26 St Martin-in-the-Fields, www.smitf.org, accessed 30 Sept. 2016.

27 Bishop David Jenkins (died 4 Sept. 2016), in memorable personal conversation, 1975.

28 Genesis 1:27.

29 Acts 17:28.

30 John 20:25, general.

31 Quoted in John Donohue, *Eternal Echoes, Our Hunger to Belong* (Bantam Books, 1998), 379.

31b Caspar Henderson, *Monotheism and its Weapons*, Granta 2017

32 Acts 10:34.

33 Paul Tillich, quoted in John Robinson, *Honest to God*, (SCM,1963).

34 Exodus 3:14.

35 Romans 12:3–8, New Revised Standard Version Bible, copyright © 1989 the Division of Christian Education of the National Council of the Churches of Christ in the United States of America

36 William Shakespeare, *The Merchant of Venice*, Act III, Scene 1.

37 KSIMC, Clifton Road mosque, 5 Feb. 2017.

38 Timothy Williamson, *Tetralogue: I'm Right, You're Wrong* (OUP, 2015).

39 John V. Taylor, *The Go-Between God* (London: SCM, 1972).

40 Micah 6:6–8.

41 John Donne, 'Meditation XVII', 1624.

42 Hans Kung, *On Being a Christian* (Collins, 1977,).

43 The Golden Rule, Matthew 7:12.

44 Acts 17:23.

PART IV

CHAPTER 5

Challenges to Christianity:

Five Challenges to the Church and Christianity Arising from the Inter Faith World

1. Sectarianism
2. Conceptions/understanding, and misconceptions/misunderstanding
3. Confusion and incomprehension
4. History: rightness and strife
5. Abuse of power

Preamble

Every faith and every faith member probably have challenges from within and without. These partly arise from the perceptions of others and from changing contexts and personalities. Who, though, in any times, has not found it difficult being a Christian? I do not find it surprising that some people ditch the name for themselves. Increasingly now, people say they ditch God, Jesus, the Holy Spirit and prayer because of the image, stereotypes and associations the names have acquired in their understanding.

A compelling reason for this being understandable is the climate of deception and post-truth (intentional lying), misinformation and non-fact which all speed instantaneously around the computers of Britain and the world through and into the tentacles of our media. When even a man of notable scientific integrity, Richard Dawkins, since his famous book, The God Delusion, persisted in criticising Christianity and indeed God in the negative terms only used by a section of uninformed Christians, he embodied the fact that attainment of reasonable criticism, critical reasoning, Christian enlightenment and even intelligence have always been a very difficult struggle. Social media has now heightened the struggle. It is so easy to feel we have to take sides or indeed, to do so without any feeling or self-awareness.

As we have seen, about 50 per cent of Britain's population in this present decade of 2010–20 say they are not Christian. Christianity and the Church in Britain, overall, are amidst and in difficulties and ecumenism is struggling. In a sense, Christianity has been globalised in principle from its beginning through its message for all time of God's love for all, demonstrated supremely by Jesus. We read from Mary Warnock, Oxford philosopher, 'It is impossible to exaggerate the influence of Christianity on our culture and traditions …. However, no one doubts [it] has now lost its dominant position in the lives of the majority of citizens and, more slowly, losing its dominant culture. And yet religion is on the increase throughout the world.'[1] What have been its obstructions in Britain? Why does it not now deliver in Britain more successfully, at least in terms of increase in numbers of churchgoers and in its estimation by the general public? Why can dogmatic belief be so obsessive? How far

228

are Christians and Christianity itself, part of the problem? What are their virtues, not just their difficulties?

Such questions require exploration, because if religion is not part of the solution, it will assuredly be part of the problem, *as voices become even more strident and religious voices ever more violent*, as Rabbi Jonathan Sacks has said in his powerful and timely book, Not in God's Name: Confronting religious violence[2]. *Grace Davie, doyenne of the sociology of religion, states in her* Religion in Britain: A Persistent Paradox[3] *that a strong case can be made that Britain has a deeply embedded Christian culture and that its secularism is rooted in Christianity. Christians do well to recognise their own history and consider from which elements it might beneficially liberate itself.*

All the five challenges noted here, sectarianism, conceptions/ understanding and misconceptions/misunderstanding, confusion and incomprehension, history, strife and rightness and abuse of power, are mentioned here. They are largely from my own experience, limited to the Church of England rather than from wider knowledge of the whole Christian Church and the international scene. I hope they are relevant to the Roman Catholic and Free Churches. While these challenges are about the British Christian scene, they are relevant to Christian relationships with other faiths and in other countries and to those faiths and other countries themselves. They are predicated on hopes for unifying rather than dividing humanity, unifying in attitude and mutual respect rather than in differences, including among and between Christians themselves and the different world faiths. They are an attempt to look at the evidence of Christianity's situation and effect in Britain and lead to the argument of what the Church might do with such evidence in order to be true to itself. According to Berthold Brecht's play The Life of Galileo (1938), *Galileo and the Church in the 17th century had the same problem. The following* *includes live examples from my own experience but aims to be sufficiently general so as not to be limited by them in their being quickly outdated and too specific.*

1. Sectarianism

I begin with a question: music, is it religious or secular and in what respect and circumstances? Take Debussy's ravishing symphonic poem, 'Prelude a l'apres-midi d'un faune' or Bach's overwhelming cello suites or Taize's monks' uplifting chants, are they holy music; or the spirit of a joyous Big Band? They surely merge the religious and secular. They raise, for me at least, the question of their theological content, that is, what they convey of God. Inter faith music is a whole exciting area explored by, for instance, Pandit Ravi Shankar, Hindu classical musician, late British violinist, Yehudi Menuhin and 'Ex Cathedra', the Birmingham international chamber choir.

Sectarianism is a general issue for every faith. It is also specific, as it is for Christianity. Christians in British society and probably further afield still seem reluctant in this age and in their separate domains and traditions to take seriously alternative theological ways of understanding Christianity and being Christian. In this light I offer an arbitrary selection of books and movements on this theme. I welcome *the Christian atheist*, title also of a book[4] by the recent vicar of Oxford that builds on previous stands for Christian humanism and search for meaning, as in an old book by Viktor Frankl, *Man's Search for Meaning*,[5] which incorporates recognition of unconscious religiousness. Such imaginative thinking shows respect for those who feel they cannot go on any longer with the institution of the Church, with its imposed identity and what they consider its traditional Christian dogmas and closed-shop mentality.

To be constructive, such thinking and such peripheral movement has prevailed in many quarters throughout Christian history as essential indicators that the body of Christ is always alive and always in need of creative, open and generous thinking. The Quakers have been going strong in Britain for over three hundred and fifty years. The Progressive Christianity Network, Britain,[6] founded in 2003, is part of an international movement originating in the USA. Modern Church, the Sea of Faith, Free to Believe, Greenbelt, the British New Church Movement and Restorationism are broadly interdenominational, progressive or charismatic. The innumerable others are fit for research. There have always been potential new clothes, invaluable gulps of fresh air, life-saving ideas, books and leaders worth a look and a following, all to be taken seriously, tested and abandoned, abhorred, tolerated or welcomed with open arms.

However, in the present multi-faith scene in Britain and particularly in some medium- and large-size cities and their areas, Christianity is in danger of being seen at least by outsiders as a sect. According to the *Oxford Dictionaries* a sect is 'a group of people with somewhat different beliefs from those of a larger group to which they belong'. The online, American *Free Dictionary* defines a sect as 'a group of people forming a distinct unit with a larger group by virtue of certain refinements of belief or practice'. Outer-city estates may well have this problem. It is hard to find trustworthy evidence; research of the whole ground of belief and faith can be very selective. This is not least because as we have noted already, about half the country - people and places - has no truck with institutional Christianity any more than it has with politics. That does not prevent Christianity and good faith from thriving in particular minority settings. I would strongly regret any genuine offshoot of the Church being widely labelled a sect because of possible inappropriate and derogatory associations in public, especially media minds. Nor, broadly-speaking, do I see Christianity of the Anglican Church fitting into such definition. However, it is a warning for their developing context. Prevention is usually a worthwhile preference.

A sect is worth analysing for its distinguishing features. It is likely to indulge in careless use of pronouns of separation, signally *we* and *us* and *they* and *them*, even without realising it. For example, 'We are the people of God' is a ready sentence of worship leaders. True, but then who is/are 'we'? and who is/are not, and why say this except as a dubious boost to Christian identity? Insensitivity to outsiders in our midst is not loving behaviour. Then there is lack of clarity about expressions, words and their meanings. Examples are easily found, for example, Jesus named as Son of God, which few can define, and Handel's *Messiah*, with *Messiah* meaning in Greek 'the Christ' - literally, the Anointed One, the expected King and deliverer of the Jews is another title that for some has grown to mean 'Saviour of the World'. We could all check the real meaning of 'prophet' All are welcome in this place' is a common hymn but is scarcely true when, in some churches, those not confirmed are denied Holy Communion, and maybe not when gypsies/travellers and Muslim women in niqabs or at least hijabs 'come to see'.

What divisions help construct the kingdom of God? There is a tendency for churches to be oblivious to artistic, sensitive and flexible imagination, as in any reluctance to try out new forms of worship through poetry, music and the arts, dismissiveness of the value of compromise and alternative views and practices and attachment to potentially false dichotomies, as between the religious and the secular, science and religion, spiritual and material and tradition and progress. It is inadvisable for me to generalise too much.

'The Future Shapes of Anglicanism'[7] by Martyn Percy, Anglican dean of Christ Church, Oxford, has its own outspoken take on this issue. The author in his Afterword vouches that the Anglican Church 'is being slowly kettled into becoming a suburban sect, corralling its congregations, controlling its clergy and centralising its communication. Instead of being a local, dispersed, national institution.' Instead, there needs to be 'a broad church, capacious and generous. Narrow Anglicanism [I wish to enlarge this to Christianity] is almost a contradiction in terms. It is the breadth that defines Anglican polity [Christianity likewise] and it is the breadth that will save it.'

Concerning those who declare themselves to be nonreligious, Percy says they 'will not be won over to return to the church by increasingly organisational, theologically narrow and vogueish sectarian expressions of faith'. Christians in British society and probably further afield need to take seriously alternative ways of understanding Christianity and being Christian to what is standard at present. This is particularly the case in the context of our relatively new multi-faith scene in Britain. I have at times personally felt Christianity in danger of being seen as a sect because of its declaration of being 'the one true faith' and its consequent religious exclusivity[8].

Christianity in Britain in the past has not been seen as a sect. A literal understanding of the Bible and liturgies, combined with Christianity's entrenchment in the authority and support of monarchy, Parliament and the priesthood and eventual acceptance of Protestantism and Roman Catholicism has meant that up to the mid-twentieth century - within my own lifetime - Christianity was naturally accepted as the religion of the whole country. Henry VIII changed its earthly authority but not its comprehensiveness, which it has never lost. It has even had a universal element because of its physical reach into most of the world through the British and other Christian European-based empires and missionary movements. Confidence and sense of Christian identity overseas has been high, particularly in Africa, amongst deliverers and receivers.

And today, when Christianity looks ahead or outside itself to the needs of the world and those of outsiders to Britain - be it, for example, global warming, scientific advances in gene therapy, care of all creation, care of refugees or peace and reconciliation among the nations - it is *far from* behaving like a sect. It grows and prospers far more overseas than it does in Britain, reasons for which being another topic. In a new approach, public 'secular' involvement of Pope Francis with *Laudato Si'* about climate change and care of the planet, inspires British Catholics while, 2016/7/8, Archbishops Welby and Sentamu provide strong non-sectarian leadership concerning refugees, Zimbabwe and President Mugabe, climate change, local British squalls following Brexit uncertainties, the miscalculated election and the appalling London Tower block fire. Pope Francis's visit to the Holy Land,[9] where he vehemently supported peace between Israelis and Palestinians, was a telling act of Christian leadership.

Priorities are very difficult to determine and settle. Churches within the Church have enviable freedom of thought and action. They have so much to be concerned about and public attitudes can be so fickle and ignorant in the face of even more ignorant and unprincipled media. Yet the Church and individual churches can appear to cause some of its own problems as in some of its narrow increasingly sectarian attitudes towards sex and gender and other world faiths. Religious intransigence and public perception can be implacable and give a bad impression to many of Christianity, just as Muslim violent extremists do with Islam. The sectarian issue remains. Generalisations and ignorance can be my problem here!

The most relevant sectarian danger in our context is exclusion of different faiths. Martyn Percy's cry is a timely aid to my argument. It would be a move against the increasing sectarianism that he decries were Christians to aim, as a priority, to recognise and accept their own diversity, both in practice and principle. Thought through, that probably would encourage Christian partnership and mutual friendship, firstly with varieties of Christianity with secular faith and secondly with different world faiths at every level, including the theological. It would be grievous were the new national ecumenical mission *Thy Kingdom Come*[10] to be charged with fostering a threatening attitude to those of different faith, of 'us and them', intended or otherwise.

2. Conceptions/understanding, and misconceptions/misunderstanding

Conceptions can demonstrate difference, sheer incomprehension and/or disagreement. Perceptions I am defining as more personal and telling of one's impression, as of Christianity.

First, I give a positive foundation from which misconceptions can arise as challenges. God is the most important concept in all life and inevitably the subject of endless conceptions. At the Council of Chalcedon in 451 C.E. following the Church's Council of Nicaea in 325 C.E. which fathered the Nicene Creed and consequent male domination of the Church. Jesus was named 'truly God and truly man' with two natures, one divine and the other human, distinct yet united in one Person, a conception that somehow stuck. Such understanding about Jesus and God is not held in the other world faiths, so this particular traditional orthodox Christianity has a particular conception of God. A question arises as to how much that has been

235

due to Christian insistence on its own separate identity. However, the Christian conception that Christ died 'for all' might well be accepted gratefully by members of these different faiths.

A further conception is within that of faith itself. In my understanding, faith embraces more of our whole than does belief. Christians have all sorts of beliefs, whether in assertions in the Nicene Creed, as above, in the Bible, in life after death, for and against homosexuality, in the Pope and on we go. It depends partly on one's definition of Christians. Scientologists now institutionalised here in Moseley, Birmingham, are a challenge to Christians with their conceptions of Christianity. Belief in 'way of life' following Jesus's example seems to me the most valid and widely supported conception.

Misconceptions are a different matter, and perhaps Christianity's chief problem: a development from ignorance and incomprehension on the one hand and error and deceit on the other. It can be extraordinary how perceptions can also be powerful and irrational misconceptions. This applies especially when they are attached to violent religious history such as perpetrated in our times by Muslim violent extremists, supporting Isis in the Middle East, or the Christian Lord's Resistance Army in northern Uganda said to be caused by theological differences or, more likely, by shared misconceptions arising from misinformation, confusion and false certainty. I have heard Hindus, Sikhs, Jews, Muslims and Buddhists commonly claimed to say that Christians believe in one God but actually they have three Gods. I regret that the Church seems rarely to succeed in communicating a personified concept of God, or a God in relationship, or a concept of personas, masks or faces that within one human being is entirely compatible. Without such explanation, misconception remains constant, even among some Christians.

This Christian doctrine of the Trinitarian God gives easy rise to misconception. It is strongly challenged by many people of different faiths as an illegitimate view of God because of its incorporation into God of Jesus as the Son of God as the second person of the Trinity. It is indeed challenged by some Christians, particularly when meant in simple literal terms, which lead to misconception of the meaning of the 'Son of God'. If it is taken, very acceptably, to mean God was and is *in* Christ, a Jew so close to God that he could be called 'God's Son', that is not the same as 'God is the Christ', nor that God and Jesus as the Christ, meaning the Messiah, are one in God. Each word above, 'person', 'God', 'one', even the word 'is', requires analysis of possibly different meanings. Different interpreters might call it disagreement, not misconception. Whichever, its most serious consequence has been the assertion by many Christians of old that the Jews murdered 'the Son of God'.

How astonishing the power of words can be. 'You are from your father's desires'. Such words, according to John, 8.44 and put into the mouth of Jesus, have much to answer for in fostering appalling prejudice of Christians against Jews. Consequent violence and tragedy have persisted throughout the centuries, with murderous pogroms in Eastern Europe culminating in the Holocaust instigated and wrought by Nazi Germany in the 1930s and the 1940s. Such prejudice as there is lies mostly suppressed in Britain and western Europe, but given the opportunity, when people feel the chips are down, it remains potential dynamite to peaceful Jewish–Christian relationships.

It is easy for Christians themselves to have misconceptions about the beliefs of other Christians, traditionalist, liberal, progressive,

Catholic, Protestant or Pentecostal, to name some existing divisions. Ignorance, assumptions and prejudices about the other have been rampant in history and remain so though with less violent outcomes than say in the 16th and 17th centuries. It is easier still for those of different religious and nonreligious faiths to have profound misconceptions about the nature of the Bible. Failure to understand metaphor and to distinguish literalism from likely factual history causes profound misconception about the Bible and its purposes of conveying human perceptions of the history of God in Jewish and Christian terms and its unique records of Jesus's life.

Textual criticism reveals many a discrepancy as in the four different accounts of what Jesus said on the cross. Additionally, there is possible alternative interpretation of such difference simply through the *literal* acceptance that the four Gospel writers were different people who lived at different times, had different information at hand and had different imaginations and even purposes. And why not? The Bible's truth lies in its writers' honest presentation of different experiences 'for God's sake', not - on the whole - in literal photo and/ or audio records. Stars cannot come down to earth and rest above cowsheds, and even Jesus cannot ascend to heaven or descend except metaphorically if the Nicene Creed is allowed to be metaphorical. Both phenomena assume a literally false three-decker universe of heaven above and hell beneath. It was ever misconception to think otherwise even by Popes of Galileo's early days.

I know Muslims from the nearby mosque who who assert that Christians and Jews are people of the same book, as if 'the book' is an end in itself. That is double-edged. Even if that does give a bond of unity it can also be a means of excluding other faiths rather than a means for them and other faiths, with their own scriptures, to know God. Understandably, the subtleties of translation, faith and interpretation of any faith's scriptures are hard to comprehend by an outsider, especially for a literal, fundamentalist, black-and-white mind, whatever the background. I have been told at my local mosque for example, that I don't believe in Jesus. It depends on what perception the interlocutor has of Jesus and my own perception of Jesus. It provides, though, a chance for dialogue! I have heard many a Christian making the same mistake in a simplistic judgement of another's faith.

3. Confusion and incomprehension

The traditional concept of the Trinitarian God produces an example of confusion as well as misconception. Often it only takes words themselves for all of us to confuse one another. Approaching fifty years of marriage, my wife and I still can have that problem, especially when we each are certain that we were quite clear. Use of words, their meaning, our different understanding and interpretation, the context heard, spoken and read, their purveyor and the purveyor's authority, the language itself and its translation, spoken or written—all are a deep wet bog.

I often long for music and silence, freedom from words, especially in church. It's hard to disagree with either! Words certainly have their ability to communicate, confuse, lie, cheat, delight and provide enjoyment ad infinitum. An understanding of paradox is instructive, of Greek nisi........nisi, 'not this ... not that', of 'yes and no' and in, say, relation to God, but it does not solve imposed and ignorant contradiction.

Endless questions can promote and provoke confusion. It depends on the audience. Yet in the world of thoughtful inter faith dialogue they really are essential for the sake of clarity. For if words and terms used by the first speaker are not understood similarly by that same speaker, how can the second party be expected to understand? What did Boris Johnson say to Jeremy Corbyn? My point is exemplified by three unconsidered assertions that provoke three questions:

Assertion	Question
All religions believe the same thing.	What is that same thing?
We all believe in the same God.	What do you and I mean by the word *God*?
All Christians believe Jesus is the Son of God.	What does 'Son of God' mean?

Metaphor is a vital tool of biblical writers, poets and theologians, but its recognition requires language training and imagination if literalism is not to cause havoc. Confusion can be the name of the game - not least, for example, in varying accounts of the resurrection of Jesus and of his life in the Synoptic Gospels, and indeed of our own 'resurrection of the body' in the Nicene Creed.

Incomprehension is a different matter. A prime example comes again from the Trinity. When seen in a rigid way, the notion of God being three persons in one seems to contradict traditional understanding - even Christian understanding - of God being ineffable, 'unimaginable, loving intelligence'[12] that is indescribable, beyond human categorising, and 'than which nothing greater can be conceived'.[13] 'How then can it be ...? Ah, it is a mystery created by God,' as Mohammed Amin-Evans recounts in his Perception in Chapter 1. Most mystery about it is created by humanity, not by God, although, in a different way, it still conveys truths about God. Cheap mystery may only add irritation to incomprehension. Yet the Trinity has been mainline inspiration for Christians over the centuries. One resolution offered by progressive Christians is to understand Trinitarian language as poetic, metaphoric and symbolic, so it is therefore fluid, relational rather than fixed in brass that is rarely rubbed. Another is to take a metaphorical comparison with water: it has three aspects, liquid, ice and vapour. And ourselves: how many selves do you and I have?

4. History: rightness and strife

Christianity and Christians have a history of 'rightness', especially in the perception of others, that is 'rightness' in the sense of 'we are right, you are wrong'. It can readily signal arrogance or a sense of superiority. Christians might well find this in Scientology -very understandably to my mind. They, we, certainly do regarding IS extreme murderous islamists - but then non-Christians find such rightness in Christians hard to stomach too, Right judgement is so difficult but so essential. A sharp issue that cuts into good relationships at some Christians' insistence is when Christianity is pronounced by occasional church noticeboards as 'the only way'. This can amount to an assumed superiority especially if the assumption is that Jesus is God, that the Church has the one true answer to God and life and that God himself is actually in the body of Jesus. I imagine toleration and acceptance would be hard for non-Christians if they experienced intransigence in the certainty of Christians who declare, 'We are the people of God,' 'We are God's newly chosen people' in the steps of St Peter,[14] and even 'We are the New Israel,' as uttered by members of one twentieth-century Russian Christian sect. Natural selection led to the social danger of Christians considering themselves as of a superior religion of a superior white race. Read William Sumner 1840-1910, Darwin's contemporary.

A new BBC TV series,' Civilisations', early in 2018 followed on from a 1969 previous series 'Civilisation', which was presented by one very civilised white Englishman, Kenneth Clark. In the first series which I remember, he presented an assumed superiority and rightness of Britain extended to Europe as the epitome of 'civilisation'. The three presenters of 'Civilisations' related how the 21st century recognises it is no longer appropriate even to suggest such a distortion of the truth of world history. China for one does not allow it. Civilisation and civilisations have always been worldwide. It is just that Britain and Europe have taken centuries to give up their self- congratulatory navel gazing.

Throughout Christian history, there has been crazy strife between Christianity and all the major faiths with Judaism being the prime target of Christian bigotry. Self-rightness has no doubt played its part, but strife has many causes, some of which are social, military and personal, not theological. The British Empire has a lot to answer for despite its constructive mission and economic, political and structural achievements. Christianity was entwined with it in many ways; theology and perceptions of theology were integral to it, whether recognisable at the time or not. I have mentioned that I grew up greatly respecting a most friendly bishop who lived next door whom I often visited when he had black 'overseas (colonial) bishops' staying. I did learn to respect his black friends. As a young man in the 1950s, I ignorantly took for granted British history of imperial exploitation, sanctioned and blessed, to different degrees, by Christianity.

Old and not-so-old perceptions of history in matters of theology, faith, ignorance, power and identity still linger within members of all the world faiths. Intermingled with powerful emotions they can last interminably. They are worth thorough analysis and due understanding for everyone's benefit. It is invariably an unbalanced picture with the powerful coming out on top – practically speaking. But that is not to be the aim for inter faith dialogue.

Missionaries like my same neighbour Bishop, 'Mrs Bishop' and colleagues in my youth had, I think, considered themselves inheritors of 200 years of what they saw- arguably justifiably - at the time as the great and good mission of Christ bestowing undoubted benefit to the recipients. Christian education in method and content contributed much to the leaders of African nations and more selected areas of India and the Far East, for example, to Julius Nyerere in Tanzania and Kwame Nkrumah in Ghana before the early decolonised 60s. However, mutual and trusting reciprocal relationships were rare and not comparable with the like of those of 19th century Bishop Colenso in Natal, South Africa and 20th century Bede Griffiths in South India as suspicion of both in Britain and 'in the colonies' indicated. Many a memory in reality and folklore is a vast and disputed subject. However, selective British history can easily point to the religious influence exerted by its political hierarchies bearing the imperial virus from which too many, including Christians, suffered long. Many non-Christians and Christians have a broad perception that British imperial history reinforced that situation not only with 'the Word' but with bullets hailing from the military might of the British Empire. Archbishop Desmond Tutu has asserted: 'When the missionaries came to Africa, they had the Bible and we had the land. They said, "Let us pray". When we opened our eyes, we had the Bible and they had the land!'[15]

Old suppressed memories have not made for good relationships. Resurgent animosities, for example in Iraq and Syria at the present time, 2016-8, now have appalling effect there and even in Europe, and China is reacting strongly against Christian missionaries from the United States seeking to convert its citizens. Sunnis and Shias can celebrate their ancient historical victories against each other without overdue effect here in Britain but the assumed certainty that crashed murderously out of presumed 'rightness' in the new Islamic State (so-called I.S,) could still be an ironic lesson. Twenty-first-century strife, raging on the world stage and dripping flaming fat onto British shores, is likely to rekindle old perceptions and memories of violence that people of different faiths have known, whether, say, in Iraq or Afghanistan. It is a warning that all is not forgiven, forgotten or reconciled by members of our population even in relatively peaceful Britain. Perversion produces progeny. Roman Catholics still do not officially share Holy Communion bread and wine with other Christians despite otherwise good relationships. And that is said to be no less than 'the bread of life'! The good national and Western European ecumenical climate of the 60s-90s between different Christian denominations has collapsed[16]. Faith relationships in war-torn areas affect faith relationships of all countries involved, including Britain. Righteous anger is understandable whether erupting on the streets, in prisons or in mental hospitals. On the positive and hopeful side, Britain still has a role as a European leader in this area and as a good example of vulnerable fallible harmony; Birmingham, to a degree, has a similar background and role. May we urge the Birmingham Council and all our city leaders to speak out in the name of racial and faith justice and try to do the same ourselves.

5. Abuse of power

Power itself is fraught with tensions, practical, moral, personal, national. The Faiths are subject to the same tensions, or at least their members, all of whom have played their part in squalid and violent history - a sorry unity. Yet we have to hope that it is not timeless, for we are all God's people and in our different ways God beckons us all. We are not wild boar and deer at the wilderness watering-hole nor lone blackbird and robin at the winter food-table! Our human task is to survive together not deny or deprive the other. However, a last problem, unlikely to go away, is abused power, state, religious, individual or corporate, power to win and dominate. My experience of the Church and of clergy - including me - is that we can take our own power very much for granted. Then, when times are rocky, there can be in all of us an inclination to uphold the powerful inside or outside church rather than the powerless. It's easier that way, gets things done! In a spiritual setting, in the name of Jesus Christ, that is ironic for it is not the Christian path. We may hardly be aware of the power we have, while others are all too well aware when they do *not* have it.

I wrote an article about this topic as an ordinand (trainee priest) at Theological College that was not appreciated! It was not objective: I had my own agenda. As a mature and experienced student and former university teacher, I resented my *own* self-imposed powerlessness. I know that those of other faiths can feel this with Christians, especially with Christian clergy, though other faith leaders, I know, are not immune to the problem. At its most theological and dangerous, it can be assumed by clergy and laity (non-clergy) that clergy have, if not the power, the authority, to some degree, of God. That is potentially a huge trap and spiritual abuse can easily arise. Such exalted status is hard to surrender despite clergy knowing of the humility of Jesus. It might be more than claiming that 'I am right; we are right, and the others are wrong.' I gave a short talk about this the other day and only just remembered to acknowledge my own power in giving it.

Human power, prowess and identity seem often to hold stronger sway than actual beliefs, which for many may be incidental. That is a fair description of brash religious politics. New initiatives by clergy - but so common with new guys in any walk of life - can by a snare and delusion for them and their congregations as they are means for the Church or the church minister to accumulate power in the name of Christian mission. Motives are often complicated. Hierarchical lines can be drawn so easily and quickly and *the dignity of difference*[17] so hard to accept. Prejudice, ignorance and thoughtlessness can swell so rapidly when topped with crude power-seeking. All of these things may explain why clergy and elders may find it hard to quit supposedly superior status and why younger juniors find ministry hard going. Churches are not the only places of worship to suffer such human problems which can inhibit free association with those of different faith. Party politics is hardly different

It may be that 'I am in power and you are not; we are not equal and do not wish to be.' It may be the reverse: 'You are in power and I am not. God is on your side, not mine.' 'you are too right: God is on my side!' Remember Fanon *Black Skin, White Masks* (quoted Chapter 4). Such are the easy negative contortions of those who have power and those who do not. Not all those in weakness and subjection find the strength of God found by St. Paul, as he told the Corinthians.[18] The Genesis story conveys a powerful truth about such pride in power leading to the downfall of Adam and Eve. The biblical prophets and the Gospels are very much about hope of something better. One hopes always for humanity's spiritual and moral progress, but we rise and fall with the tides, so powerful in themselves. This decade, 2010–2020, has already taken humanity backwards as say through the devastating civil and proxy warring years in Yemen and Syria and forwards, as say, in success with millennium goals of worldwide poverty reduction, both situations subject to different power and easily confused with faith, even religious faith.

Assertion of power by the institution bearing his name would have brought grief and shame to Jesus. *O Jerusalem, Jerusalem,*[19] he sighed. It is hard for humankind to rid itself of ancient behaviour patterns. We never in reality start from scratch; there's always a context. Take Syria again since 2010 and still continuing 2018! The very assumption and expectation of the necessity and inevitability of violence in 2010 rather than continuing peace talks has been a constant disaster for humankind. It was so in 1914. Israel and Palestine know the problem too. The cheap media can horrifyingly stoke many a fire.

Conceptions, misconceptions, confusion, disagreement, historical memory, superiority, exclusiveness and love of power, no doubt all the faiths share such problems, always similar, always different, but none of these is to take priority over God. By my definition, God remains supreme transcendence and immanence, 'the infinite ocean of being', love itself.[20] This book always carries an intended implication that this truth is above all truths and tries to work out what God means for Christianity and the faiths of the world, their relationships, how they will all respond and with what hope. The stakes are already high; unless the faiths learn to work together in our increasingly hard global times, they could get much higher.

It is a tragic truism not to be neglected that members of different faiths who are 'recipients of Christianity' in Britain and elsewhere can themselves be exclusive, 'superior' and self-righteous themselves, in or out of turn. It is worth considering the extent to which they might, in taking such attitudes, be responding to similar Christian attitudes attacking *their* faith and lives in the past, or elsewhere in the present. And so on, ad infinitum. Have a further look at our *Perceptions*. They are mild but they remind me of vicious downward spirals which are the responsibility of those of good faith, Christians included. According to Matthew, one of Jesus's key messages in his Sermon the Mount[21] declares that if anyone has a problem with us, we must drop any idea of worship and first go and make our peace. That is Christianity. Cycles of love can defeat cycles of violence, at home and abroad.

1   Mary Warnock, Oxford and public philosopher, introduction to Dishonest to God (Continuum, 2010).

2   Rabbi Jonathan Sacks at the award ceremony for his Templeton Memorial Prize, 2016, and author of Not in God's Name: Confronting Religious Violence. In this powerful and timely book, Jonathan Sacks tackles the thorny issue of violence committed in the name of God, and draws on arguments from science, philosophy, and many other disciplines to show how religion, rightly understood, is hardwired to be part of the solution, not just the problem.

3   Grace Davie, Religion in Britain: A Persistent Paradox (Wiley Blackwell, 2015).

4   Brian Mountford, The Christian Atheist (O Books, 2011).

5   Viktor E. Frankl, Man's Search for Meaning (Beacon Press, 1946).

6   www.PCNBritain.org.uk. Also see the websites of the other movements mentioned.

7   Revd Dr Martyn Percy, dean of Christ Church, Oxford, author of The Future Shapes of Anglicanism (OUP, 2016), quoted in the Observer newspaper, 14 Aug. 2016.

8   Birmingham demonstrates great varieties of churches but succeeds well, to my mind, in generally not being sectarian.

9   25 May 2014.

10   May–June 2017.

11   E.g. John 8:44ff (31), 5:18, 7:13, 20:19.

12   Rowan Williams, quoted in Church Times, 30 Sept. 2016, from St Martins-in-the-Fields autumn lectures.

13   Anselm, eleventh century.

14   Epistle of Peter, 1 Peter 2:9.

15   Archbishop Desmond Tutu quotations, www.goodreads.com.

16   Keith Clements: Look Back in Hope. SCM 2017

17   Ibid, Jonathan Sacks, The Dignity of Difference (London: Continuum, 2003).

18   2 Corinthians 12:7–10.

19   Matthew 23:37, Good News Translation.

20   John of Damascus, quoted by David Bentley Hart in 'We Need to Talk about God,' Church Times, 12 Feb. 2016.

21   Matthew 5:23, 24.

PART V

CHAPTER 6

Ways Forward

Understanding our perception of our own faith: believing, belonging, behaviour and being; planting seeds of transformation. The universality of so much of our basic human existence and experience, whatever our faith.

Preamble

After the three Introductions about content, process and the book's development, the central Perceptions and Responses and their review, an account of the present-day context of Christianity, my perceptions of my own journeys and how my background has influenced my theology and attitude to Christian relationships with different faiths and an account of possible challenges to Christianity that may be obstacles to Christian inter faith relationships, the likely question is obvious:

Where do we go from here?

In the foregoing text I have offered many questions and made many implications and even direct suggestions about people of faith and our own understanding of ourselves and our own faith. In this chapter these are laid out more explicitly but I experience a personal tension: on the whole I am not into conclusive conclusions. These may be what you the reader wish to make. Nevertheless, I do feel strongly about many of the issues I raise so I am documenting my own opinions and proposals. Before I suggest hopes for future seeds of transformation within a potential inter faith context, we take a look at ourselves, our believing, belonging and behaviour. Examples of people of different faith working together are numerous throughout the book.

There is some inevitable overlap.

- Awareness of moral and personal/spiritual values relating to equality; attitude; confidence; being truly human; compassion.
- Acceptance of collective responsibilities: the one human family; inclusiveness; upholding universals; making a difference
- Valuing Partnerships between faith and the secular; the different religious faiths; in theological discussion; with ourselves
- Five tasks for Christians

Moral and personal/spiritual values relating to the following:

Equality

The equality of humankind is rightly the persistent shibboleth of humanitarian and religious society. It is therefore a prime basis for interfaith relationships. Baroness Shami Chakrabarti,[1] past director of Liberty, upholds 'the equality of all people' as basic to her personal doctrine of human rights rather than her religious view. Laws in Britain against discrimination with regard to sex, gender, race and faith were not established without a struggle and are now the bedrock of our predominantly secular society.[2] What they uphold is the abolition of the concept that in the eyes of the state one person is superior to any other. At least that's the intention. According to St Paul, more unifying thinker than secular spokesman:

> There is no longer Jew or Greek, there is no longer slave nor free, there is no longer male and female, for all of you … are one in Christ Jesus. God created humankind in his image, in the image of God he created them; male and female he created them. Truly I understand that God shows no partiality.[3]

That is the moral imperative of God's Holy Spirit, shared by all the world faiths in principle. It is shown in their support for the golden rule, which in the Christian wording of St Matthew is 'in everything, do to others as you would have them do to you; for this is the law and the prophets'.[4] However, there exists a marked discrepancy by way of worldly wealth, cultural and educational privilege and social, employment and housing situations. which is probably ingrained in all societies where formal social equality exists - or tries to - alongside gross inequalities. Social revolutions, French and Russian, for example, have seen violent contests between powered rich and disempowered poor, only for inequalities to return in a very few years. Just in this decade, 2010–20, comparisons of wealth within and between countries and people have attracted common disapproval, but inequalities remain the likely even inevitable outcome of our capitalist world system of winners and losers. This means that religious and moral equality are all the more important, unable to offset material inequalities but able to provide alternative means of justifying human worth and existence.

There is but a small step from deemed equality in morality and truth to relativism. For many people, the moral truths of Christianity and its 'fruits of the Spirit'[5] quell very helpfully the argument about endless relativism. For others, it is not so easy. Context and meaning are relevant. All faiths and their members cannot legitimately always be considered equally morally good or bad or of equal credit to God.[6] Together and separately, in small degree and large and at some time or other, we all face the issue and decision as to who and what is right or wrong, whether or not that is a valid question, and, what leads people into hostile darkness or into inspirational light, call it with St John and Jesus' 'abundant life'.

Moral good, truth, justice and love within humanity do exist objectively. Though they may be hard to define, they can be reached for, even if early Christian fathers[7] saw God as *nisi ... nisi*, neither this nor that—the apophatic approach. They can be recognised by their opposites. When reasons for our awareness, perceptions and recall are taken into account, untangling both the arguments and the processes of argument is fraught with difficulty in the exercise of human power and authority. Circumstances and personalities are crucial, and both, in connection with the world faiths in Britain, may throw up legal, practical, and pragmatic resolutions to disputed issues.

Like any family large or small, faith members and participants have, eventually, to try to get on together. It is tragic in this 21st century whenever peace appears unattainable for the foreseeable future. Human relationships are again a crucial issue, whether between Israel and Palestine since 1948, between Donald Trump, president of the USA and Kim Jung-un, ruler of North Korea since 2011 or after 2016 within the British government. Between and amongst them, God is there to be found, even in issues in which danger and suffering are horrific. Regarding achievement of God's love, justice and peace between and among people and nations - people again - their relationships are more than ever an issue for our survival. Even short-term failure can be disastrous. Kindness is a start and can be a wonderful healer. Different faiths have the opportunity, so they can set some example through their relationships. 'Like any family large or small, faith members and participants have, eventually, to try to get on together'.

Attitude

I think it was Carl Jung who said that if one has the right attitude right things happen. I believe that the greatest threat to other faiths and interfaith relationships lies primarily not in opposition to Jesus as a person but in negative and even bad attitude, distorted state of mind, what traditionalists tend to call 'sin'. It lies not just in those who express it but also in those who cause it. Three million Europeans living in Britain and 1.2 million 'Brits in Europe' have to some extent been fearful as a result of the vote for Brexit, demonstrating how even the British government can cause institutional fear. Rank bad attitude has spread in post-Brexit Britain, expressed in the shocking continued increase in racism, hate crime and consequent fear in several British people of 'foreign origin' whom I know. One fear spawns another. And fear can spawn violent attitudes and behaviour as the campaign 'Hope not Hate' knows well. Then too, little fish like ourselves, probably, and big fish – mass murderers, child abusers, the 'monsters' of some Press - should not be left to fate. Likewise, nuclear weapons whose very existence is a moral outrage. If all the Faiths, their members and those of good faith took the attitude of NO WAY to nuclear weapons that might be really powerful. Yet our attitude can be apathetically to leave such Big Fish issues to political Big Fish, which may be disastrous. Little fish, at first just right- or left-wing violent extremists, have a history of turning into big fish. Who knows the consequences.........?

One of the main objections from those of other faiths to the Christian approach to other faiths has, in my experience, been this 'bad attitude' of superiority - our contributor Mohammed Amin calls it 'gaze' - which Christians, even unwittingly, often adopt. Such attitude is the opposite of the humility, vulnerability and wisdom of Christ. Amongst our five perceptions of Christianity we have seen a striking unity in this reaction. As was clear in their 'perceptions', there are those of different faith who feel that Christians themselves can be Christianity's worst enemy in this very way, especially when they set themselves apart. Our faith contributors have noted - however generously described - their own problems in this way at times with Christians. Here indeed is a Christian weakness. Such attitude is the badge of sectarianism especially when it plays on worst fears rather than best instincts.

Attitude, both broadly positive and broadly negative, is very significant. It is a manifestation of our theology. The Archbishop of Canterbury, Justin Welby, has referred to 'Christians' insecure tolerance'. In a speech to the Board of Deputies of British Jews[9] he said:

> We do not as faith groups in our society always exhibit that secure tolerance to each other that enables us to speak powerfully of secure tolerance to the world around us. Christians are as bad as anyone at this. In fact, ..., I think we're worse.

Tolerance is a weak cousin of love and acceptance and a minimal moral demand on Christianity, but it has a role. Such insecurities and attitudes of Christians are to be taken seriously to heart. What are they about? Most markedly, these displays have sometimes portrayed bad attitude, intentionally or unintentionally.

One demonstration of bad attitude lies in the tendency to hypocrisy: saying one thing and doing another. That is ironic, for Jesus was particularly critical of hypocrisy[10] and Christians set themselves up *not* to be hypocritical. Naturally, members of all faiths may at times be hypocritical too. A commonly amoral media is a dominating example of in our time. Hypocrisy is generally deceitful and dishonest behaviour, destructive of the confidence of others and of a faith's own integrity. Christians aim high but often fail to deliver. Aspiration to superiority commonly collapses into hypocrisy, fouled relationships and trouble.

Coping with 'bad attitude' is a major priority with which we all need one another's help. Christianity claims to be transformative but personal change can be difficult. It helps to find out or at least listen to others' perceptions of what we get wrong or where we could do better. Mutual encouragement, confidence, observation, self-awareness and a discipline of Christian faith practices, do not come easily. It is nigh tragic when young people miss out from whatever source on such natural discipline and openness appropriate to their age. The decline of institutional Christianity does leave this problem. I have talked with Muslims about this worry about future generations.

Attaining understanding of the appropriate degree of freedom in our lives, mine and anybody else's, is not an easy task.[11] I accept that as human beings we do have a measure of responsibility for our thoughts and actions, how much, I rarely know. The above values are easier said than achieved. They are issues of shared as well as personal responsibility and how we encourage, criticise, praise and indeed, love one another. The same applies to issues of responsibility, negative and positive. Try this test: ask yourself what attitude you have to recommend to someone wearing a niqab (a full face covering except for eyes). I realise you might be a Muslim woman yourself.

Confidence

Positive attitude requires confidence, which lies in a strange no man's land of morality, spirituality and responsibility. 'Christian insecure tolerance', in Archbishop Welby's words, has already been lamented. Sam Wells, vicar of St Martins-in-the-Fields, Central London, has written that the church should have 'confidence in the completeness and ultimate fulfilment of Christ's ministry and the work of the Holy Spirit in transforming individuals, neighbourhoods and nations'.[12] Such confidence would be well-directed to Christian partnership with different faiths. A first priority would be to analyse the Christian situation and context in relation to different faiths and to know and accept, in the first place, in what ways Christianity, is generally appreciated. Christianity, like all faiths, can undoubtedly provide much benefit for everyone, not least comfort, belonging, security, community, moral grounding and spiritual appreciation. If a sense of faith and belief is lost, it is worth finding confidence to ask others and check what is meant by both and what to believe about anything.

Consider our relationship of love and respect, or not, of children, for example. Doctrines can be very detached from our relationships. We do well to check what actually is the honest difference between us with our faith and others with their so-called 'no faith'. Sharing Jesus is about sharing his love and life with others, far more than just his name label, in a way that is likely to be freely and joyfully accepted. Signing up to be a Christian is not the only way to do so, least of all pressing others already confident in another faith or kind of faith. I doubt Jesus wanted any Jesus army to capture anyone. Sectarian faith is as liable as religious faith to possessiveness of idea and people. Christianity has been said to be better caught than taught, though learning can be caught from other people's ways. Sharing faith in Jesus may be but does not have to be about converting anyone to your faith but rather about inviting mutual human relationship through what is vital to you and perhaps for the other too. 'Making disciples' as in Matthew 28.19, sounds very one-sided to me except with the few who seem really lost in life. Their self-determination still has to be enabled.

We are not to deny the insistent and symbolic death that we human beings, whatever our faith and background, can and do perpetrate on others. True confidence seems to entail recognition of human wickedness whatever its tragic causes; but also of perpetual resurrection, transformation, redemption, all these, which we can call the ultimate gift of life. True confidence would encourage Christian recognition of Christianity's common weaknesses. The seductiveness of the label *Christian* can promote the power, the glory and the urge for identity via assumed superiority, but that would be to turn on its head the priority of humility and weakness to which Jesus gave his life. Paradoxically, therefore, refusal to promote Christian superiority, except one's own choice, would be a true Christian strength. Other faiths have the same problem: their members are as human as anyone else! Religious and spiritual bullies, clergy or lay, can be the most ungodly variety of their breed and, actually, they maybe least confident of true heart and soul. I have found them hard to cope with.

True confidence would also come to Christians from recognising and seeking to alleviate human inconsistency in their practice of ideals. Perceived failure can be damning in outsiders' perceptions. One area not often explored in such a context is Christianity's traditional theology. Theological journals, such as the *Church Times* series 'Theology Now 'left the unfortunate impression that theology remains unaware of the injustices and inequalities it perpetuates.' All world faiths and most human beings, have found difficulties in the practice of their ideals. Present global-in-the-local challenges test authentic faith very severely, whether at first or second-hand. Immigration, homelessness and refugees are, in Britain, persistent cases in point.

We can all seek to be clear to ourselves and others about what it is we stand for by sharing confidence with others to look behind our outward show of faith, however plausible and ingrained that might be. What was behind Jesus? What did he stand for? Was it not the principles of love of God and love of neighbour as oneself from which came the law and the prophets that have guided us to the primary life tasks of seeking justice and peace for all. I doubt any faithful people doubt that, whatever their background. It is an ironic weakness that Christians have so often spoiled and wasted these eternal principles for the sake of superficial worldly power. Jesus's paradox is that his true strength arises from assumed weakness.[14] Over such universal values, there is every need and good reason for discussion. True confidence would encourage a blessing of others to live out their lives in a multi-faith world and celebrate that reality in order to be true to their faith, finding reciprocity for oneself and trust in God's love for everyone. It would recognise that 'all real living is meeting' and that God actually meets us in human meeting. The twin bed-mate of confidence is hope, hope especially in the transformative power of the Holy Spirit and constant resurrection.

Being truly human

Issues of positive attitude and confidence are part of our human agenda, their opposites included. There is hardly need to search far and wide for our common humanity. 'What a piece of work is man'[15] (that is, humanity, to avoid sexist favouritism). Confidence in God, confidence in Christianity and confidence in ourselves are all interwoven and interdependent. Interfaith relationships and our personal perceptions come down to our own individual humanity - who we are in our own eyes. 'Know thyself,' said Socrates. 'I am who I am' are words naming God, given by the Exodus writer[16] we have met already. Chief Counsellor Polonius says in Shakespeare's *Hamlet*, 'This above all to thine own self be true.'[15] These three famous quotations ring true to me. They do not say how we are to go about these things. And some are deprived even of the opportunity.

I return to my youthful forays into Viktor Frankl's insights about finding ourselves through meaning, best achieved via tasks, meetings and relationships outside ourselves.[17] Created by God, we always have meaning from God enmeshed in us, just as we have our parents. I've gradually learnt it is inescapable in both cases and to be accepted. In his wisdom of living for God and other people, Jesus Christ knew it naturally. Interfaith work is a dynamic way to discover that we find ourselves and our own true faith by losing ourselves in others. It is often us and our own view of ourselves in relation to 'significant others' that inhibits us, despite our external faith, from relating to others, especially to strangers. Christopher Cook, doctor and psychiatrist believes 'Science now seems to affirm that stigma, marginalisation and exclusion are … harmful to human wellbeing.' Suicide often tells us that, even if we have long known it. Our own son's suicide endorsed it for us.

How often have I heard a surprised, 'They are just like us!' Hesitancy, even rejection, may have nothing to do with our faith or anyone else's; it may have much to do with us and our personal, social and economic situation, past and present. I am enormously grateful never to have encountered IS warriors fighting in Iraq and Syria, but I suspect the faith of many of them in themselves without a gun is as minimal as their faith in God. However, we are who we are; we cannot be anyone else, nor they us. Our present and our future are ours. We carry in us our unique and precious personal experience, however creative or destructive, beautiful or savage and with it our self-acceptance, self-love, belief and respect, and/ or their lack and loss. Therein lies our authenticity as persons.

Our own loss or lack of holy confidence in ourselves so easily inhibits the positive and produces fear from insecurity, rivalry, egotism and bigotry towards others known and unknown. I have at times been asked about someone who looks and is assumed to be different, 'What do you want me to say?' Much of the hesitation of the initial inquirer is likely to be based either on what fundamental loss and pain might or might not have been suffered, or on simple lack of experience. Loving ourselves as well as our neighbours can be far easier said than done. Still, our empathy for ourselves has, in all justice, to be extended to those of other faiths and what they might possibly, like anyone else, even us, have lost in *their* lives, individually and corporately. Loss and pain can on all sides be a prime cause of reluctance on all sides to accept similarities and differences, as well as our own failings, limitations and refusal at times to learn about ourselves. Again, someone has to take the initiative in breaking the bonds asunder. This is simple but crucial to recognise. If we really are God's creation, then it is a fair assumption that we are all in some way holy ground, temples of the Holy Spirit of God,[20] to be revered equally as such. Clear confident, loving foundations, corner-stones, are fundamental to our human well-being.

All such problems in human life actually unite us as human beings and strangers across the faiths. Our hearts, minds and bodies, from emotions to imagination, from toenails to kidneys, from smiles to brain cells, have remarkable similarity in strength and vulnerability. We all share them not just DNA. It is constructive to cite and share problems and what we have in common but our similarities as human beings so massively outweigh our differences that we would do well to respect and treasure differences, even our own, *more* highly - except when I start running slower than my nine-year- old grandson! In music however, differences of note and sound are designed to be melded into one. We can't have everyone singing tenor. When I taught about racism, a common metaphor for unity in difference was the black and white keys of the piano. In the inter faith world an orchestra is a better picture, different instruments, superficially different music all combining into one work of art.

It may profit us to remember that probably everyone at some time suffers severe pain in one way or another whatever their faith or belief, mothers included, maybe others more than we. We are united with and without problems, just by being human. Loving our neighbour leads to a reciprocal partnership and mutual benefit to whatever degree. It can be as simple as that, though it is not always. Rowan Williams has said, 'The deepest condition of our humanity is recognition, interaction and the exchange of life.'[19] That realisation is fundamental to our existence. It crosses all boundaries including those of faith. We are all a presence to one another. The challenge of compassion is to click the right keys.

Compassion

Compassion is one unbounded quality. It epitomises the qualities required to follow the way of Jesus. Jesus's compassion, as reported by all four writers of the Gospels, is a model not just for Christians but also for those of our five faiths and for those with no nameable religious faith, including that of humanism. Christian humanism, while reasonably recognised as such within Christian circles, may be no more compassionate than the humanism of anyone else, except it is inspired by the example of Jesus Christ.

Compassion involves equal respect shown to all people. It is the universal potential quality of all people and the value which can be applied across any boundaries. It is immensely positive and creative of itself in relationships and hugely healing in its practice at every level of humanity, professional and voluntary, young and old, able and disabled. Compassion is the heart of God and of God in humanity, whether named as such or not. The theologian and ex-nun Karen Armstrong is a famous international proponent of compassion through her initiative of the Charter for Compassion.

Compassion comprises small everyday kindnesses and inspires international intent and generosity. Yet it is rarely talked of at that exalted level! Ex-President Obama was/is its best political exponent I know of. The challenge to humanity is how to relate to compassion and tie it in to political, governmental and international behaviour. It would indeed be witness to a vision for compassion to recognise the equality in God of every major faith and to bear it out at street level. And for young people? Compassion is surely their prime need from their society: the 'love God and love your neighbour' policy towards them is just as crucial as for adults, even though they might not admit it! It can become a habit.

Collective responsibilities related to:

The one human family

It is one thing to think, believe or trust that all human beings are one in God, but to behave as if this really is true can be a different matter. All people in one form or degree have naturally belonged physically to a mother and thereby a basic human family. This is fundamental but can fail to be consciously accepted openly into our experience. There is that within us all that is holy, for we are all to be revered as God's creation, holy ground, temples of the Holy Spirit of God.[20] I admire the custom of taking off our shoes when entering another's home but it is to be remembered that it is primarily the people there who make it holy. Even those labelled monsters by the cheap media, such as Jamie Bulger's two child murderers (1993), have that potential holiness along with the 80,000 plus people in our shameful British prisons. Even the doctor I once met in Brixton prison who had murdered his four children.

The label *Christian* can be seductive, as can all our group loyalties and 'additional families', whatever the label-Manchester United or Scottish, even 'Made in China'. The label can mean believing in a name and additional family for its own sake. Facebook is at this time, 2017, the prime modern example. A relationship with Jesus may look good, feel good and be good and exemplary too, but perhaps because of our human passion for celebrity we can still mistake the label for the product, the name for the true relationship. I imagine members of other faiths can have the same basic problem with their central characters. Loyalty with a sense of belonging to one's own family, clan and faith is understandable; betrayal is logically derided. Yet other priorities exist, even co-exist.

Wise judgement is called for when it comes to priorities of purpose and personal and community identity. Jesus's loyalty is clear: according to Mark's Gospel, Jesus considers all people equally to be his brothers and sisters, even his mother and not just those by birth, even children ('teenager-hood' is a recent worldwide development). 'Who are my mother and my brothers?' Jesus asks. He answers himself: 'Who ever does the will of God is my brother and sister and mother.'[21] That is a supremely idealistic view of humanity for how in reality can we ourselves uphold the family of the human world, as well as that of our own birth? We may do what we can to embrace our own different parental family generations. It is becoming increasingly necessary for it looks as though now, for the world and our families to survive, we have to uphold and respect both those close, in here, and those, distant, out there. Closeness and distance have through modern communication become such relative terms whether we live in the heart of Zimbabwe or that of Britain.

Inclusiveness

Inclusiveness is a basic principle of much of the Bible and Christianity. Christian principles have their roots in the Jewish Bible and the New Testament. God - in my understanding - is in all and for all and is from whom all the world's faiths stem. What Christians call 'the fruits of the Spirit', are essentially the inclusive gifts of God, namely love joy, peace, patience, kindness, generosity, faithfulness, gentleness and self-control,[22] and let us add goodness. Within this understanding of inclusivity, Christianity can retain its unique differences and traditions as can other faiths retain theirs. This could mean inclusivity of Christianity and Christians and other faiths and their members as of equal worth to God, both in their theology and relationships. Christianity[23] and its Church exists not just for itself – to do so would be an alarming definition of having become a sect - but to enable in God, the moral and spiritual well-being of everyone, outsiders as well as insiders.

In this century, Christian inclusiveness by the Church has been publicly measured in relation to sexual orientation. For some, including myself, it is still wanting in relation to equal opportunity, pay and rights for women and men for the same work, not least in the Church. Inclusive Church is a Christian organization founded in 2003 which aims to 'advocate the full inclusion of all people in the Christian churches including the threefold order of bishops, priests and deacons and regardless of ethnicity, gender and sexual orientation', This book proposes Christian inclusion of those of different religious faith, not within the Christian churches but within the compass of Christian theology and recognition as being equally within God's love, all in the same ark whether sailing north, south, east or west.

'Christ died for all' does not mean that everyone has to become Christian, but it does mean that Christ's life and death have universal significance for everyone in their equality in God. Tony Bayfield, senior rabbi, believes that 'Christianity has been a fundamentally pluralistic religion all the time'.[24] Within itself and its denominations, that is a valid statement of inclusivity. If and when, however, Christianity is in any sense and in practice perceived as 'superior' in relation to different world faiths, then both inclusivity and equality are surrendered. Our local vicar[25] invited a group of Muslims, women and men, to the church's confirmation and lunch, and in between to have their prayer time in the Lady Chapel. In response to my encouragingly raised eyebrows, he simply said, 'My job brief was to be inclusive and inclusive means inclusive.' Everything went serenely ahead, led by two lay Muslim men, with the Muslim women participating in the prayers and Christians sitting by - an immensely moving expression of inclusivity.

On one level, inclusivity does not necessarily exclude expression or belief that personal preference, or even sense of it, is better for me or even for others, whether children and adults. Another level which to me is a matter of my faith seems entirely compatible, that is recognition that in the mind of God, the other is of equal worth and therefore to be equally regarded, loved and included in Christian hearts and minds. Is that any different potentially and in principle from inclusion of our own close family and friends? No one said that living both levels was easy. Jesus found that out.

By way of example, the following was broadcast on BBC 4 's Thought for the Day:[26] "Christians focus not on a tribal god who favours people like us, but on the universal God who, in becoming human, chose solidarity with the whole human race ... In the kingdom of God there is no us and them." 'Yes and no' was my response! Yes, certainly yes to the inclusivity but maybe the speaker spoiled her own point in her choice of language, because to me at least, concealed in the exclusive statement that God became human was the inference that Christianity is best and it alone has the universal message. I once heard virtually the same words from a Baha'i leader, but he concluded with the advice to 'therefore come and join us'. I did tell him that

270

with me that spoiled his case because he had an agenda. One is entitled to believe what one says, but that means being honest about it and recognising that what is meant does not necessarily produce the same perception and interpretation of others. The process of communication is many-eyed.

Christianity and its Church exists not just for itself - that would be an alarming definition of having become a sect - but to enable, under God, the moral and spiritual well-being of all. In principle, which is what matters, there are no outsiders, all are one and included.

Upholding the universal

Universals are particular expressions of inclusivity. To seek the universal basics in all or most of the world faiths is to seek inclusiveness. The way forward may again be to look behind the faith's outward show, however genuinely attractive that show might be, and see what the religion stands for, what it is all about and its purpose. Christianity, like all faiths, can undoubtedly provide much to everyone from a long list of benefits that includes comfort, belonging, security, community, moral grounding, spiritual inspiration, social justice and subtle combinations of love and beauty. However, I suggest these are not intrinsically Christian but universal values, common to all our roles of being human.

Every world religious faith honours the golden rule, again a favourite, as exemplified by Jesus: treat others as we would wish to be treated ourselves. No faith possesses this rule as its own. Christianity cannot, in God's name, possess Jesus for itself, to the exclusion of others, any more than it can possess God. John's Gospel says that Jesus came not just for Christians or potential Christians but because 'God so loved the world.[27] Other faiths wish to share more of Jesus, provided that Christianity allows him to remain a universal man for all seasons, a human symbol of God, in God but not God. Jesus is revered as a prophet like Isaiah in the Qur'an, second only to Mohammed. Progressive Christians would share with other faiths on those same terms. Jesus stands for everyone to live under whatever label they wish if they will love God and love their neighbour as themselves, however hard that is to put into practice.

The present-day international Movement for Compassion and the Charter for Compassion are an admirable lead based on first Christian principles, instigated and supported by many world faith leaders, including Archbishop Desmond Tutu. How far these principles are relative or absolute to religious *truth* is a subject too large and fascinating to debate here. Suffice to say that Jesus and great leaders of other faiths - Buddha, Isaiah, Confucius, Mohammed, Guru Gobind Singh - all stood for the same absolute ideals of love rooted in our humanity and worked at the primary life task of seeking justice and peace for the poor and unprivileged. In their wisdom, they discerned what really matters - the universal principles of life within which we are created and by which we are born to live and die. Spiritual awareness comes and goes: The Compassionate Frome project, Somerset county, launched 2013/14 for 3 years was set up by a G.P, who discovered from data - common wisdom too, I trust - that when isolated people with health problems are supported by community groups and volunteers the number of emergency admissions to hospital falls spectacularly, in this case by 17% compared with elsewhere in the county as rise of 29%. The relevance of faith of any kind is not recorded. Humanity in such cases, comes first, again.

Members of the Christian church and the different religious faiths have now in our globalised generation the unprecedented opportunity in Britain to recognise and practise through their daily lives what is universal in their own teachings and in those of the other major faiths, compassion for example. Inclusiveness may come to incorporate specific contributions of each faith, complementary to one another, religious and otherwise, to be shared for the common good. Persistent and trusting interfaith dialogue has aimed at that in this book. Authentic religious differences sensitively perceived and acknowledged add a storehouse of dignity, insight, distinctive truth and appeal to each faith, as they do to all human affairs. Over and within us all there is a universal and transcendental reality of life - known through mystical human dimensions or by whatever name - seeking our love and respect rather than our greed and selfishness. The issue of what happens at death democratizes all faiths.

There is a strong case for praise of universals as rational inclusive truths because they are perceptions of human experience and observations on a vast geographical and historical scale. Faith in them is a natural consequence of their personal and community worldwide significance. Plato, 3-400 years before Christ, on a smaller stage, described them as archetypes. Such faith seems to me entirely reasonable and rational compared to what can be labelled superstition, particularly if it can prove more meaningful to many. It would be in the same way that love, the supreme human experience, is accepted as a major motivating power in all our lives. Such acceptance seems common-sense wisdom - rational even. It might do religion a considerable service in the eyes of many objectors.

Making a difference

Rebirth, transformation and repentance (metanoia) have at heart the desire to make a difference and are basic to Christian teaching. Making a difference is more than change: playing in tune at a concert can make more difference than just changing your shirt. It is worthwhile to examine what it is about difference that can cause problems and what it is that does not. Partly it depends on how it is introduced and implemented and by whom. At St John's Ladywood our redevelopment entailed removing the old pews and installing a new window, gift of our local synagogue. The changes contributed to the church artistic and worship potential and to our Jewish/Christian relationship. The church's inter faith education programme with local schools and Muslim, Jewish, Buddhist and Christian places of worship and their teachers created a new feeling of partnership within the church itself and those involved especially the children. (See Chapter 2) Making a difference through change may be positive or negative. Both may even strengthen our genetic survival!

Making a difference is likely to involve the taking of initiative. After the Brexit referendum, June 2016, a small group of people inspired by a humanist who wrote to the Bishop began the movement of Love your Neighbour, LYN, producing long-term banners for the city and used by many of its institutions. A local mosque distributed about 2000 roses to shoppers in the Birmingham Bull Ring at Christmas 2017, not done 10 or 100 years ago. Pope Francis has clearly wanted to see change and new openness in the Church. Campaigns against smoking, modern slavery, sexual abuse, women's social inequalities, over-use of plastics, gay rights etc have all begun from the bottom – excluding Pope Francis or not - even if good action has not necessarily meant good theology. Likewise, inter faith activities such as inter faith forums, campaigns, intellectual challenges like 'scriptural reasoning' or demonstrations for 'Hope not Hate' against violent extremism, racism, islamophobia and anti-Semitism. Examples are of course endless but they are still worth learning from. That can be a theological lesson in itself in making connections. 'Christianity from below', the way ahead? Most of these discussions are informally structured in a variety of partnerships, the most fundamental one being with God which we have already recognised in God being with us.

Partnerships

N.B. 'Partnership is a wonderful ideal but, realistically, people are complicated, contrary and unco-operative'.[28] Partnerships are basically about making human connections for public wellbeing. The European Union has developed since 1945 partially in 1957, fully since 1993, as one of the greatest political, personal and social partnerships in history. I mention this as a context for my hope still in the future of Britain in Europe.

Destroying such a partnership would be a huge grief to me and, I believe, an act of tragic irresponsibility.

Different inter faith partnerships are increasingly commonplace. This is an exceptional example:

On May 22nd 2017, a suicide bomber was responsible for a terror attack at a young people's concert in which 22 people were killed. 'Manchester Together' is a priceless example of partnership: people uniting in love and spirit across all faiths and backgrounds in the face of horrific adversity, especially through 'coming together in song' exactly one year later.

From the outset it is crucial to recognise the imperative of friendships, flexibility, adaptability, imagination and creativity. First meeting, then dialogue and partnership - one leads to the other. All three require a listening to others, acceptance of the human rights to live and be heard. Models and experiments are valuable, but probably not as inflexible blueprints. Much depends on personalities, histories, situations and need. Partnerships vary in their nature from say, business to sport, artistry to education, space travel to mountain rescue, artistic productions to marriage. It is to be hoped that individuals of different faiths, Christians or otherwise, will naturally be in informal partnerships through the normal courses of life. Mixed partnerships/marriages producing dual heritage children seem to me a great advance for those who can brave it - though our youngest and dual heritage adopted son always found his identity difficult.

Partnerships between faith institutions are of a different order and less common. There are notable examples of organisations having priorities and structures that work well together. The environmental Jubilee Debt Campaign struggles here in Birmingham to facilitate 'Footsteps', an interfaith support group stemming from the Paris global warming coalition in late 2015. Christian Aid, Islamic Relief and Muslim Aid are visible local organisations with similar goals to each other. Faiths for Fun has since 2009 been an admirable annual Birmingham scouting initiative with the Birmingham Council of Faiths for youngsters to learn and play together. The door is open locally and nationally to new needs, confidence and initiatives.

There were 340 Christian denominations in 2010, 20 per cent more than in 2005.[29] How many still go it alone, as might be surmised because many Councils of Churches have declined in strength. And how many team-up with other faiths' places of worship? Again, there is the need for organisational and individual thinking and planning to exist on different levels. Ideals of the kingdom of God can operate at the local, the national and the global/universal level. Here's another boat to be pushed out.

Partnerships between those of religious faith and those of the secular realm

The most exciting dimension of our 21st century New Age is the expanding universal realisation that, actually, we all united by human experience, however diverse or similar it may be. Scholars may say that it is on those ancient grounds that Islam rejects any division between the religious and the secular. Christianity could well focus afresh on making bridges between the two. Within the bridge might come for example in their own minds, the Christian humanist, Quaker and non-theist, and within the secular minds, the universalist, Unitarian, atheist, non- theist too, all labels convenient but potentially misleading and divisive. Christianity might though have to change some of its way-out clothes to which I have referred in Chapter 4.

The most far-reaching area of bridge-building has been and remains that of health and well-being, especially in social and prison care. Hospitals in principle and usually practice are inspired examples of wholistic thinking. As far as I know, to date they are nearly all of Christian base. Prisons seem rarely have the resources, political and economic to have much chance. I once lived for a week in a borstal - a young men's treatment centre - one which was very positive in theory and practice. Yet between liturgy and prayer in one box, medical care in another, and then further division between spiritual, mental and physical care there can be an unimaginative and destructive demarcation. Creation of a truly wholistic approach is a huge achievement. We are all body, mind and spirit, interdependently in inevitable need of one another. Young men and women of whatever faith and background – and poverty can naturally take its toll- are increasingly found to be desperate for attention and secure identity, needy of encouragement from whoever is willing to give them time and unselfish attention so that everyone's future is to everyone's benefit. That attention constantly requires fresh wisdom and understanding of its practice whether in the secular, liturgical or social world; likewise, within the life-and-death practices of other faiths. There is scope for mutual support and learning in this area.

Christianity's effect on society over generations - supporting, initiating, and managing countless voluntary movements, such as the general benefit of churches and church schools throughout Britain, the National Health Service and the birth of the Labour Party - has, since the mid-nineteenth century especially, given British society as a remarkably moral public aspect of the two working together. David Cameron, prime minister from 2010 to 2016, expressed his hope that Britain would educate for and encourage a real 'one nation' democratic and egalitarian approach;[30] Mrs May in 2016 similarly. Christianity, in my understanding, is logically democratic not least in relation to the health of those of different faith. Hope dies hard! That is potentially an expectation for other faiths too, as their family structures change in the British context.

Grace Davie, professor of the sociology of religion, states in her *Religion in Britain: A Persistent Paradox*, previously mentioned,[31] that a strong case can be made that Britain has a deeply embedded Christian culture and that its secularism is rooted in Christianity. I find that reassuring. It would be wise for Christians and leaders of different faiths, not to diminish what in effect is the context for most of their lives and arrogantly dismiss those with no religious faith as aliens who may well have a faith of a different kind, besides a morality as good as another's. About half of British people consider themselves not to be Christian, as we have observed earlier. Such proportions would have been inconceivable when I was a kid singing to full churches. This scale of ineffectiveness is therefore likely to be absolutely vast. Christians - and this particularly means the Church - would, in principle do well to listen, understand and respectfully aim to communicate with the those of 'no (named) faith' - 'nones' we have called them already. They may be the unvoiced non-voters of any survey. They may well be local and national leaders from all walks of life seeking meaning to life, perhaps even God. Who is to say they are not! I have commented on the increased and increasing numbers of international citizens in Britain with secular as well as religious commitment, most conspicuously in the National Health Service. Their overall goodwill is essential for fostering good faith, morality and social unity.

Secular society has to be taken into an all-embracing heart and mind: everyone lives in it and depends on it. While on the one hand it does contain destructive elements, not least on the commercial, general and social media and online front, on the other hand, commercial adverts can suggest new ways forward through mixing social salvation, peace of mind and security into advertised products. The fashion store Benetton has done this. What aid to beauty is not supposed to court love? or breakfast food be love's object? British Telecom told us, 'It is good to talk.' I know of those who see themselves as secular but willingly value their own faith, religious or not.

Old, unnecessary and often spurious divisive barriers are still regularly revisited between faith and science, the religious and the secular, reason and faith. That is more than unfortunate. I do not accept any inherent antagonism. These are different entities that enrich each other. Each may counter outmoded tradition in their observation and experience of change but tradition may best be re-interpreted in preference to being discarded. That can feel personal. People of tradition do not take kindly to being discarded. Christian theology can be seen to lag behind secular society in ideals such as anti-discrimination, gender and racial equality and in urgencies such as climate change, prison conditions and 'over-population'. Both at their worst, may sanction untruth, destruction, bigotry and egotism; both, at their best, are resources of accumulated human wisdom, experience and loving practice. Scope for collaboration is endless. The Malvern Faith and Science week-ends since 2014 stimulate partnership in ideas. I recently visited a public exhibition in Berlin entitled 'Jews, Christians and Muslims: Scientific Discourse in the Middle Ages 500-1500 CE.

The secular is not all exploitative, selfish and immoral, as the Church is in danger of assuming. The Church exists for the world and not vice versa - the only institution that exists for the sake of others, as Archbishop William Temple[32] is famously quoted for having said back in 1942. He also supported 'emergent evolution'[33] as having naturally spawned human consciousness for everyone. Christianity has long been called the most materialistic of all religions and is in theory very body-conscious too. So much so, and so 'down to earth', that traditional Christian orthodoxy maintains that God even became man as proclaimed in the Nicene Creed back in 325 CE. Christ's real body and blood are said to be present in the Roman Catholic Mass and are constantly revered. Christians may sing 'O Lord, All the World Belongs to You'.

'Two things fill the mind with ever new and increasing admiration and awe, the more often we reflect upon them: the starry heavens above me and the moral law within me,' wrote Immanuel Kant. 'All creation, including all people and faiths, reflects the creator God.'[33] There is no temple in John's biblical Revelation of a heavenly city; it is for people. Goodness and beauty are both secular and spiritual values. Mediators of transcended reality, human and otherwise, are all around us if we but open our eyes.

Faith communities, through their common opposition to all things secular - which in turn can provoke secular opposition - are in danger of hastening further decline already seen in churches and future decline in other places of worship. They would be foolish if they foster a besieged religious mentality by arrogantly, even hypocritically, ignoring the obvious merits of secular society for everyone, including themselves. In particular, the natural pluralism of the anti-discrimination secular world can offer example, legality and hope for the multi-faith world. 'Religionless Christianity', in terms of Dietrich Bonhoeffer in his *Letters and Papers from Prison*,[34] is about faith in Christ without the formal institutional non-essentials of religion. Faith truly exists in the secular world - faith in life, faith in love, faith in having babies, faith in death, faith in healing, endless faith wherever, faith in winning as displayed by the footballers of lowly Leicester City in winning the English football Premier League, 2015/6 and those of tiny Iceland beating England in the 2016 European Cup. Faith in the Parkrun, suggests for some that ' it is a new church. Here you come together and you feel embedded in the local area' . So is quoted a runner from the 5 km run, Saturday 9 am sharp, with the national charity, Parkrun. Other sports may understandably make similar claims.

Partnerships between the different religious faiths

So many such partnerships happen constantly on the British scene. More can always be made on basic levels of relationships, policies and theology. This could mean central official leadership; encouragement and blessing of theological discussion and partnership with those of different faiths through their chair, church moderator, bishops and archbishops, democratic assemblies and synods. I remember that the People Next Door discussion groups of 1966 urged on us by the World Council of Churches were all about denomination [35]. That same local spirit of mutuality and joint learning could be replicated instead by different faiths and with it a willingness to encourage young people in such a style.

Britain could be an international model through Christianity and all those in whatever good faith, taking the lead in enjoying and respecting differences and similarities, publicly pledging to work in peace together. Other faiths have their share of responsibility, but in my experience, Christians are often seen by the formers' members as expected to take the initiative, despite obvious dangers of undue power and self-perpetuation. With relative newcomers to Britain - that status can stick for too long - the different host communities have for over a generation had major responsibility for initiating kindly welcome. That is changing fast. Responsibility is often shared for enhancement of good community relationships. Power may be best used to empower others.

Birmingham, despite its limitations, is ever the city of immigrants. Some citizens work on it being a model for Britain, enhancing worthy expectation and hope for the future. Put negatively, interfaith antagonisms in Birmingham could bounce around Britain, harming prosperity and well-being. They do exist, for example, in 'Britain First' and the 'English Defence League',[36] Until now however, 2017/8, they have been largely kept at bay or in the case of National Action proscribed in 2016 by the Government as terrorist.

Christianity needs the other faiths as partners in seeking the kingdom of God for everyone, rather than the kingdom of the Church for relatively few Christians. Christianity is not homogeneous any more than are the other major faiths. Partnership and collaboration are imperative - state with church, church with mosque, synagogue, gurdwara, and temple, secular with spiritual. In the centuries around the first millennium the House of Wisdom established in Baghdad in 1004 C.E symbolised the cultural and religious richness of areas of Spain, northern Italy and southern France through Jews, Arab Muslims and Christians meeting one another. Such cultural heights are an inspiration even now. Successful efforts of cathedrals could be stretched to involve fresh interfaith relationships, as previously sought at Birmingham Cathedral by the dean Catherine Ogle, from 2010 to 2017, and Westminster Abbey's multi-faith annual Commonwealth Day Service, headed throughout her reign by the Queen. She spoke in 2017 of the need for 'true celebration of each person and the value of their uniqueness and contribution which involves reaching out, recognising and embracing their individual identity'. Yes, indeed, such a combined approach might usher in a real sense of reformation in society as a whole, a real one-nation approach for the long term.

There are countless examples of groups of Christians prioritising interfaith partnerships. By no means are all of these members of the Inter Faith Network for the UK, which I have mentioned as supporting the 250 - plus interfaith groups around Britain, all developed over the last 30 years. They are all part of an invaluable framework arising from and from which arise seemingly small acts of kindness, individual and corporate, that have profited from the butterfly effect sadly without the butterflies. Such partnerships can grow additional identities without losing existing ones.

Birmingham interfaith groups play a part. See Introduction 3 on Birmingham. My impression is that the city takes its political and religious responsibilities to heart, not attempting to keep politics out of religion or religion out of politics. That is practical reality, but the theory does need discussion and clarification of meaning. For example, 'Not in Our Name' was an international political/religious cry around the world following the Charlie Hebdo massacre in Paris in January 2015. Our two local interfaith groups quickly planned a rally with the same title, in our own city square, inviting Birmingham's mayor and local citizens. Several of the contributors to this book, including me, were speakers. There was good and wide publicity in the name of faith harmony.

What happens in one city can set an example. The informal interfaith movement, besides the Love Your Neighbour movement mentioned, fostered Inter Faith Tea and encouraged Hope Not Hate parties with the aim of 'doing something kind' in response to Brexit anti-immigrant scaremongering. Our Moseley inter faith group has been as a team to a local madrassa to talk about working together. The Faith Encounter Programme has organized annual visits of usually six members of different faiths to Pershore School out in the West Midlands countryside. I strongly recommend such educational team approaches to different communities. An initiative from a city councillor which our local interfaith group is working on is for members of different faiths to visit together local disaffected areas/people and offer kindness and reassurance under the Love Your

Neighbour banner. The movement continues. Europe's apparently largest iftar was held a Birmingham' Central Mosque on 24 June 2017, and the increasing enjoyment of iftars as interfaith events during and at the end of Ramadan has been a leap forward in interfaith relationships throughout much of Britain.

Since 2016, the Birmingham Anglican Diocese has sponsored a six-month Conversation between thirty established and emerging leaders from a variety of the major faiths in Birmingham to discuss how to 'contribute to the city's active flourishing and social, spiritual, and economic prosperity'. This was another impressive initiative. There have now, as of September 2017, been four 'Conversations' of this kind. I select a few of their recommendations:

- Religion should not be excluded from 'city discussions', though its voices should not be prioritised above the nonreligious.
- Schools should accept their natural multi-faith benefits as centres of different faiths and engage with young people.
- Inner-city white populations and black churches in particular should be encouraged to participate in interfaith activity.
- Attention should be given to public respect for all of different faith background; different faiths should put the well-being of the whole community before themselves. The Inter Faith Network for the UK, www.interfaith.org.uk is the most fruitful resource of enquiry.

For many outside a city like Birmingham, these suggestions can be of interest and a source of encouragement that so much has been achieved through community integration and friendship. For many inside Birmingham, they are encouragement on a practical level. Birmingham's long tradition of migration and integration, assisted by its strong Christian roots of nonconformity, Quakerism and Unitarianism continues, two hundred years on, to set expectations and norms of the new imperative of creating respectful interfaith relationships.

Good relationships in Britain between the many different faiths are of vital importance not just for the faiths themselves and interfaith life but also for the peace of Britain. Whether on climate change or religious matters, their effect can be either positive or negative or both. Butterflies still beat their wings, indifferent to the outcome they create. One new outrage, like that of twenty-two people, largely children, being killed in Manchester in 2017 rapidly breeds new labelling through the media, stereotyping fears and an endless chain reaction almost around the world. Laced with trumpery in our alarming era of non-fact and immoral propaganda, a negative, destructive atmosphere can develop all too quickly. The good can be lost sight of. Incidents in Germany and France of different levels of horrific murder, such as in Nice in July 2016, immediately broadcast by world media, set off wild assumptions about Islamic extremism, often with very limited evidence. Fear is a terrifying weapon in the hands of unscrupulous minds. It can be simply the toxic recipe for more and more security as I witnessed in a mixed faith visit to Palestine/Israel early in 2018 but it can be a motivation. That is how it is, and Christianity and the faiths, preferably together, have to respond with alternative conviction and hope.

The political scene is a strong component of interfaith relationships. It offers a different context and priority, mostly positive, sometimes negative. The priority may be to win and not to lose, to enjoy the struggle and even the fight, because pride and identity, possibly laced with misguided patriotism and faith, can determine priorities. Priority may *not* be to seek to understand the other party or understand who 'they' are, however helpful in the long run that would probably be, for the heart may refuse to understand the other party or make friends. Brexit has been a good - or bad - example. Good hope feeds on the whole idea of love being so basic to everyone that it may be harnessed to make a bridge for those who otherwise separate heart and mind. That is the genius of Judaeo-Christian teaching for it shows that the two cannot ultimately be separated and promotes love in experience, love in principle and belief and love of God and neighbour.

Partnership in constructive politics is an essential means of living with otherwise rivals, advancing friendship and trust. Partnership within the bounds of Christianity is similarly essential in constructive faith so that alternative progressive forms of Christian thinking may complement the more orthodox and traditional. Both partnerships can lead to plurality of thought and action. Politics and the Church know the reality of compromise, 'good disagreement', as Archbishop Welby constantly advocates.

Partnerships in theological discussion

The contents and processes of this book require discussion and partnership in discussion. Yet in many a church circle, discussion and partnership at appropriate different levels seem rarely found. There tend to be certain closed shops in church life that are not helpful at all for consideration of obstructions, let alone accepted and possibly encountered by adoption of relevant practice and theology.

Archbishop Justin Welby, speaking not just of Britain but also of Europe as a whole, has commented at the World Economic Forum in Davos discussing religious extremism, that Christians have 'lost the capacity ... to use theological values to discover our differences in society', to which I would add, to discuss very much at all theological and personally meaningful in church or within its hearing or within its hearing. It can be so ironic. Some clergy devoutly wish to do this and some congregations/members likewise, yet apparently not often in the same church or at the same time despite impassioned separate efforts by both clergy and church members. Those who succeed deserve great credit. This is likely to mean that consequently, many Christians hold back theologically, that is in discussing issues about God, particularly alternative views about God. Good examples of such discussions need good publicity because their absence disempowers reflective, searching and experienced Christians and those who know less but might wish to know more.

Whose responsibility is this? All church leaders could take a lead themselves in fostering theological discussion, even within Sunday service itself. Straight Sunday services and sermons alone may offer great benefit but may also fail in their educational method; potentially absorbing, spiritual and enjoyable at the time, but not very good for discussion and long-term inspiration unless alternative opportunities are offered. This failure may betray a lack of trust in relationships between clergy and laity which inhibits discussion and partnership and, therefore, motivation for learning from one another.

It is grievous how often Christian adults and enquiring children report their frustration at being left in the dark by church ministers about their questions on life, liturgy, scripture or theology, with little encouragement for them to learn or have discussions about God and Jesus, of whom they otherwise have to hear so much in church. When did you last discuss a sermon in church? Do many, for example, know what they mean themselves by calling Jesus unique, divine and the Son of God? Christians require rechargeable confidence that through Jesus

Christ, they can find a whole new way of life. That is how Christianity began for Jesus's early followers, on the highways and byways without having taken a pew. In personified terms, both God and Jesus seem to long for open discussion not dominating dogmatism.

Despite church support in principle and practice for individuals of different faiths just as was offered eventually to those of different race or nationality, many people simply may not have the educational tools with which to meet and discuss. The numerous Friendship Circles triggered by the national Inter Faith Network are proving an enjoyable intimate way of improving both knowledge and relationships. Theology with God at its heart has harvested time-honoured glories, hazards and conflicts. Regrettably, however, theological thought is often considered a separate and highfalutin order of understanding, irrelevant to human life and relationships. Sacred theological beliefs of members of different faiths can often be discounted without definition or quarrel. 'Better to stick to practical matters'! That's practical advice but highly uncreative. It is unfair to over- generalise. I suspect that there is neither ready means nor motive to employ Archbishop Welby's theological values.

This is a very regrettable mistake. Theological discussion is essential, however initially awkward it may be. Reasons for this are to be explored, especially Christian assumptions such as the literal truth of both Bible and Qur'an, Jesus as the Son of God, or the so-called gods of Hinduism, or the denial of God by Buddhism. The heart needs the help of the head for its beat to be heard and inspire.

Many churches seem to find discussion hard, despite new-found willingness, because society itself finds it hard and because learning to discuss is not educational, media or intellectual priority. Interfaith education is probably very patchy around the country, despite my argument that interfaith activity is a desirable feature, in some form, for the whole country. Evidence is bound to be partial. When discussion is practised, it is probably about cultural details and religious education and not about theology and a uniting God. Muslim madrassas – voluntary Muslim schools - have had the chance in the last generation to prove their excellence in the face of the demise of much Sunday school activity.

It is worth further note that democracy in Britain suffers from the same general educational problem. This is a major omission in principle. Theological roots arguably underpin all moral, secular and institutional contexts, all human relationships and therefore all interfaith relationships. This is because these contexts are all, in my understanding, about God, the God of all creation. Construction of bridges between bodies of thought that are categorised differently can lead to creative developments that liberate God's Spirit in and for us. It is a feeble admission of failure, guilt, inferiority or superiority, for Christians and members of the different faiths not to venture into or have any opportunity for discussion about God when prayer and any communication involving God is so basic to most faiths. It is worth the attempt amongst other faiths when it can be more relaxed than between those of the same faith. That is a gift of inter faith relationships in themselves. I find many Muslims, for example, very open to theological discussion. It is worth reflecting how far the love your neighbour principle based on human equality before God is the height of democracy and therefore combines Christian and secular views of life.

Open, patient discussion is especially vital to mature interfaith relationships. For example, the key concept of Christians having 'the Son of God' on their side is not necessarily about assumed power, arrogance and superiority, but it is essential for the issue to be fully discussed between the faiths. In this interfaith era, it behoves members of all the faiths to be secure about what they mean themselves when they speak about their faith. My experience of the last twenty-five years indicates that the British interfaith world and related discussion has had increasingly positive effect on individual church members and whole congregations. This may appear initially to have little to do with clearing their paths to salvation through personal relationship with Christ. It has though everything to do with a new incentive to enhancing their knowledge of the plurality of God's work and especially with the joy of their playing their part in creating further respectful, even loving, experiences and relationships.

The dialogues recounted early in this book are felt to be within that category. Another budding example, already referred to briefly, is that for the last three years in 2015, 2016 and 2017 in Moseley, Birmingham, a party of youngish Muslims - first about 40, last time about 100 - have come from a local mosque to St Mary's church for Christmas Eve, midnight Holy Communion. Having just turned up in 2015, in 2016 they were invited by the clergy in to an Easter service meal, and the same number came to the Easter morning celebration beforehand. Then at Advent 2016, The Service of Confirmation by the bishop of Birmingham and a meal was followed by Muslim prayers in our Lady Chapel. All the visits have been reciprocated with a meal and prayers at the mosque in question. True, this is not common in most churches, but such exceptions are very inspiring. Analysis is still for the future but has so far been superfluous. Further discussion is growing and all seems very relaxed. According to St John in his Gospel, it was an ultimate prayer of Jesus to God that all people who follow him 'will be one with each other'.[37] Humanity's prime goal is for all to be respected and respectful members of the whole human family. If that is accepted, then if we join a religious family, we do so, inevitably, within the context of that human family. The prayer of Muslims alongside that of Christians in a church and mosque is a stirring example of this unity.

Prayer and discussion may lead to action and action to discussion and prayer, whether the focus is on climate change or justice, peace or poverty, inequality or immigration, economic injustice or warfare, or just cricket. To still recognise the world as God's creation, the Church has to be open to the transformation through resurrection that God brings to the Church and to the whole world. The job of theological discussion is to open the door not just to more good theology but to enable response and action through new relationships.

My analysis of the Perceptions introduces the issue of Christian interfaith education. It is probably very patchy around the country, despite my argument that interfaith activity is so desirable throughout the country. Evidence is bound to be partial. When discussion is practised, I surmise that it is probably about cultural details and religious education, not about theology and a uniting God. Birmingham's Standing Advisory Council for Religious Education, (SACRE) has since 2007 been exceptional in establishing and practising its 'Agreed Syllabus' in its Birmingham schools, a very go-ahead joint interfaith educational model. Since 1997/8 it has been foremost in fostering the Ladywood Interfaith Education Project mentioned earlier.

There is an aspect of Christian theology that is sometimes called 'exclusivism'. It is a root subject for theological discussion. I largely leave the subject to others except for a brief comment. Exclusivism matters because it does not acknowledge the inclusive way of Jesus Christ that recognises members of different faiths, religious and secular, as equal partners in the loving of God and humanity. I as a Christian see my relationships with members of the different faiths as intrinsic to Christianity itself in today's world. I would have liked the books, *On being a Christian* by Hans Kung, 1977, and *Being Christian* by Rowan Williams in 2014 to have included more words about why and how such inter faith relationships might be integral and crucial for their own sake now, for Christians and for future world harmony. A dynamic interfaith theology seems to me indispensable for the churches. 'In our modern world ... to be religious is to be inter-religious'[38] amongst those of different world faiths and with those of faith for the common good of humanity.

Encouragement of one another to discover and employ our own spirit from God to serve God and one another is its own reward. So much practical living and theological discussion comes down to partnerships and relationships. I believe that it is in personal meeting that God is present and even created. Networks of small cells of any size, two or more, consisting of people of different faith sharing friendship and being alive together, are to me the best proposal - though in certain places maybe nothing new - that arises from this book. It might mean extra effort and encouragement, but the reward may be to discover God in new ways, not least with different faiths. It is just that we find it hard to believe that life and faith can be so simple. That's a new challenge.

Partnerships between our different selves

These imply that whatever we wish for and seek out for others, we need first or simultaneously to seek out in ourselves. It is for us, in friendship with others, to make partnerships connections between our body, mind and spirit. we may have confidence in the rules of 7 a side rugby, but not singing Jerusalem, in visiting a church, say, but not a mosque or in our different identities. For example, we can be both parent and child, cricketer and musician, practitioner and teacher, Christian and scientist, even Christian and humanist/atheist. British and European (British for us might mean being English, Scottish, Welsh and Irish depending on circumstances, though in rugby it might not!) I am personally Christian and pluralist in matters of faith, as you 've probably picked up. There are experiences, differences, tensions and gifts within ourselves which may or may not clash that are worth our efforts to comprehend for the sake of Christ's 'abundant life' in us and others.

We may live with apparent contradictions in ourselves and have to hold our own tensions between love and hate, darkness and light, patience and anger, scorn and understanding, being right and wrong. Sometimes we are *us*, and sometimes we are *them* to ourselves as well as to others. In love you might mix up 'you' and 'me'! We may do well to accept that we ourselves may have two or more points of view. I have, for example several points of view about God, Jesus and the Church, which I reconcile together without being at all confused. I do though accept that can seem confusing to others. I hope this maybe doubtful ability helps my understanding of others. Donald Trump, 2018, though, oozes confusion.

This all means there is need for us all to understand our context, what we have to face in order to free ourselves to be who we want to be, whether it is understanding our perceptions or accepting that we are stammerers, disabled, childless, orphans, not-as-bright/ brilliant/bonny-as- we-would-like- to-be or often have difficulty in relationships with people superficially different to ourselves. Our past, present and future are important to each of us. However, trying to suspend our own problems for the sake of others has become a community necessity too of our times, not just a nice idea. That is really about loving ourselves in order that we can love others and therefore maybe ourselves. The Spirit of life is around wherever we can see it, in others, in nature, in worthy challenges. Try to watch a film of a baby being born!

Five tasks for Christians

Throughout the book I have aimed at a non-didactic and dogmatic style even if I have sometimes failed. These five tasks are serious suggestions addressed to Christians though they may be of interest to non-Christians.

1. *In the light of Christian unequal treatment, past and present, of different faiths and their members* - to recognise our institutional, corporate and personal failings concerning equality, unagreed power and presumed superiority in our relationships with others, rather than continuing in denial, ignorance and indifference. In the light of the biblical statement that 'God created all people in his own image', to practise human dignity and respect for others, support increasing work against any historic imperial domination of inequality enacted between Christians and those of different faiths, particularly on the theological front; to learn from Finland where 'you don't look up at people and you don't look down at people, you look level.'[39]

2. *In the light of limited Christian success in twenty-first century Britain in reaching out to half the British population and the different world faiths* - to recognise possible need for variation in interpretation and priority from mainstream traditional Christianity; to accept into that

mainstream - what has been the reality from Christian Day One - the varying but equally principled study and interpretation of scripture, tradition and mission, particularly of the four different Gospels; to recognise different understanding of what, for example, it means to call Jesus 'Son of God'. It may entail looking inwards, call it processing ourselves and our spiritual foundations. It will mean valuing present contributions to society through, for example, imaginative Fresh Expressions, Renewal and Reform and prayer movements like 'Thy Kingdom come' fast becoming world-wide. It may mean trusting those who see life differently in *their* integrity and experience, encouraging established Christians to open up to additional alternatives of a transformed theological and biblical interpretation based on non-literalism and our perpetual new understanding of the Spirit of God.

3. In the light of considerable ignorance about that 50 per cent and those of different faith and a growing moral and religious vacuum - to take initiatives to recognise the priority of listening to others and learn from them, especially young people and others who may be outsiders to us. This might get at what that that 50 per cent of nones (non-churchgoers) may see as the heart of their problem with Christianity and/or the Church. It may prove appealing to young people too, otherwise absentees from Church but to be trusted as working things out for themselves. The generation gaps are increasingly apparent but not to be frightened of. Whether so-called 'outsiders' are so-called atheists, secularists, agnostics, free thinkers, 'nones' or of another belief or faith - labels are to be carefully watched. We are all God's people to be listened to as allies on life's journeys, especially the younger travellers. ...and to treasure honest differences. You and I are probably a bit different too, and the better for it, whether in the same business, family, jazz group, church or whatever, something like the fish in the sea. If we think they – not the fish but just 'others' – are talking nonsense, we may want to tell them so, but it is better to ask for explanation and the same possible treatment for us.

As outsiders are often good at honest insights., to recognise one another's gifts, be grateful for them and share them for our own benefit and the benefit of others. Truly confident communities, including communities of faith, do not need to bolster themselves and their power. Truly confident Christians do not usually have to constantly tell others of, or even convert others to, our particular doctrinal beliefs; rather, to do our best to recognise and appreciate how we may each may assist and learn from one another on the art of living. Teaching and learning to connect are essential skills in our tangibly shrinking world. Connections are increasingly advisable, particularly with people who at first sight and without thought seem very different from us. (Recently I felt antagonistic to some ultra-orthodox Jews, men, in black and white and big hats and ringlets. I regret I failed to create any human contact, usually my solution to any sharp prejudice. I admit too, that the niqab is not my favourite female dress but I fully accept it is a woman's right and a British value to wear what she wishes within professional boundaries.) Social media is easier for some to handle than others. Generations could learn from one another. Our life-task is to accept both the past and present as we know them for the benefit of the future.

4.   *In the light of lack of confidence or over-confidence as to what being Christian actually means* - to encourage one another to trust ourselves and our experience, especially regarding matters of faith, truth and relationships, and what we might have tried to get away with at both public and private levels, always accepting we can get it wrong; to

test ourselves out on a different plane in a different market with different customers and aim to make a difference where we can to the prevailing mood of the day. Bad and fake-news is only partial and does not have to win. Situations at the macro and micro level can be similar in need and personal dynamics. In practice, the public level, the media, business and established institutions in particular, can fall shamefully short of integrating spiritual and emotional values.

5. *In the light of our uncertainty in our possible private and public understanding of God, Jesus, different faiths and even ourselves - to* recognise and openly discuss what personal internal changes may be desirable and possible in our own understanding of Christianity and the Church and how we might possibly better serve their purpose of loving Jesus and what he stands for, humanity and, supremely, God. This may mean discussion of the nature of change and its difficulties; how we may cling to existing power and authority – even fail to recognise it - and be fearful of unknown people and change itself; selfish about our own apparent needs and blind to those of others and the common good; blind to those who feel and experience serious loss of their own identity, community cohesion, and even faith; blind to the mutual enjoyment and benefits of good inter faith relationships; blind to the inevitability of British and international social change; blind to God being with us always, even in reading this book; and to consider the difficult challenge as to what we might actually give up in terms of what we may have assumed to be God-given theology. As surrender and sacrifice are marks of the Christian life, to consider how we might connect and integrate any revised understanding of God in a new way that might open doors to would-be followers; basically, to feel we may have to make fresh or renewed priorities in our lives.

All Bible references in this chapter are from the New Revised Standard Version, copyright © 1989 the Division of Christian Education of the National Council of the Churches of Christ in the United States of America.

1   Lecture to Birmingham clergy, Birmingham Cathedral, 2015.

2   For example, Race Relations Act 1965, Disability Act 2005, and Equality Act 2010.

3   Galatians 3:28.

4   The golden rule, e.g. Matthew 7:12.

5   Galatians 5:22.

6   Basil Scott, God Has No Favourites (Primalogue, 2013).

7   Fourth-century Cappadocian fathers, including Basil the Great and Gregory of Nyassa.

8   The Brexit vote in Britain was and remains very divisive.

9   Archbishop Welby, in a speech to the Board of Deputies of British Jews, 6 May 2015.

10 Luke 11:42ff.

11 Isaiah 58:6.

12 Sam Wells, 'Reform and Renewal in the Church of England', the Church Times, 4 July 2016.

13 Linda Woodhead, letter to the Church Times, 4 Mar. 2016.

14 Paul in 1 Corinthians 11:9.

15 William Shakespeare, Hamlet, Act II, Scene 2, and Act I, Scene 3.

16 Exodus 3:14.

17 Viktor Frankl, Man's Search for Meaning (Washington Square Press, 1948).

18 Rev Dr Christopher Cook, Spirituality and Narrative in Psychiatric Practice (RC Psych Publications, 2016), quoted in the Church Times, 16 Sept. 2016.

19 Rowan Williams, lecture series Who Is My Neighbour? St Martins-in-the-Fields, 2016.

20 Cf. I Corinthians 3:16.

21 Mark 3:31–35.

22 Galatians 5:22.

23 See Chapter 4, 'A Christian Context'.

24 Beyond the Dysfunctional Family, editors Tony Bayfield, Alan Race, and Ataullah Siddiqui, (Createspace, 2012)

25 The Revd Duncan Strathie, Moseley Benefice, Birmingham.

26 The Revd Dr Jane Leach, principal of Wesley House, Cambridge, BBC Radio 4 Thought for the Day, 3 Apr. 2017.

27 John 3:16.

28 United Society Partners in the Gospel, Lent Course 2018

29 UK church statistics, Peter Brierley, 2010.

30 See note 2, above.

31 Grace Davie, emeritus professor of the sociology of religion, Exeter University.

32 Quote from Archbishop William Temple, Christianity and Social Order. Penguin 1942)

33 Immanuel Kant, 1724–1804, world famous philosopher, Wikipedia Quotations.

34 Emergent evolution was founded by C. Lloyd Morgan, 1885–1936.

35 Dietrich Bonhoeffer, Letters and Papers from Prison (London: SCM, 1967).

36 The English Defence League was founded in 2009 and advocates for an anti-Islam, anti-Muslim, pro-English, and pro-Christian way of life.

37 Quoted from the World Economic Forum, January 2016, in the Church Times that week.

38 John 17.

39 Andrew Wingate and Permilla Myrelid, Why Interfaith: Stories, Reflections, and Challenges from Recent Engagements in Northern Europe (DLT, 2016).

40 Quoted in The Guardian Weekly. 16.2.18

CHAPTER 7

HOPES FOR THE FUTURE: CONCLUDING SUMMARY IN TEN CHALLENGES

For the sake of immediacy, significance, and emphasis I have included references within the text.

Preamble

These ten points are not intended to be dogmatic statements; if they were, they would be unsuitable for the subject matter and my approach to it. They are personal to me and foundational to this book. I need hope too. They are proposed as representing and symbolising the experience, in my observation, of ten other people of faith and of my own as opened up in this book. They arise from evidence of the severe need of our British society presented in Introduction 1 and the perceptions and responses, from all ten contributors in chapters 1 and 3, my analysis in chapter 3 and my suggestions and examples in chapter 4 re inter faith relationships and throughout the book. They point to a potentially transformational movement aimed at the heart of Christianity, from which a reformed love may flow in inter-weaving channels with other faiths.

1. The potential source and symbol of the love that sustains us and gives us purpose and meaning will be recognized and loved under whatever name.

I call this source the idea of God or, simply, God. God is the symbolic name for love which is demonstrated by Jesus through his whole being, presence and way of life. I see Jesus as a symbol of justice, harmony and well-being for everyone, in which he stands for what he calls in metaphorical language 'the Kingdom of God'. The God in my mind is 'one' and not and could not be divisible between the faiths or divisive on theological grounds. If and when that disunity prevails, it seems appropriate to rethink our idea of God.

This love for others as well as for ourselves is the foundation of all good human experience. It includes acceptance of all others in mutual respect. Such love I choose to call love from God. In a divine cycle, it promotes love of God, love of neighbour and love of ourselves. At heart, everyone is to love and be loved for we cannot love without others. In reality, love is the practice of enabling human dignity and respect to others. Without love, evil destroys itself. With love, goodness is infinite despite often severe even impossible obstacles. With love, disagreement, transgression, aggression have the potential for being not only acceptable but transformed into human harmony and unity.

2. Every possible cause of the decline in both numbers of churchgoers and in the moral and spiritual

framework of the country will be considered, including Christianity's theological and liturgical expressions.

Over at least my conscious lifetime, say the last sixty years, there has been a decline in both numbers of churchgoers and the moral and spiritual *framework* of the country especially in relation to young people, though not necessarily in personal morality and spirit. I cannot tell. Who is to say? Comparisons can be meaningless. We can however sense imbalances of Church tensions and priorities at least on its public wing. My sense is of imbalance between:

identity within doctrinal belief experienced in liturgy and Bible reading and the practical living-out of the love of God demonstrated by Jesus;

conviction of one's own truth and awareness that others - whom we can no longer ignore - have their own understanding of truth with potentially equal conviction;

the Churches' own traditional practices and those of others living alongside us;

evidence of the Churches' own authentic good news and that of others who contest this with their own fake-news of non-facts and post-truth;

and between calm and peaceful ways of seeking justice and more strident ways of demonstration and collective or strike action.

3. The economic, historical, theological, literary and social context of Christianity, Christians and the

British Church will be taken to heart and mind both on the local and the international stage.

'The church is the only society that exists for the sake of those who are not its members,' as Archbishop William Temple famously said in 1942 and I repeat again. (Perhaps it was for my own sake, too, because I was born, churchless, in that year!) This would mean that in Britain, churches are called to face the major realities of potentially overwhelming change, from yesteryear's different national order and disorder to today's twenty-first-century globalised world order, divided as it is unified outside and inside our front door. Besides global warming, nuclear threats and the communication revolution over the last sixty years, these changes have increasingly included mass immigration into Britain. Gross figures have increased from zero in 1993 to the present 230,000 in the year to June 2017. The Church is fundamentally about people and relationships and therefore may duly see inter cultural and inter faith relations as its priority and a prime responsibility.

The British indigenous population, including Christians, has been brought by the media, by housing, by work and by modern communications into personal, geographical and electronic contact with people of different faiths and backgrounds. Most of these people, to Britain's great credit - despite the shameful Caribbean Windrush fiasco, very rightly and likely completely to unravel, 2017/8. Before attitudes and closed minds become fixed, and before dangerous drifts and then rifts develop, the situation cries out for prevention through increased urgent and honest analysis response to this multi-faith situation. A vision, a movement, at different levels, starting small and with different priorities of a new spiritual understanding of our existence from all people of goodwill, religious faith and none, has already urged analysis, response and possible transformation of state and church. Such vision and change seem to me to be the Church's loyal duty and care in the name of Jesus Christ, who himself urged openness to transformation in his followers. It has already begun in the last 30 years or so but it is an ongoing task of increasing importance for Britain's well-being.

4. All people of different faiths will be generally accepted to be people of equal worth in God to everyone else.

I have aimed to elucidate both possible need and feasible response by seeking out and examining five perceptions of Christianity and of Christians ventured by five people of different faiths, Muslim, Hindu, Buddhist, Sikh, and Jewish, and five responding Christians. Together, in a hazelnut-ish kind of way, their responses could suggest the merits not only of a new process but also of a new paradigm, a new attitude of listening to others, a new British outlook on others and ourselves, our thinking and our behaving - in other words, a transformation. An initial inspiration would be a refreshed Christian theology and practice which recognises publicly that all people of different faith are of equal worth in God. Increased recognition and reflection on others of different faith with our differences and similarities has been an essential beginning. This book hopes to give further support and stimulus to that existing momentum.

Current progress in change could be developed further in cells and networks of mutual and respectful religious, social and theological relationships and partnerships on a corporate and individual basis. This would entail respectful and open re- prioritising and recognition of old and new, local and universal and human and godly values from across the traditions and beliefs of Christianity and the world faiths. Further, this would entail more than superior and simplistic assertions about so-called 'British values' potentially over against those actually similar values of other faiths and nationalities. It would mean learning that our need to understand otherness is not far from our need to understand God. Inter faith Friendship Circles and Birmingham's neutral Places of Welcome are more very encouraging examples.

Jesus was clear about this. According to the Gospel of Matthew, 5:23–48, you are to 'be reconciled to your neighbour, even your enemy, above and before all else' and according to I John 2:4ff, 'you cannot love God and hate your neighbour' (my wording). Our getting our hearts and minds around such essential presumptions as Christian priority would be a leading foundation for partnership and peace between the faiths and even for British and world peace. Diversity and difference, similarity and sameness, beauty and fascination, in the world are God's creation. They are ever the foundation of creation for our growth, interest and enjoyment, not for the foolishness of deadly rivalry.

5. In Britain, this means generous recognition and acceptance of the four branches of Christianity – always a debatable division – other than denominational, that is Traditional Orthodox, Liberal, Progressive and Evangelical/Pentecostal and what is problematic to them all inside and outside the Church.

Labels are applicable to attitude, alternative/additional perceptions and interpretations of Christianity, particularly of God, church worship and liturgy. They are not usually cut-and-dried divisions any more than we are cut-and-dried ourselves. All our British identities are incredibly mixed in past origin and present reality. I ask where each branch and everyone is going in order to find heaven-on-earth without this mutual recognition, offered with equal respect and trust to each as a God-given reality, experience and vision. We have never had to look far. Our globalised society simply confirms that 'heaven lies about us in our infancy'. The poet, William Wordsworth, knew that!

My first positive acceptance would be of the Christian Church's apostolic, traditional, Catholic and evangelical Protestant type of orthodoxy as invaluable to many for community life, particularly for children's and young people's upbringing. Church ecumenism is not to be mired and left behind because the British Church may now have other priorities. At its best, the Christian Church offers the beauty of holiness, a spiritual, moral and structural framework, clear comprehensive certainty and practices of learning and appreciation of God, Jesus, our natural environment and the mystery of life. It has invaluable threads connecting this present generation with previous generations and their old traditions, even centuries of Christianity.

Whatever flowers as a generous blessing to all is to be honoured by all. I used to love sums but life is not maths at least not at that level. Listening to the other, especially *by* the clergy, asking questions of one another, enjoying and valuing difference as much as similarity, learning to trust our own experience and integrity, seeing agreement and disagreement as only one issue among many in new relationships - all these would be paramount. Purpose and means, human experience and Christian worship, would be integrated. Good, open-minded education for all ages is fundamental whether in educational establishments or places of worship.

A negative priority would address whatever obstacles seem to cause Christianity and good religion to be seen as problematic in society. This is clearly a demanding proposal to be explored. Arrogance, religious absolutism and supremacism - love of power and authority? - which naturally infect attitudes to Christianity, may indeed be the prime problematic targets for rejection of the Church by members of different faiths, religious and otherwise. These are cited, however generously dressed, in our five Perceptions from individuals of five different faiths. Similar infected attitudes may also be just as much a problem amongst that broad half of the population that has grown to reject the Church and even Christianity.

6. Mutual partnerships between and among all the faiths and at all membership levels will be sought after with respect, compassion and appreciation of shared benefit as cause and consequence of meeting and discussion.

All the faiths share this responsibility. Dehumanising polarisation between *us and them* creates destruction on both sides and inequalities may become more pronounced with scientific, genetic, and robotic advances in every sphere of life. They might not if people's equal worth before God is accepted as human priority and put into practice at the same time. So much hinges on motivation, trust and integrity. Mutual partnership between Christians and those of different faiths, formally and informally, fosters the process as well as the purpose. Such partnership would as never before in Britain fulfil the specific Christian commitment to love God and our neighbour on a national scale. Britain offers this perhaps ultimate opportunity because of the intermeshing of its world faiths for Christians to choose with whom to collaborate with full hearts and minds. There will be endless opportunity for Archbishop Welby's 'good disagreement' within mutual acceptance of one another which is, I feel, one of Christianity's gifts to the world. Partnership might be initiated by honest Christians exploring the barriers that Christianity itself presents and the particular responsibilities of Christians past and future. I have made suggestions for this in Chapter 6. In July 2017, in Moseley, Birmingham, for example, our local inter faith group and the Birmingham inter faith climate change group 'Footsteps' held a symbolic meeting in the local Anglican church on Climate Change: Faiths Working Together. In September 2017, a similar meeting was held in the Progressive Synagogue.

7. Listening partnerships could unlock acceptance and healing of past religious hurts and unlock respect for different theologies and alternative ways to God inside and outside Christianity.

The pain, fear and anger that some people of faith carry, inherited from past generations and stemming from perceived violation of mind, body and spirit by members of other faiths, is akin to that from sexual abuse nowadays publicly contested. Emphasis on listening would be creative and educational for all ages and situations, family, friends, work, leisure, in school, in church, whoever and wherever. Proposals for inter faith connections, friendships and partnerships are, I believe, one element in increasing Christianity's public appeal. So many people I have met from many spheres have declared the obvious need and value of this action. Attempts at unity across faiths would be a telling model for our society. They would broker new friendship and mutual patience with those who find church changes unnecessary and threatening, particularly maybe for some convinced traditionalists, evangelicals and the black Pentecostal community, who can be none too enthusiastic about theologies other than their own. Such hopeful ideals apply equally across the other faiths as across the breadth of Christianity.

It would all amount to re-energising Christianity for this new century and a contrast with what appears to be perceived by the majority of the British public, fairly and unfairly, as a fearful and deadening attitude of mind and simply total irrelevance of the Church. It is the urgent task for Christians but so it is for all people of good faith. We might encourage one another not to be constantly and fearfully looking over our shoulders at what might be; instead trying to understand those with different sexuality to ourselves and why non – violent and violent extremists might think, whatever their reasons, but the positive pursuit of the love ethic, experience and commandment in the cause of a new and renewed mindset. This is primarily and in practice about presence, with no other agenda than learning to listen and to share the love of God together.

8. Understanding and confidence is required in treating the causes of both anger and aggression and our own often fearful reactions.

I have lived and worked in inner-city/city centre London and Birmingham for nearly forty-five years so I hope this book offers some compassion and practical sense rather than naivety in the face of angry, aggressive, even murderous greed, jihadism and conspicuous evil. Unreal? I think not, Britain isn't Syria so we have the responsibility of making it work in peace for mutual benefit. It is likely that the problems, individual and community, began with a context only known by those involved and a long way back in life-times. I accept that alongside the continual fear and anguish at first-hand of others I have known and lived amongst, I am an innocent concerning extreme violence. I do, though, acknowledge that there are many different levels of relationships open to us all. Times have changed from the 1960s - brought to my mind by the delightful TV programme, *Call the Midwife* - to the 2010s. Relationships in Britain's black and white relationships and the Irish communities have changed for the better over the last 50 years but lessons are not necessarily learnt from history. Difficulties in interfaith relationships, unless resolved in good time, can go downhill with compound speed. The 'far-right' is doing too well in many a European country, 2017/8; evidence is that Brexit has not helped. Hate crimes escalate. It is one thing to try to understand causes there and here, quite another to live with and cope with negative knock-on effects.

9. Achieving an ideal of transformation is possible and, to different degrees, does happen visibly in many of our lives, but not always.

Christians like others, but especially clergy, often have hectic agendas often contrary or irrelevant to harmonious relationships. 'All partners in inter religious dialogue … must be ready to reform, change, perhaps even abandon, certain beliefs and missionary impulses in their own religion,' say editors, Tony Bayfield, Alan Race and Ataullah Siddiqui in *Beyond the Dysfunctional Family*, 2012. Jesus's life and death showed us that love demands just such a sacrifice. We may continue to hope that Resurrection will continue to arise out of the ashes because the nature of God is always present.

We are all God's incarnation as conscious beings of creation and need nurture through loving human partnerships. Sacrifice to varying degrees in the name of the cross of Jesus is an age-old Christian aspiration. We may all do better if the churches sacrificed some of our favourite church practices and old theological certainties. We need to realise their possible effect on others. How much better is the local pub and public health for all without cigarettes -an unbelievable change to my generation! Syncretism is an old aunt Sally; no new world faith, sticky amalgam or pecking order is proposed. 'All real living is meeting,' wrote Martin Buber in his famous book *I and Thou*, of 1923. Andrew Wingate wrote in 2005 of *Celebrating Difference, Staying Faithful*, showing its possibility within personal difference, truth and dual identity. We may well each enjoy our own but learn and grow from the other. Young people do well to realise this early in life; their parents and teachers too. Schools have wonderful opportunities which would take another book. Many have moved a long way over the last thirty years regarding integration and opportunities for good inter faith relationships. So have many churches and I have myself since *With All God's People* in 1989 - which meant 'Christians alone' - was published by the World Council of Churches. Alan Race and colleagues, as above, recognise 'the necessity for twin tracks of theology and dialogue'. I simply attach a third track which our new century needs: that is 'loving relationships'.

10.   God will be seen always to be central and present and never divisive—otherwise beyond category.

The separate faiths tend to create their own separate claustrophobic division and category of God. Personal preference, *my* and *our* church, theology, opinion, music, context, tradition and loyalty - all can be means to God, but, ultimately, they are not ends in themselves. Our different faiths, with all our similarities and differences, are the gifts of God and every single person to a degree has a different context and every faith likewise. We are all just humanity, potentially enabled to live happily and peacefully as one human race.

We do already, to a degree; but now, paradoxically, since our twenty-first-century oneness through globalisation, our natural oneness in God is challenged in new ways. However, 'the cosmopolitan impulse that draws on our common humanity is no longer a luxury; it has become a necessity', concluded the 2016 BBC Reith lecturer Professor Kwame Appiah. I have the hope that under God we can step up and take responsibility for the world around us.

The alternative could be 21st century self-destruction and disaster. That is no negligible matter! If we are together to save humanity, acceptance and appreciation of this reality is the major task for our 21st century. That is a worthy contribution of faith to peace in Britain and to the world peace envisaged by Hans Kung quoted earlier (p.217). It would mean change, likely public sacrifice and loss of much-loved sacred cows. Hindus know about such sacrifice, as do Christians through Jesus, our human centre point. It is not, though, to displace love, which is humanity's and God's agent for being human and faithful to God. Such love is available for the task ahead because God is available, always with us. Will this aim of the recognition of overall oneness and threats to it, require big change? Possibly, but it could well energise transformation of priorities in the world and within Christianity for the sake of God and humanity. Unity of purpose wherever we explore and find opportunity is one aspect of oneness, worked at on a multitude of levels.

There is a profound battle going on over the nature of truth and reality and over right and wrong. Let us as people of faith together, religious and non-religious, seek and live out the common good, both the universal and the personal. They are interdependent and in their apparent limitations I choose to believe they have the power of God ever present. Jesus knew, as John tells us, 15.14, this may be best known to everyone through loving relationships for, 'you are my friends'.

Questions from each chapter

Preamble

Questions have arisen directly and indirectly from within the text. However, you may not like questions. This is not a legal or doctrinal tome; nobody is laying down the law, despite strong views being expressed. Answers are not predetermined.

Despite Britain being a democratic, free and open society and despite Hyde Park's 'Speakers' Corner' of which we need more, the scale and level of questioning, debate and discussion is seriously damaged by mod cons and decadent attitudes. This applies in politics and elections, in the media and even in schools and universities. It applied pitifully to the Brexit referendum in 2016.

It also applies in churches, which have a very mixed background in this regard. In my experience, voiced questions in church are fairly non-existent, such as to sermons. Answers are assumed and discussion tends to be top down rather than bottoms up, to quote President Macron's linguistic slip. The Church and its guardians have tended to lay down the law, which may be seen as the law of God, or of the Church, or of the clergy, or of all three. Gentle authoritarian dogmatism can still pertain in practice as well as in theory. Granted, it has its place. Appropriate teaching and *learning must not go missing. The questions here, therefore, are intended to promote open and honest discussion.*

The multicultural and multi-faith society that is now twenty-first-century Britain and reflected in this book provides opportunity in Britain for unique and willing discussion. The questions here are not, in my experience, commonly raised in church or street conversation - often for understandable personal, community or faith reasons. They are meant as a further guide on our different yet similar life journeys.

Introductions, 1, 2 and 3

1. Do you feel that this book might be for you?

2. What appeals to you about the subject?

3. What do you think of the description of the state of Christianity?

4. Is its vision one that appeals to you? Why or why not?

5. What is your own context in taking up this book?

Chapter 1: Five Perceptions of Christianity

1. Do you think this process of perception and response is worthwhile?

2. Do you know any people of different faiths? How is that so or not so?

3. What do you know about them and their understanding of Christianity?

4. Have you learned anything new about any of the five faiths themselves?

5. Does anything come across as similarities and differences they all have in common?

Chapter 2: Five Christian Responses to the Perceptions

1. What are your own perceptions of Christianity and Christians?

2. Have the five writers, to your mind, understood Christianity?

3. In which ways are your perceptions of Christianity different or similar, and why do you think that is so?

4. Whether you are Christian or not, what do you most enjoy about *any* interfaith contact you have, whether first- or second-hand, and what do you find most difficult?

5. As a Christian, or not, how would you most wish to respond in thought and practice to those of different faiths?

Chapter 3: A Review of the Dialogue, Perceptions and Responses

1. Do you find evidence here of fundamental difference between members of the five major faiths and Christianity?

Will your answer affect your relationship as a Christian with each faith?

2. What would feature in your own review?

3. Do such differences and similarities matter to you and do you enjoy them or not?

4. Is it easier to respond to people of different faiths simply as human beings together and disregarding your faith rather than seeing yourself as a representative Christian? Why might this be so?

5. What do you think of the idea of contributors to this book communicating openly and honestly about their beliefs?

Chapter 4: The Author's Personal Journey, Reflecting on my inter faith journey, a Christian Context and a Christian Theology for inter faith Britain.

1. In what ways has your life experience influenced what you believe about religion and Christianity?

2. What might you do if your experience of life and faith does not match what you have been taught?

3. How much say/freedom do you think you have had in your life and in what you believe? Does that matter to you or not?

4. What has your life journey to do with God or not and vice versa?

5. So far, have your beliefs and priorities of life, even your prejudices, changed during your life journey?

Chapter 5: Challenges to Christianity

1. What do you mean when you might say that Jesus is 'the Son of God' or divine?

2. If and when you find Christianity hard to fathom, what do you do about it? Are you aware of any aspect of Christianity that obstructs you in potentially mutual relationships with people of different faiths?

3. Do you need encouragement to emphasize the goodness, wisdom and love in Christianity when it might be scorned for other reasons?

4. When it is said in church 'We are the people of God', do you think anyone is excluded? Who to you are *us* and who are *they*? When do you use the word 'we' exclusively? Does this require action?

5. Who is to speak for Christians and take responsibility for declaring and acting out that love is the foundation of Christianity, of all faiths, and of everyone, and when appropriate declare that anything less is 'not in my name'?

Chapter 6: Ways Forward

1. In the light of your own experience and perception of Christian priorities, how do you see Christian relationships with the major world faiths?

2. What to you is the heart of Christianity applicable to making changes in the new British context of multi- faith relationships? Does the idea appeal to you of 'Christianity from below' rather than/ as well as, top down?

3. Which neighbour are you best at excluding from your own security, perhaps at their cost and your false benefit?

4. How do you connect your experience of globalised life with 'your' Christianity?

5. How far are you aware that many people of different faiths, religious and secular, acknowledge the love, peace and justice that Jesus stood for in the name of God, even if they do not see Jesus as divine?

Chapter 7: Hopes for the Future

1. How far are you as a Christian/'none' prepared to (a) acknowledge and (b) discuss in church or just your circles your multi faith involvement and attitudes?

2. Are you prepared to respond, possibly in new ways, to your current understanding of God, Jesus and

theology - especially if you see the evidence of response coming from outside the Church?

3. What understanding do you have as to why about half the British population are/are not churchgoers and of their similarities and differences with those of different faiths?

4. What is your opinion of the Ways Forward proposed in Chapter 6? What is your own vision of the future of Christianity amongst the different world faiths?

5. What do you hope for from yourself for the next ten years?

Overall

1. What have you enjoyed most?

2. What have you found most difficult to grasp?

3. Is there anything you strongly (a) see differently or (b) disagree with?

4. What has been omitted that you would like to explore?

5. Over what is your heart most encouraged?

Epilogue

I have speculated whether I and some other 'progressive' Christians sometimes have the wrong end of the stick about Christian theology and practices and that we may not help the Church to do itself justice, although that is not one of my aims. Yet you may consider that is the case. I can only say that we all have to be a very broad Church to address our 21st century context. My experience is that in inner-city Southwark and inner-city Birmingham and mixed- class Lancaster and Moseley, the Church does wonderfully well within a limited circle but has been often unnecessarily limited in its imagination, church outreach, theology and worship and therefore in its influence. Over half of British people apparently say they have 'no religion'. I have suggested that were Christianity perceived as more from below than from above, more flexible, generous, open-minded and respectful of others who may consider themselves of 'no religion', or 'on the brink' in thought as well as in person, that would be to the good. As for other faiths having their own challenges too, naturally they do, but that is not our subject. I hope this book may encourage the followers of other faiths and none to continue to ask their own questions and work out what they see as their priorities in adding to their own well-being and recommendations for the British Church and Christianity.

God and theology are ultimately both personal and communal, about you and me, 'us and them'. I hope my flexible understanding of

God is constructive. To me what matters most is not a name, a title or a label but what these terms may stand for and, in this regard, the name, God. We carry around our own experience and understanding. I have aimed to uphold the ten writers in their perceptions, responses and faith, different from that of one another and from me. It is easier for us all to accept difference when we know one another. Not always! That is much of the point of the whole book - to demonstrate perhaps a fresh way forward to listen to and learn from one another, about not just knowledge but about creating harmonious and just relationships. We all have body, mind and spirit to integrate together, individually and corporately. The British context has simply widened through new people of other nationalities and faiths coming to live here potentially for everyone's benefit. New priorities have consequently surfaced for our time.

My prime question in this book is about how Christianity and Christians contribute to, and even as appropriate take the initiative in creating good relationships with others of different faith, religious and non-religious. I consider finding purpose as the major essential characteristic of our lives, the best purpose being for us to work out for ourselves with and for others what is best. I hope my purpose has been clear: to rediscover, find or encourage new or old ways for us all to save ourselves and renew heaven and earth, with God certainly. That has long been an ambition of humankind in Britain. From the16th/17th centuries' Reformation to the Enlightenment of the 18th and 19th centuries to the physical progress of the Industrial Revolution to the 20th century national utopian ambitions of Russian Communism and German Nazism, ambition has flared up for visions of heaven on earth and died down, frequently causing hell in the process. History though is more than fighting. York and its castle inspired me as boy to move to reading history but so did beautiful, peaceful, engaged

Fountains Abbey. More death but more resurrection. And so we have gone on. Back to the beginning, start again. 'Return to Go' the game, Monopoly, instructed us.

It is so ironic that all the time there has been the inspiration of love, truth and justice, faith, hope and love, waiting their cue in the wings. Mary, Jesus' mother symbolizes that calling from Jesus's birth to his death on the cross. Meantime, others started again. Christmas, with its love to and from family and outsiders, symbolizes that love which is our due right from conception. And now in the 21st century there are more fears of domination and strife from one quarter or another. T.S. Eliot knew about this tragic but reflective circle when at the apparent end he recognizes the beginning for the first time. Sometimes too late? My Welsh - in spirit- poetic mother, knew it too. Loving God and other people as ourselves is a Judeo-Christian practical principle from 5th-3rd century BCE, not a grand utopian theory imposed from above which Christianity sometimes also sought after: to be 'right' and in control. 4th century CE Roman Emperor Constantine creation of a Holy Roman Empire was not a good omen.

I am now at the end of my written contribution to this book after its nth amendment. I have agreed with myself to have no more. This is the last day. Quite an occasion after nearly five years. Tomorrow I go climbing hills in Snowdonia. In the light of its recommendations for trustful inter faith relationships, I'd like to remind you of the context where the book started in hope with five quotes from notable sources as expressed in Introduction I about 'The current Christian church in Britain',

Professor Linda Woodhead, professor of religion, 'Britain is undergoing the biggest religious transition since the Reformation of the 16th century,'

The Church Times, leader, 8/9/17, 'the chief task.... of the Church...... is to encourage and equip individuals to communicate their faith in ways that mean something to the 'nones' (those who say they have no faith.).

Justin Welby, Archbishop of Canterbury: 'We do not as faith groups in our society always exhibit ....secure tolerance to each other. Christians are as bad as anyone at this........ I think we're worse'. His book published in 2018, 'Re-imagining the Future', is above all about hope, 'realistic and positive.'

Richard Chartres, previous Bishop of London: 'the Church of England (is)- possibly a legitimate marker for all churches'—rooted within the context of our rampaging contemporary world, needing 'to rediscover its heart .... There is need for narratives capacious enough to permit development and to accommodate new themes.'

Rowan Williams, previous Archbishop of Canterbury: hopes 'above all else that the years to come may see Christianity ... able to capture the imagination of our culture ... plaiting together a single strand of all kinds of diversities'.

Final reference: Holy Communion Order One, Common Worship (Church of England, 2000): Jesus according to Matthew's Gospel, 22:35ff.

The first commandment is this: 'You shall love the Lord your God with all your heart, with all your soul, with all your mind and with all your strength. The second is this: Love your neighbour as yourself. There is no other commandment greater than these'.

And yet it declares on behalf of its communicants that we have not have loved God 'with our whole heart' and that 'we have not loved our neighbours as ourselves.'

We are all just extraordinary human beings trying to make life work for others and ourselves, enveloped by the Spirit of Life some of us call God. You may not agree nor with much I have written nor see life in the way I do. Why should you? Our experiences of life are not the same. We have our own story. We have had somehow to make our own priorities of life. Maybe we might meet one day. As for now we might accept together that a simple practical aim would be to be kind to anyone we meet today.

Richard Tetlow 13th September 2018

Bibliography

Books recommended and/or used

Alker, Adrian, *Is a Radical Church Possible? Reshaping Its Life for Jesus' Sake*, (John Hunt publishing, 2016)

Generous Love: the truth of the Gospel and the call to dialogue; an Anglican theology of inter faith relations, Anglican Communion Network for Inter Faith Relations, (Christian Alternative Books, 2008).

Bayfield, Tony, Alan Race and Ataullah Siddiqui, eds, *Beyond the Dysfunctional Family: Jews, Christians, and Muslims in Dialogue with Each Other and with Britain* (Manor House, 2012).

Berg, Jonathan, *Positively Birmingham*, Birmingham Picture Library, 2015

Birmingham Anglican Diocese, *Birmingham Conversations 2016.*

Borg, Marcus, *The Heart of Christianity: Rediscovering a Life of Faith* (Harper One, 2003).

Braybrooke, Marcus, *A Heart for the World: The Interfaith Alternative; Widening Vision* (Lulu Press, 2016),

Buber, Martin, *I and Thou* (Germany, 1923).

Catholic Bishops' Conference of England and Wales, *Interfaith Dialogue: The Teaching of the Catholic Church* (2005); *Meeting God in Friend and Stranger* (2010).

Chinn, Carl and Dick Malcolm, eds, *Birmingham the Workshop of the World* (2016).

Cracknell, Kenneth, *In Good and Generous Faith* (Epworth, 2005).

Crossan, John Dominic: many titles include *The Power of Parable*, Harper Collins 2007

Davie, Grace, *The Sociology of Religion* (Sage Publications, 2007).

D'Costa, Gavin, *Theology and Religious Pluralism* (Basil Blackwell, 1986).

Deacy, Christopher, *Christmas as Religion: Rethinking Santa, the Secular and the Sacred* (OUP, 2016).

Diamond, Jared, *The World until Yesterday* (Penguin, 2012).

Disbrey, Claire, *Listening to People of Other Faiths* (Bible Reading Fellowship, 2014).

Dawkins Richard, *The God Delusion*, 2006, from Amazon

Ehrman, Bart, *How Jesus Became God* (HarperOne, 2014).

Firth, Tim, *God's Favourite Colour Is Tartan* (Lulu, 2012).

Greenfield, Kent, *The Myth of Choice* (Bitback, 2011).

Griffiths, Bede, *An Autobiography: The Golden String* (Medio Media, 1976).

Griffiths Paul, *Christianity through non-Christian eyes*, Orbis 1990

Harari Yuval Noah, *A Brief History of Humankind*, Penguin Random House, 2011

Hick, John, and Knitter Paul, eds, *The Myth of Christian Uniqueness* (Wipf and Stock, 2005).

Hooker, Roger, and Christopher Lamb, *Love the Stranger: Christian Ministry in Multi-faith* (SPCK 1986).

Iqbal, Karamat, *Dear Birmingham* (xlibrispublishing, 2013).

Ishiguro, Kazuo, *Never Let Me Go* (Vintage Books, 2005).

Kermani Navid, *Wonder Beyond Belief: On Christianity*, Polity, 2017

Kinnaman, David, *You Lost Me* (Baker Books, 2012).

Knitter, P. F., ed., *The Myth of Religious Superiority: Multi-faith Explorations of Religious Pluralism* (New York, 2005).

Masuzawa, T., *The Invention of World Religions; or How European Universalism Was Preserved in the Language of Pluralism* (Chicago and London, 2005).

McLaren, Brian D., *Why Did Jesus, Moses, the Buddha and Mohammed Cross the Road: Christian Identity in a Multifaith World* (Hodder and Stoughton, 2012).

Race, Alan, *Making Sense of Religious Pluralism* (Modern Church Series, 2016).

Radmadhan, Tariq, *The Quest for Meaning: Developing a Philosophy of Pluralism*, 2010, Penguin Global.

Reiss, Robert, *Sceptical Christianity: Exploring Credible Belief* (Jessica Kingsley Publishers, 2016).

Sartre, J. P. *"The Look": Being and Nothingness* (New York, 1956).

Schmidt-Leukel, Perry, *Transformation by Integration: How Inter-Faith Changes Christianity* (SCM, 2009).

Scott, Basil, *God Has No Favourites* (Primalogue, 2013).

Spellberg, D. A., *Thomas Jefferson's Qur'an: Islam and the Founders* (New York, 2013).

Spong, John Shelby, *Biblical Literalism: A Gentile Heresy* (Harper One, 2016).

Spufford, Francis, *Unapologetic* (Faber, 2013).

Sudworth, Richard, *Encountering Islam: Christian-Muslim Relations in the Public Square* (SCM, 2017).

Sugirtharajah, Sharada, *Religious Pluralism in the Modern World* (Palgrave Macmillan, 2012).

Tacey David, *Religion as Metaphor: Beyond Literal Belief,* garrett publishing 2015

Vosper, Gretta, *With or Without God* (Harper Collins, 2009).

Watts, Alan, *The Wisdom of Insecurity* (Rider and Company, 1954).

Webb, Val, *Stepping Out with the Sacred: Human Attempts to Engage the Divine* (Continuum, 2010).

Williams, H. A., *True Resurrection* (Mitchell Beazley Ltd, 1972); *Tensions* (Fount, 1989).

Williams, Rowan, *Being Christian* (Eerdmans, 2014); *Being Disciples* (S.P.C.K., 2016).

Williamson, Timothy, *I'm Right You're Wrong* (O.U.P., 2015).

Wilson, Brian W. J. G., *Lost Certainties* (The Memoir Club, 2012).

Wingate, Andrew, *Celebrating Difference, Staying Faithful: How to Live in a Multi-Faith World,* (DLT, 2008); with Permilla Myrelid, *Why Interfaith: Stories, Reflections, and Challenges from Recent Engagements in Northern Europe* (DLT, 2016).

Websites:

www.PCNBritain.org.uk;

www.theinterfaithnetwork.org.uk

www.NetworkforInterFaithConcerns.com